Concorde Diplomacy

Concorde *Diplomacy*

The Ambassador's Role
in the World Today

by

Sir Geoffrey Jackson

HAMISH HAMILTON
LONDON

First published in Great Britain 1981
by Hamish Hamilton Ltd
Garden House 57–59 Long Acre London WC2E 9JZ

British Library Cataloguing in Publication Data

Jackson, *Sir* Geoffrey
    Concorde diplomacy.
    1. Diplomacy
    1. Title
    327'.2   JX1662

ISBN 0–241–10524 2

Printed in Great Britain by
Willmer Bros Ltd
Rock Ferry Merseyside

To Anthony

Contents

Preface

Despite the heading of my first chapter, this is not a book of memoirs. If it were, even more reminiscence, instance and quotation would have intruded. Where they do, they simply serve in lieu of illustration, in a brief exposition of diplomacy's present and past state, and likely destination, as seen mainly through British eyes.

I have not imposed on departments of the Foreign and Commonwealth Office, or individuals of HM Diplomatic Service, for any of the opinions expressed in this book. But I certainly did consult some functional departments for factual help, and to refresh memory on occasional technical and administrative matters. To them, and particularly Miss Blayney and the staff of the FCO Library, who helped me unstintingly with research material, I am deeply grateful. They most generously exemplified Lord Home's farewell when I left the Diplomatic Service – that 'every door in Whitehall would always be open.' As indeed they proved to be. Without that reassurance I should probably not have launched myself on this venture.

I am also indebted, for a second time, to Mr John Dickie, the distinguished diplomatic correspondent of the *Daily Mail*. His early encouragement to pursue these reflections followed on the support his professional understanding and discretion meant to my wife during my long captivity in South America. Now my 'memory-person', her indispensable cooperation during the writing of this book has always and unfailingly retrieved for me that which I was certain I had forgotten.

I am particularly grateful to my publishers, Hamish Hamilton, for their help in providing me with invaluable research assistance in the person of Miss Anne Gray, and to the numerous publishers whose books I have cited.

Finally, I confess to a special debt of gratitude to President Giscard d'Estaing of France, without whose intervention this book might logically but lamentably have been birth-marked 'Jumbo Diplomacy'. Most of the neo-summiteers do after all reach their destination by jumbo-jet; though I gather that the British sub-species still prefer the quiet and comfortable VC10. But summitry only went supersonic, or as supersonic as its image, when President Giscard, to his great credit, actually flew by Concorde to the Tokyo summit of 1979, thereby providing me with an analogue and a title. Meanwhile it is gratifying to see that Lord Carrington too endorses the practice.

And my apologies to the Foreign and Commonwealth Office – or FCO – which I shall affectionately but indiscriminately refer to as the Foreign Office – or FO – a compact and seasoned designation that I, and most people, stubbornly forget is momentarily out of style.

Part One

TODAY

Chapter I
'I, The Diplomat'

The 'I' in 'I, The Diplomat' should be read very much in its inverted commas; it has no autobiographical significance. This book deals with a particular change in the exercise of the diplomatic profession; so the first person singular will intrude only as a point of reference and when useful. Of necessity it will do so fairly regularly, since the writer is himself a by-product of a particular transitional generation in British diplomacy. Starting out representing a Great Power, we finished up reminding ourselves that we still represented at any rate a great nation, even if at times its grandeurs seemed in suspense, or hibernation.

In the late 1950's I was, they tell me, the youngest career British Ambassador ever, if at possibly the smallest British Embassy ever. In the study overlooking our dusty patio in Tegucigalpa, the capital of the little Republic of Honduras, my wife and I one autumn day were listening, over my big short-wave Pye radio, gothic and walnut veneered but very efficient, to the United Nations radio transmitting direct and live from New York.

Instead of the usual Security Council diatribe, or the set speeches for home consumption of minor Heads of State addressing the General Assembly, a beautifully modulated voice was speaking from, by all the evidence, the earlier caverns of mankind. To the drip of adjacent stalactites the 'Old Man' of some Cro-Magnon family unit was briefing the world's two first ambassadors, to go forth and negotiate the limits of their foraging-grounds with the tribe from the cave next door. We listened with some sympathy as it emerged that only one of the emissaries ever returned. The other envoy had been eaten, which was why diplomatic immunity had to be invented.

A succession of equally famous voices then played the roles of their not always more fortunate successors. Some of these early envoys were flayed. Some had their ears cropped, or on arrival

3

at their post had to be purified by leaping over hot coals – an incipient presentation-of-credentials ceremony, no doubt. At later stages more acceptable hazards followed. One envoy was welcomed by the siren voice of the receiving monarch's favourite, enchantingly singing 'Voi Che Sapete'. An intimate bilateral negotiation culminated in a manner politically most rewarding to the ageing but indefatigable ambassador, though financially ruinous and, so it seems, medically even more so.

The long procession of the diplomat down the ages reached its goal, at any rate for the purposes of the broadcast, in the new international-style diplomacy of the United Nations. For it was a birthday programme, celebrating the anniversary of that then still new, exciting and hope-filled body. And I, being by that time an old United Nations hand, an actual exponent of the New Diplomacy, had friends in the glassy new skyscraper of Turtle Bay in New York. So the Secretariat gladly let me have a record of their programme entitled, as above, 'I, The Diplomat', then as now a true collector's item.

I can borrow no heading more appropriate – and I acknowledge it most gratefully – to convey the genealogy of the diplomatic species, and function, right from those early hungry caverns to the air-conditioned supersonics of today. Yet is the diplomat's truly a history of indispensability and survival? Or has the diplomat at last outlived his usefulness to his country and to mankind?

Here I must confess that I found some special pleading in the dénouement of this UN epic. In it the diplomat of the future is, not surprisingly, a Secretariat man operating out of New York, hurrying and bridge-building the wide world over in the name of FAO, WHO and UNESCO. Such a function presupposes a World Government rather than a diplomatic brotherhood of nations. It poses the question whether there will even be a diplomacy when diplomats are all on the same side. So far they are not, the maximum refinement to date being the mobile summit-diplomacy personified by the former United States Secretary of State, Dr Kissinger. Though this innovation seems to dispense with the conventional apparatus, if not all the retinues, of traditional diplomacy, it still operates on the principles of 'us-and-them', of rivalries and alliances, and of negotiation.

Others have asked themselves such questions, and at different points in history. Certainly much of the content of my cherished

4

'I, The Diplomat' United Nations anniversary programme was inspired by Sir Harold Nicolson's between-war reflections, either serious or, when irreverent, all the more effective for that. In his book *Some People*, the creatures of his imagination walk side-by-side with the flesh-and-blood pioneers of a nascent summit-diplomacy, as the ineffectual pathos of poor Titty co-exists with an authentic if fledgling Gladwyn Jebb.

It was the wholly fictional Titty whose one boast was of owning at his early age the longest and most varied entry in the FO List. It never occurred to him that it proclaimed to the world that no chief had been able to put up with him for more than weeks; Nicolson even has him die young. The very real-life Jebb of the stories happily survived, to be a founding-father both of the United Nations and the European Community, an exemplar of the diplomat's response to evolutionary pressures. His memoirs are a principal insight into the early development of conference diplomacy and summitry, if – to his discomfort – still by flying-boat and converted bomber, with the Jumbo-jet and Concorde yet to come.

Long before Nicolson, only a year after the death of the first Queen Elizabeth, Sir Henry Wotton had lodged an indelible question-mark against the legitimacy of the diplomat's calling, with his famous aphorism – 'An ambassador is an honest man sent to lie abroad for the good of his country.' Many have believed, as I do, that a crucial word is missing, or even suppressed. If he is seen instead to 'lie hard' for his country, the whole subsequent stereotype, of the wily and cosmopolitan functionary hedonizing far away in his duty-free comforts and immunities, is corrected, and his less-publicised trials and discomforts brought into focus. The new summitry is to the contrary by its nature spared the monotonies, and sometimes the perils, which line the daily road that the diplomat must plod, in between the peaks of international encounters.

But does a jet-set world need the pedestrian any more? With the immediacy of the hot-line and the communications satellite, is not the diplomatic bag, plus the author of its contents and its attendant Queen's Messenger, doomed to extinction? Must not the spectacular, the exceptional, necessarily dispense with and bypass the continuing and the routine, and the new then wholly supersede the old?

Not so long ago the Far Eastern correspondent of the BBC was offering – probably by satellite – a personal opinion on this very theme. Certainly he saw the need for a complete reassessment of the diplomat's future role. According to him the species lives an encapsulated life, in a pleasant ambassadorial ghetto. In consequence diplomacy has no contact with reality or real people. On this analysis he contemplated a handover of future international relations to a consortium of journalists and political leaders, objective information being supplied and interpreted by the press, and thereafter acted upon, occasionally and succinctly as and when needed, by summit meetings of leading statesmen.

But the opening recollection of my dusty Honduran patio reminds me that human relations are as obdurately unpredictable at the international as at the domestic and personal level. It was never my own experience that my official function kept me at a distance from my flesh-and-blood fellow-men – to the contrary indeed, if sometimes disconcertingly, yet on balance almost always finishing on the credit side of the human ledger. Once, during one of our Central American coups d'état, my wife and I were woken in the small hours by a tapping on our bedroom window. The shadowy figure poised on the step-ladder outside explained that he wished to take political asylum with us. 'Hombre!' I whispered back. 'We British haven't even signed the Havana Convention' – an over-simplification, but true. 'So I can't protect you. But if you climb the big mango at the bottom of the patio you can get through our neighbour's garden – he won't bother you – and by-pass the patrol.' 'Gracias, amigo embajador!' And he slipped away through the darkness without my ever knowing who he was, let alone on which side.

My BBC friend might answer that, if the conduct of diplomacy were handed over to pressmen plus occasional summit-meetings, such incidentals to international negotiation need not occur, and so would be immaterial. Yet friendships, international just as much as personal, need tending, and the fostering of incessant care-and-maintenance. The French say rightly that friendship is composed of small considerations; and it has been my experience that much of negotiation can consist of unconsidered bread returning on the water after many days.

For negotiation is in essence an exercise in mutual confidence, in the recognition that 'win one, lose one' is a sounder settlement than sweeping the board against a thoroughly trounced opponent. So the question arises whether there can ever be such a thing as instant confidence, or whether it can only be attained through the old-fashioned procedure of 'keeping in touch'. In the newly fashionable terminology diplomacy probably rates as an 'interface'; but whatever it is, confidence counts for as much as cunning, and in the long run for more.

In another analogy, diplomacy has over the millenia evolved into a marriage institution of sorts. As in matrimony, the high points, the humdrum, the ecstasies and parturitions are all part of an enduring and uninterrupted relationship, and have their rules, written and unspoken, for quarrel and for reconciliation too. With nothing but a summit diplomacy the nations risk exchanging marriage for a mere mating, an intermittent rut in which a frenzied collision of the parties briefly and single-mindedly interrupts long intervals of mutual aversion.

To such an analogy it may be objected that with traditional diplomacy the protocol and ceremonial of international courtship and matrimony have all too seldom worked, or resulted in that permanence which is the main purpose of the marriage institution. The new-style summits do to the contrary seem to work. Arguably then, a more functional analogy for the hot-line and the overnight jumbo-jet would be not so much for example the grizzly-bear, briefly sacrificing his habitual surly monasticism for the survival of his species, but rather the dedicated business executive, briskly cutting out the cackle for a necessary quick return, or for the fulfilment of some meticulously planned critical-path target.

Perhaps too Hegel and Marx have taught not only the faithful to see human progress as a swinging pendulum mounted on a forward-travelling vehicle, so that alternation becomes progress. In such terms therefore we may be witnessing an advancing compromise of old and new, leading to a new diplomacy altogether. In British terms, for example, it might emanate from some permanent Whitehall or Downing Street secretariat, dispensing both with the plenipotentiary function and the diplomatic panoply corresponding traditionally to it, and simply servicing past and future summits between their convening. Would however this low-profile compromise be adequate? Could it lend real substance to the superficial intimacies of great men meeting at rare intervals briefly and in crisis? Would it substitute for an international network of on-the-spot ambassadors, ministers and under-secretaries who, over the years and around the world, come to know each other well, even to trust each other within the limitations of pre-scribed loyalties and separate articles of faith?

A caricature stereotype of this network is the much-maligned diplomatic cocktail circuit, presumed to exist at best as national propaganda, a mere high-echelon show-off, and at worst for the promotion and exploitation of alcoholic indiscretion and low-level mutual espionage. Instead, of course, its main function is one of familiarization. The inevitable free-loaders and eminent or de-corative lay-figures are just a part of the furniture, incidental to the melting of professional ice. Officials for whom the all too recurrent monotony of the official roundabout is relieved by the bonus of regularly encountering each other, do not as a result meet in their offices as strangers, but as acquaintances, even friends. No negotiating time is wasted on personal skirmishing and breaking down the barriers of mutual suspicion.

Underlying such traditional externals of diplomacy is a ques-tion which will come up again and again. Is summit diplomacy compatible with, or does it even require, the plenipotentiary status which an ambassador has always enjoyed, and required? This vicariously almost regal aura surrounding him – and at times assi-duously appropriated by his lady – has lately become a little thread-bare, even vestigal, as diplomacy, the are and profession of international negotiation, learns to function in a new dimension. Created for a wide world with slow and extended communica-tions, its world has contracted in a generation. The time-scale of the mail-boat and the ocean liner has shrunk to that of the jumbo-jet, and that of its communications from the overnight cypher-cable to the television satellite at the instantaneous service of the mass-media. Already by the turn of the century the diplomat was represented as having become a mere postman, for all his ostrich-plumes and gold braid. Have the electronic surrogates of com-puterized technology crowded out even that modest function?

If so, then the life-span of the career-diplomat will have been a short one indeed. Even within the brief history of civilised man it is comparatively recently that the diplomat acquired a set of immunities and a standing, while the hierarchy, the uniform and – not to be overlooked – the pay-cheque came even later. It was incidentally the pay-cheque of the permanent official that gave him the professional objectivity that comes from immunity to political jobbery.

The ancient Greeks had had their envoys, as no doubt had the Hittites, the Mayans, the Pharaohs and others whom diplomatic historians have found it less confusing to ignore. Such 'legates' were not yet however ambassadors, with due deference to my 'Old Man' in his dank cave and his all too edible envoy. Nicolson, Satow, Cambon, and several Latin American students of the ambassador, all agree that Byzantium trained him, Renaissance Italy named him, and Enlightenment Europe organised him. Already the seventeenth century was giving way to the eighteenth before diplomacy was finally taken over, and staffed, by a transcontinental network of professionals, for the most part gentlefolk and well-to-do in their own countries, and with everything in common with each other. The 'dear colleagues' were thus an international fraternity then, much as now they are still sometimes alleged to be. Even more was this true once the Congress of Vienna had, with the dawn of the nineteenth century, firmly ascribed to each his due rank and station.

For all this there are some who claim that the consul is, as an established species, yet older than the diplomat; indisputably the oldest inhabitant of the old 'F.O. List' is Richard Forster, Consul at Aleppo in 1583. Having myself been a consul too, I approach this thesis with some sympathy. In practice, of course, Britain's consuls are now all diplomats, members of a single unified Diplomatic Service. So they always were, I suspect, in everything but name – certainly when Macbeth's witch chanted 'Her husband's to Aleppo gone, Master of the Tiger.' For the Tiger's cargo, and master, were going to need much support and protection in the Ottoman Aleppo of Queen Elizabeth I's day, let alone King Macbeth's. Such aid and comfort would be provided by the British Consul, bearing the Queen's Commission but paid – by results – from the local British merchant community. A successful operator would accordingly live in princely style. Of another Aleppo consul I read that he did his community – and himself – so proud that when he rode abroad on his white stallion, splendid in his scarlet cloak, tipstaffed janissaries ran before him, laying about them and crying 'Place à Son Excellence le Consul!' And you can't get more diplomatic than that!

Strangely enough, some hundreds of years later there was to

9

be another famous Tiger, whose effective Master, Prime Minister Harold Wilson, was aboard her to experience some of the buffets that direct diplomacy can administer, not least when the adversary is an Ian Smith of Rhodesia. Meanwhile, between these two historic Tigers, life had gone on. Consul Forster and his successors had evidently not neglected one of their prime overseas duties – the well-being and morale of the local British community. For in 1673 the first overseas game of cricket on record was played, by the English expatriates of distant Aleppo. A far cry from the Concorde, the jumbo-jet, and the shuttle-diplomacy of Dr Henry Kissinger.

Chapter II
The Kissinger Phenomenon

Consul Forster in Aleppo long ago, and Prime Minister Wilson, Master of the Tiger only lately, both testify by their respective roles in history that in knowing where we come from we best know where we are, and are going. Another man, very different yet in their direct lineage, symbolizes in his person the continuing challenge of the remote, strange and dangerous which Shakespeare conveys so well, and the human urge to confront it which underlies all summit diplomacy. Henry Kissinger's repeated girdling of the earth represents a new fusion of the two incentives, by the application to them of modern technology and his own particular abilities and temperament.

The conduct of foreign affairs has not always come easily to United States presidents. It was to do so even less after Vietnam, with both Congress and the State Department seeking to reassert their role in it. Even Presidents Roosevelt and Truman, who took better than most to life with foreign commitments, had needed always to look over their shoulder, with one eye for the smooth running of the monstrous political machine that sustains a successful president in office. The domestic and international impact of this concentration of power has since their day been even more intensified. The burden of the presidency, already immense, has been multiplied many times over, by the advent of nuclear fusion as a weapon of war, by the revolution in the speed and efficiency of physical and electronic communication, and by the polarization of political and military might between the two new super-powers.

No one was more conscious of this ever sharper focusing of power, or looking forward more to manipulating it, than Richard Nixon in late 1968. He was also conscious that his lack of preparation in foreign affairs was even greater than his fascination by them. It was presumably to make up for this deficiency in formation that he had earmarked in Henry Kissinger one who shared his passion for achievement in world statesmanship, but also had a proven record of intellectual eminence in the domain of foreign policy.

In many countries a top-ranking career ambassador can become foreign minister. Neither Britain nor the USA follow this practice; though Lord Carrington had been High Commissioner in Australia before becoming Secretary of State for Foreign Affairs, his had not been a career appointment, albeit his experience as a Head of Mission has evidently served him in good stead in his later capacity. Unlike the British Diplomatic Service, however, United States diplomacy has for some time had its own ample tradition of interchange and mobility between government, business and academia – something approaching a foreign affairs equivalent of what President Eisenhower had in the defence area termed the military-industrial complex. Kissinger already belonged to this foreign affairs 'establishment', but only after a fashion. He was in it but not of it, used by it but, till then, not allowed to use it. With his thrusting ability, plus his awareness of it and ambition to deploy it, he must have resented this subordinacy, to the point no doubt of sharing Nixon's own complexes towards the 'eastern establishment,' and his dislike of it; to this extent they were two of a kind.

To an Englishman the East Coast American 'wise-man' variant of the familiar 'mandarin' type that Nixon and Kissinger detested is by no means the 'toffee-nosed cooky-pusher' that it must first have seemed to them; an Englishman tends to see the likenesses in Americans rather than the differences between them. Thus one Harvard student of my own Cambridge days managed to combine every archetypal WASPish characteristic with an impressive if at first disconcerting talent for noisy precision-spitting, western-style; I recall him striding alongside a bed of long-stemmed tulips and virtually decapitating every other one *en passant*.

So in due course the 'Boston Brahmin' element in the American Delegation at the United Nations, so strangely lacking in the mellowness and style appropriate to a tradition of responsibility, was to come as no real surprise to me. Paradoxically, and to our life's great enrichment, my wife and I were instead to encounter these attributes elsewhere and later, among the Americans of the newer cities and universities farther west.

Another initially startling characteristic of the home-spun East

Coast aristocracy is that it does not at all speak as it writes. Your British top-man, be he diplomat, don, trade unionist, businessman or statesman, has one single vocabulary; he tends to speak very much as he writes, if perhaps a little less so. Very often however his American equivalent is on paper a model of erudition, but in tête-à-tête, or even in conference, a master of profanity. Roosevelt's characterization of President Castro's infamous predecessor Batista as 'a son-of-a-bitch, but our son-of-a-bitch' is historic. This execratory conversational trend is even more marked down the Johnson-Nixon years, and abundantly recorded in the growing literature of Kissingeriana.

As a type diplomats, any more than your average Englishman, are not like this as a rule – a rule to which the American career diplomat, as I remember him, is also no exception. He tended to be more sedate than his non-career ambassador, and in fact had much in common with his European colleagues, save that for long his chances of ending up as an ambassador were far more slender than theirs. Career minister was at one time his theoretical ceiling; this was in fact the title originally intended for his memoirs, he assured me, by Willard Beaulac, a pioneer career appointee to the rank of ambassador; and he too thereafter had to submit his resignation on a change of president. I believe that this convention is still mandatory, even now that career United States ambassadors are less of a novelty.

American ambassadorial appointments are often of course political *quid pro quos*, of the style immortalized on stage in that amiable musical, *Call Me Madam*. In Latin America they go a step further; in many cases the offer of an embassy may equally well be a reward for political services rendered, or a polite exile to keep a political adversary out of mischief, if not indeed an alternative to some less humanitarian mode of disposal. Under the less Byzantine American system it is the contribution that tells for the appointment, either in political leverage duly applied or to party funds in straightforward cash. Oddly enough the bidding is often steeper for the more arcadian but comparatively minor embassies, where local status and amenity are high and the outgoings modest. The great world capitals apparently come comparatively cheap as regards the down-payment. The true cost comes later, when the social and representational demands of such posts call for a subsidy which can only be met out of really great personal wealth. For Paris, even perhaps London, it is not enough to be only what the late Lord Beaverbrook reputedly classified as 'a poor rich man.'

I recall one such case where an eminently successful entrepreneur had contributed a small fortune to the party's campaign, to be duly rewarded with his chosen microcosm, and with powers and responsibilities in both of which he manifestly revelled. He admitted to me cheerfully that three distinct functions were associated with his mission. Of the other two one was self-evidently the invigilation of a specific business interest. The other I could only assume was a parallel quasi-governmental activity which ultimately foundered, rumour has it, at the Bay of Pigs in Cuba. No ambassador should be expected, or accept, to be associated with such heterodox diversions.

Nor for that matter would the traditional American career 'Foreign Service Officer.' For him – or her – the achievement of this designation and status has always meant far more than the ostensible British equivalent of becoming 'established.' Rather it seems to have some of the prestige, honour and *esprit de corps* comprehended in, say the British 'Queen's Messenger' title. It is my impression that the Kissinger legacy to diplomacy, which will be both positive and negative, must include on the debit side some disturbance, possibly lasting, but with good fortune evanescent, of this American Foreign Service tradition.

It has often seemed to me that the explanation is that in his years at Harvard, then with the Council on Foreign Relations, and working for Mr Nelson Rockefeller, Dr Kissinger had, in a very special sense, met all the wrong people. For a would-be diplomat he was starting out too near the top. The 'wise-men' or 'establishment' types whom he joined first as Assistant for National Security Affairs and then, after September 1973, at the State Department, were not Foreign Service Officers, of whom a future Secretary of State could have done with far more experience. However heretical it may seem, it is fair to question whether to such names as Rusk, Ball, McNamara, Bundy, Helms, and so on, the designation of diplomat is properly applicable at all. Though their names shone brightly in the American diplomacy of their epoch, they had always been negotiators – grey eminences, grey men, technicians, fixers, even statesmen on occasion, but not professional diplomats.

For all his brilliance and penetration the newly 'arrived' Kissinger may therefore quite wrongly have sublimated, in his later handling of State Department 'regulars' whom he probably scarcely knew, a resentment which he might more appropriately have taken out on the east-coast 'mandarin' circuit. Parallel to this antipathy a disturbing trend to the politicisation of the State Department is also noticeable from contemporary accounts. The career Foreign Service of the United States had hitherto, like the British Diplomatic Service, been rigorously apolitical. Now however, time and time again, Kissinger appointments were indicated as going to those State Department officials who had been at pains to make their political allegiance clear. It is sad enough when with each political upheaval a nation must, by their formal resignation, publicly reaffirm the loyalty of its ambassadors. It is far more grievous that at any time the bipartisan impartiality of its permanent diplomatic officials should be open to question.

Any more than with the British Foreign Office, it would be fatuous to contend that the American State Department of the last quarter of the century needed no renovation or reorganization. To the contrary, its devotees would have welcomed a fair share of the uprooting and scrutiny of which the British Foreign Office had had more than its surfeit. Kissinger had the power and the authority which would have enabled him to make full use of an opportunity denied to predecessors without his position at the very axis of power. Because of his fascination with the conduct of foreign policy he showed no interest in the machine indispensable for its day-to-day processing. As a result he left untouched and unimproved on his departure the very apparatus which he more than anyone had criticized in his time. Paradoxically this indifferent procrastination, this very failure to 'new-broom' the State Department, may well have been for the best. For by now the USA itself – as one of its statesmen had previously suggested of Britain – might well have been looking around for a role, with its apparatus of state therefore best not tampered with for the moment.

Be that as it may, Dr Kissinger has not left his country the heritage of a great and revitalized American diplomacy and State Department which was within his grasp. What he did achieve was an imprint on international diplomatic method which, whether in practice lasting or ephemeral, will at its particular point in history remain as an indelible personal signature. Even before his accession to real eminence Kissinger had been an inveterate globe-trotter – Europe, the Indian subcontinent, Vietnam – and in 1976 Rhodesia had found for him a new Southern African concern, and a new terrain – Pretoria, Salisbury, Dar-Es-Salaam – for the shuttle-diplomacy with which his name will always be identified. Its blend of summitry, diplomacy by conference, travelling circus and secret diplomacy, was at its most characteristic in the negotiation of the Egyptian-Israeli cease-fire of 1973.

On 5 November 1973 Dr Kissinger's elaborately installed Boeing 707, in effect an air-borne communications-centre, left Washington for China. The house-calls that the good doctor was to fit into the next four days were only a rehearsal for the forthcoming weeks, yet rival in sheer concentrated programming the later remarkable journeys of that other transnational pilgrim, Pope John Paul II. His stop-offs on this first brief trip encompassed five nations, and included both Israeli and Arab cities – Jerusalem and Tel Aviv, Rabat, Tunis, Algiers, Cairo, Luxor, Aswan, Aqaba, Amman, Rayak, Damascus and Riyadh. On his ensuing way to China he also dropped in at Teheran and Islamabad. This first 'shuttle' initiated the process of rapprochement between Israel and Egypt. For the peace conference which was its prime purpose Kissinger had virtually to repeat the round-trip a month later. He left Washington on 8 December for a NATO gathering and, by an approximate re-run of his earlier five-day circuit, had by 21 December assembled round one table in Geneva the foreign ministers of Egypt, Jordan, Israel, the United States and the Soviet Union – though not Syria.

On this trip Kissinger had already cemented the beginnings of a personal relationship with President Sadat of Egypt, which a further foray was to transform into a world-wide television feature. Next, on 10 January 1974, he flew direct from Washington to the unlikely destination of Aswan, site of the famous Soviet-built High Dam, which President Nixon had designated as America's greatest mistake – a shrewd second-guess with which most Britons would ruefully agree. On this occasion the shuttle alternated with all the volatility of a ping-pong ball – Aswan – Tel Aviv – Aswan – Jerusalem – Aswan – Jeruslaem – Aswan. Its product, the disengagement agreement with Israel, was personified in the famous 'kiss of peace' by President Sadat, and in his broadcast designation of a Jewish American as a friend and a brother. On Kissinger's next visit, a month later, he had become 'my friend Henry'. The easy first-name affability of the TV chat-show had thus entered into statecraft. Diplomacy by familiarity was now on view.

I have listed this particular Middle Eastern shuttle-series as just one sample, an epitome indeed, of the Kissinger technique. It could be the harbinger of an entirely new diplomacy. Equally it could be a simple updating of the late Sir David Kelly's dictum,[1] the classic fraternization process between élites being merely expedited by over-night subsonic aviation, and its outcome amplified and propagated by late twentieth-century electronics.

If so, it might well be that Kissinger's was exactly the right way of grappling with the new sources of power as he found them. The mere concept of a 'jet-set' may seem obnoxious to a traditionalist. Yet it is now a reality; and the only effective way to communicate with an unforthcoming élite, either of 'beautiful people' or of political power, may well be for their interpellator, whether gossip-columnist or negotiator, to pursue them to their chosen haunt, be it disco, dacha or desert. Kissinger was probably right therefore to take to his own jet-aircraft, and seek out his particular 'Ruling Few' on their home ground. Furthermore, Mohammed did not only go to the mountain; he made a performance of it.

So if at times his method seemed arbitrary, vulgar and tough, it was probably the best way of eliciting quick decisions from tough and authoritarian men, whether as individuals or as collective dictatorships. For that matter his own style was that of the Politburo, according to one former colleague, Senator Daniel Moynihan.[2] Here again Kissinger's individualist approach departs radically from classic diplomatic method. The career ambassador, by definition normally anything but a 'loner', has more to fall back on than his own mental and nervous toughness – usually rather more considerable than what he lets himself advertise. In his quietly implacable pursuit of the local springs of power he also has a staff to help him. His counsellors, secretaries, attachés, all represent a reservoir of pooled energy for which Dr Kissinger seemed to have no need.

To his intellectual toughness must also be added the sheer

[1] *The Ruling Few*, Hollis and Carter, 1952
[2] *Dangerous Place* (p. 9), Secker and Warburg, 1979

physical variety, when to crisis diplomacy is added the new dimension of the time-zone and the jet-plane shuttle. I have had my own experience of interference with what has come to be known as the 'circadian rhythm'. Even in a subterranean cavern or hide-out, denied the prompting of dawn and sunset, the body obeys its millenial genetic programming with surprising tenacity. Some captains of industry, men who can dispose of other people's time as well as of their own executive aircraft, have their own techniques against the notorious 'jet-lag', recognizing that it is essentially the body's protest against an inordinate extension of the previous and next working day. And, as no less hardened a traveller than that doyen of Anglo-American journalistic legend Alistair Cooke once remarked, jet-lag is not only a matter of sleep. Any sufferer knows that, as Cooke baldly put it, it is the bowels that really matter. Two large dinners in quick succession before breakfast; double dry martinis, at sunrise by the digestion's own internal clock – this is such stuff as dyspepsias are made on.

So not only a continuing deprival of sleep but also a recurrent affront to the digestion are among the first-fruits of the summiteer's aerial pursuit – near-sonic or even super-sonic – of the dawn advancing round the turning earth. Your tycoon often shrugs them off by imposing his own time-zone. He sticks to the home setting on his multi-zone digital watch, and his clients must adjust themselves to it, or lump it. Whether however Dr Kissinger would have expected or wished to keep President Sadat or Mrs Golda Meir waiting till he awoke to a mid-afternoon breakfast is questionable. Like us ordinary mortals his jet-lagged circadian rhythm was doubtless at the mercy of his alarm-clock and engagement-book too. How he mastered it is a mystery that can only be explained by some hidden reserve of physical and nervous energy, husbanded for crisis and switched on like an after-burner.

Dr Kissinger's successor as Secretary of State swore that he would never become involved in shuttle-diplomacy after the manner of his predecessor. Yet Mr Vance found himself flying more than three hundred thousand miles in two years. If indeed it is only the provisional that endures, then perhaps Dr Kissinger's adoption of crisis technique as a way of life, as against the steady pace and pressure of the resident plenipotentiary, is the memorial of him that will most endure.

For the question arises whether the Kissinger method was not essentially a diplomacy of crisis, whether therefore détente – 'the management of adversary power[1] – presupposes henceforth a permanent function for an incessantly mobile presidential intermediary; or whether Dr Kissinger was just another, if summit-level, 'Special Envoy', dealing for a while as he knew best with a succession of *ad hoc* special cases. A successful novel asked in its day the question 'What makes Sammy run?'; and equally perceptive academic studies have less personally questioned whether détente is not a system inevitable when power-groups can neither live with each other nor without each other, when the United States of America, the Soviet Union, China, the European Community, the Third World, must live together or die together.

On such a premise it could be maintained that summit diplomacy, especially in its peripatetic Kissinger version, actively feeds and thrives on diplomatic abnormality. Certainly the post-war 'shuttles' have generally arisen from crisis, from tension between apparent irreconcilables, when the traditional diplomatic 'interface' has been destroyed. If, for example, Arabs and Israeli will not speak, and have no shared and continuing channel of communication, some *deus ex machina* or 'Special Envoy' is indispensable to break the deadlock. Such an emissary might perhaps have been found in the Secretary-General of the United Nations, had the hopes embodied in the Charter been fulfilled. By force of circumstance however, perhaps by force of personality and perception, it was Dr Kissinger who invented, and possibly institutionalized, his own way to an end which without him would have been altogether different, if not inconceivable.

There is of course the converse view that, far from being a symptom of crisis, all summits – and not alone the Kissinger variant of them – are instead a sign of reassurance. It is one of the oldest of cynicisms that the professional diplomat, who prides himself on being a harbinger of peace, is to the contrary an instrument of conflict. By this interpretation of history the classic diplomacy, the 'old diplomacy', enjoyed its finest hours when the nations were reeling from one war to the next, and was at its lowest ebb when, now and then, peace seemed secure. By this yardstick of paradox, peace without diplomats should be mankind's norm, with occa-

[1]*The Diplomacy of Détente* by Coral Beel (p. 2), Martin Robertson, 1977

sional spasms of summitry correcting or anticipating its intermittent bouts of instability. To this comforting doctrine the riposte for our time might be that today's rather different 'peace' is unfortunately no more than the tightrope precariousness of a new balance of absolute terror. Recourse to the summit might thus be the nations' newly acquired survival-reflex, responding to the intermittent push of the panic-button, rather than a measure of their political evolution and maturity.

Be that as it may, the Kissinger intensification and personalization of summit diplomacy has made it an essential feature of international intercourse, and a routine function of statesmanship. Thus a new British Prime Minister, Mrs Margaret Thatcher, had within three months of assuming office found it necessary to attend not less than three summit meetings, at Strasburg, Tokyo and Lusaka. They incidentally served the useful purpose of notably asserting a personality till then a star of lesser magnitude in the international galaxy.

To Kissinger's sense of showmanship goes the credit – if it can so be called – for the element of the spectacular that now surrounds all manifestations of summit diplomacy. Precisely to ensure the participants' privacy the level of security deployed must paradoxically be all the more ostentatiously spectacular. Conversely, to ensure maximum dissemination and credibility for whatever meagre percolation of news is permitted to filter through this barrier of secrecy, the mandatory journalistic presence must be equally spectacular. Hotels are turned into fortresses; surrounding woods and gardens swarm with soldiery and bristle with the paraphernalia of weaponry and two-way radio communication. Roads are blocked, traffic is diverted, ships are delayed in harbour, jet fighters and helicopters dart or trundle across the skies. Now and then a communiqué or a set photograph is disgorged, for the propagation of which one or more jumbo-jets bring to the sealed-off summit a cargo of expensive pressmen in still more expensive luxury. Sybaritical, even bacchanalian tales are told of the jumbo-jet cosseting of the White House press-corps, along with its superlative provision of briefing and administrative facilities – all most mouth-watering to anyone who has fought his way through the hungry jungles of the earliest conference diplomacy. At one time all such fringe-benefits were 'included in the ticket'. Lately however – or so it seems – a formidable bill for them is presented to the beneficiaries' newspapers or networks, to which, by all accounts, these do not seem to object.

So there are certain human prices to be paid for the ostentatious honest-brokerage and managerial assiduity of Kissinger-style conference diplomacy and summitry. Besides such side-effects as those already alluded to under the categories of circadian rhythm and security-by-floodlight, one new penalty must be singled out, from that dangerously booby-trapped no-man's land which often barely separates the spontaneous from the farcical. I am referring to, even warning against, what might be termed the 'diplomatic hug' or 'political embrace'.

The public display of sincere emotion, let alone its affectation, is a hazardous diplomatic tool. Were it to become an accepted instrument of statecraft it could well put the professionally undemonstrative career diplomat out of business, except that he is usually a quick learner. The fact is however that any contrived pretence at sincerity invites the verdict of the television camera, that infallible exposer of the spurious. And the professional diplomat knows all too well that basic precept of his craft – falsity is always found out and its author discredited. He accordingly has misgivings about the growing application to international negotiation of techniques more appropriate to a beauty-queen competition.

There is in fact nothing new about the hazard in question, even for the British. It is merely the advent of television that has revived and publicized these flamboyant goings-on between, usually, elderly politicians of assorted nationalities. I shall be referring later in some detail to one initial precedent for all this summitry, the Field of the Cloth of Gold of 1520. Shakespeare found it a good warm-up to set the opening scene for his *Henry VIII* by headlining just such a royal embrace. He had his Duke of Norfolk regale the Duke of Buckingham – himself prevented by an ague from witnessing the encounter of the two sovereigns – with an on-the-spot account of 'Those suns of glory, those two lights of men'. True summiteers they, long before the days of television; for Norfolk

> ' – saw them salute on horseback,
> Beheld them when they lighted, how they clung
> In their embracement, as they grew together.'

Evidently both kings were good at it; as medieval monarchs they embraced as to the manner born. Today this is not always the case; and unless it is done well, the diplomatic hug is best not done at all. In Western Europe, especially Britain, the human need for tactile reassurance, inherited from our animal ancestors, has been blunted over recent centuries. In very few English families – my own happily is one of them – do the menfolk still keep the old habit of kissing each other's cheeks after separation. For the most part Victorian reserve still brands at any rate our social life with physical undemonstrativeness. And for an effective diplomatic hug national tradition and practice help. Perhaps that is why some of the most convincing embraces have been demonstrated by the two least likely candidates, Messrs Sadat and Begin. Once Dr Kissinger had melted the political ice the lively cordiality characteristic of all the Levant countries triumphed, in a number of television encounters which would have done credit to the younger end of the Montagu and Capulet families.

Soviet statesmen are, appropriately, a little bear-like on these public occasions, though evidently doing what comes naturally; Mr Brezhnev's pictures show him as particularly free from tactile inhibition. The French, surprisingly, are now less effusive, and expert, than was their former reputation. President Giscard's combined hand-shake, slight bow, and pat on the right bicep is even a little condescending, while it is hard to imagine the formal kiss of the late General de Gaulle; from one first-hand account it was evidently at its best at investitures – preferably military, posthumous, and vicarious. It is with the Anglo-Americans that the diplomatic embrace can so easily trespass across the border between informality and farce. President Carter would have been well advised for such occasions to recall Dr Kissinger. He is used to it. So much so that, during his novitiate, he ruefully admitted to unexpected misgivings about his masculine image when his new summit contacts subjected him so enthusiastically to all this embracing, and not least when one particular Near Eastern statesman repeatedly squeezed his knee to emphasize his points.

Being who and what he is Dr Kissinger understood the convention, and adapted quickly. Britain, with less current exposure, and so long as she has a woman Prime Minister, will probably be spared any such overly obtrusive affabilities. So far as concerns her travelling statesmen – Foreign Office ministers, party leaders, parliamentary delegations – it has often seemed to me a pity that there are no Latin American summits, at which practice could make really perfect. For there is nothing to equal the Latin American 'abrazo' which, even for an Englishman, by frequent repetition comes in no time entirely spontaneously. The correct hand soon slaps the correct shoulder-blades, noses are no longer at cross-purposes, cheek meets cheek without angular deflection.

Above all, a lack of self-consciousness soon evolves which safeguards all such public demonstrations of regard against either farce or insincerity. Many years ago, before various affectionate practices were legalized for consenting male adults, this very expertise on my part aroused visible suspicion in one young policeman, briefly perplexed as to his duty by the hearty public 'abrazo' of a Latin American statesman who had bumped into me, after many years, on the steps of a famous London church. The law was mystified, but turned on his heel and strode away in obvious relief, when our respective wives emerged from Mass, to join us.

So it would seem that the diplomatic hug, even on television, requires the seal of sincerity, indeed of a certain real warmth, even affection, to acquire authenticity. And it would also seem that the case arises more frequently than we might believe. If electoral advantage has often been the main inspiration for Heads of State to embark on summitry, a byproduct can be the development of a genuine regard for one or the other of their fellow-participants. They, and their Foreign Ministers, can 'get the smell of each other', as it has been put to me – even come to like each other. For this reason it is rare, I am told, for a summit to originate from the initiative of officials. It is the leaders who propose, and the officials who follow. And there is no harm, and much scope for good, in a mutual liking growing between terrifyingly powerful men, however diametrically opposed their interests, philosophies and political systems.

So perhaps the Kissinger style of personalized diplomacy, of public relations, of combining the functional with the symbolic, should be neither patronized nor under-rated. There is nothing new about 'goodwill visits', and conceivably the injection of a human element of personal goodwill can lend to a summit conference the proven added dimension of a formal goodwill visit. Certainly royal visits, which technically are purely representational, conveying undiluted national goodwill, have a much more potent impact than routine diplomatic encounters. The Crown represents the nation 'whole and undefiled'. Queen Elizabeth II can accordingly achieve a public and political effect which Dr Owen or Lord Carrington by their very function cannot. Because the Queen is spared the minutiae of inter-state negotiations, she can leave these to, or prepare the ground for, her Ministers, who may follow her or even, as in days gone by, accompany her for such useful asides.

It is perhaps the element of goodwill, of human contact, which furnishes, however tenuously, the common factor between such diverse manifestations of 'summitry' as a Royal Visit, a Kissinger 'shuttle', and a summit conference of Heads of State, Heads of Government, or Foreign Ministers. Even closed societies like that of the Soviet Union become permeable to, and intrigued by, the very societies that they aim to hold at bay, penetrate, or perhaps ultimately absorb. The growing inclination of the Soviet leaders to be 'in on the act' emerges clearly from Sir Terence Garvey's *Bones of Contention*,[1] when he deals with Kruschev's wish to reduce the areas of potential conflict – a concept of détente not that far from Kissinger's 'web of shared interests'.

'While Stalin had' – Garvey says – 'been content, except on a very few occasions during the war and immediately after it, to sit at home and leave diplomacy to the professionals, Kruschev had been to the capitalist countries to see for himself.' By 1979 this genuine curiosity, in its originator a salutary, even almost innocent fascination with the unknown, had evolved into something like an imperial progress. Success, and the ubiquity of the Soviet presence, had amplified the goodwill dimension acceptable in, say, a British Royal Visit into something which Czar Alexander I would have recognized, in which raw prestige combined with a massive negotiation function. At the SALT II deliberations in Vienna that year the Soviet delegation took over the royal suites at the Hotel Imperial in which Queen Elizabeth II had stayed. While President Brezhnev stayed at the Soviet Embassy, he was reported by the press as having had his personal Rolls-Royce limousine flown in from Moscow for the occasion.

Here again we see glamour and panache among the common factors exploited internationally by the participants in summit diplomacy. In glancing over the recent history of British diplo-

[1] p. 59, Routledge & Kegan Paul, 1978

24

macy I more than once refer to its progressive 'democratization', and to the possibility that the more lavishly the available democracy is spread around the base of the Foreign Office pyramid, the less will be left over to show at the apex. In creating freer access at the bottom, we may well be over-crowding the available room at the top. The end of one selectivity will therefore require the emergence of another, a more comprehensive recruitment demanding a more rigorous upward distillation of talent. This abandonment of the 'aristocratic' principle – not only by Britain but also by, for example, the United States and the Soviet Union – has necessitated the deliberate scrapping of certain earlier standards now judged anachronistic and expendable – private income, birth, rank, social convention etc. In the Soviet Union the process was accentuated by revolution, in the United States by the twentieth century explosion of wealth and higher education.

In all our cases, however, the surrender of the earlier standard of 'excellence' in overseas representation has called for its replacement by another. In the American and Soviet cases the new professionalism may well at its extremest have taken the form, unconsciously or automatically, of the arbitrary élitism of summitry. To fill this new 'room at the top' both placemanship and meritocracy have their part, whether it be in Dr Kissinger's 'flying circus' or in the chandeliered splendours of a Soviet dalliance in post-Imperial Vienna.

In both these types of 'spectacular' the pressure of the domestic power-struggle may not be overlooked. Nowhere more than in the Kremlin does nothing succeed like success. The Watergate scandal exemplifies much the same hypertensions in the White House. Dr Kissinger's contemporaries there showed in many cases an ambition both more single-minded and less controlled than his. Their enjoyment of sudden power was marked by an arrogance, a gluttony, a naivety almost, which Kissinger himself found amusing. He recalls in his memoirs various of their grotesqueries. One White House advance-man presumed that he could impose on Number Ten Downing Street his own version of a guest-list for the British Prime Minister's dinner in honour of President Nixon. A not dissimilar crassitude was essayed in the still more sensitive environment of Ottawa, ever wary of the giant to the south.

A combination of such shrewdness of detailed perceptivity with exceptional intelligence and energy can add up, when also allied with the grand vision of world affairs, to something akin to near-genius. Kissinger's rise to power – which it would be rash to credit has passed its peak so soon – is full of such perceptions. Thus one aspect of his shuttle diplomacy accommodates to the highest state-craft one of the most age-old principles of the prestidigitator's art – that movement, mobility, apparent ubiquity, can dominate and manipulate the spectator. It has been said that a celebrity may be defined as one who is well-known for being well-known. Dr Kissinger, who knows that illusion is more than half of reality, became powerful because he self-evidently had power. The magnification of power by movement was part of the hypnosis which created and imposed this same aura of power.

He also demonstrated immense talent; and mastery of his subject is the first essential of the negotiator. The native talent will be even greater if it is trained, and Kissinger had trained himself prodigiously, both intellectually along the book-shelves and, after assuming office, in the field also, to an extent unparalleled by previous incumbents. And even though he did not care for the State Department, it was there, and with it the whole machine of government, to support him.

At times of crisis it is remarkable how the machine can always support, accommodate, cope with almost anything; as ultimately the Suez episode of 1956 was to demonstrate for Britain, it could even absorb the shock of Anthony Eden's physical and political collapse. But diplomacy is a continuum, not a sequence of occasional crises. If personal fulfilment as a statesman is only to be found in crisis, then a thirst for the spectacular, and an instinct to dramatize rather than to pacify and conciliate, could well finish by turning diplomacy into something ominously gladiatorial. Summit diplomacy, shuttle-diplomacy, all personalized diplomacy, contains within itself the seed of what is known as 'adventurism' to Soviet diplomacy – which itself has not always resisted the temptation. Whether in the Near East or Cambodia, Kissinger however was always an advance-man, a forerunner. The novelty and dynamism of his form never over-committed its substance.

And over-commitment is the greatest hazard of summitry. If discretion is the better part of valour, preparation is undoubtedly the best part of summitry. Harold Macmillan is recorded as having said that the only way to ensure the success of a summit is to go to it with the final communiqué already written in your pocket. Even in Harold Nicolson's day he too was conscious of the risk of negotiators who only seemed to have full powers. Especially when these are Heads of State or of Government, it might seem likely that they could speed up the proceedings by immediate on-the-spot decisions on knotty problems. Johan Kaufmann says however of conference diplomacy that:

'This latter possibility is, however, rather exceptional, because in many countries the head of state has only ceremonial functions, while heads of government, even if they have special powers, will not usually be in a position to take decisions beyond the instructions given previously to the delegation.'[1]

Since those words were written ratification has become even more unpredictable. In the case of an authoritarian government it presents no problem. In the case of the United States of America, however, congressional susceptibilities since Vietnam have seriously undermined a tradition by which, over almost two centuries, only one in a hundred, out of over eleven hundred American treaties concluded, was ever left unratified by Senate rejection. Summitry may well therefore be responsible for a new laxity in negotiation, by which what should be no more than a preliminary and general rubbing of minds, and clearing of ground, either subsumes automatic ratification, or commits nations to more than the Head of State or Government can deliver.

Not less than four major instances can currently be quoted. It is possible that the 1978/79 Camp David understandings, over the future of Palestine and the Palestinians, fall into this category, as do also the SALT II and the Panama negotiation of 1979. Henry Kissinger had no part in them, but his shadow hung over them. Another instance is the Tokyo economic summit of June 1979. In an excellent BBC summary of its conclusions, the commentator remarked that he felt very sorry for the senior civil servants who accompany top politicians. The summiteers meet, disperse, go to bed. The experts stay up all night, and hammer out a compromise. Next day their masters blow it sky-high, and the experts – 'The Seven Sherpas' – start all over again.

That is what experts, including diplomats, are there for – among other things. Yet at all five previous economic summits the procedure counselled by Harold Macmillan had been followed. An

[1] *Conference Diplomacy*, Sijthoff/Oceana, 1968

agreed draft of a final communiqué had been prepared in advance, and circulated by the host government. At Tokyo in 1979 this procedure did not function. As a result, the final communiqué, of United States orientation, was an agreement to disagree. It has always been standard British government practice to drag feet and procrastinate in advance of a proposed summit, till it is reasonably certain that it can have a substantive outcome. The preliminaries are vital, so their final outcome, with any luck, is an agreeable and edifying formality. Diplomacy by summit, expedited and short-circuited by the Kissinger-style shuttle, carries the inherent risk of producing a flawed triumph rather than a broken deadlock.

These are some of the risks that the world's leaders have faced since World War II, and which Dr Kissinger has braved in his pursuit of the glittering diplomatic prizes offered by a triangular détente, to which individual regional crises in all five continents are in practice subordinate and subject. Yet it has been a balance of risks, and with a positive side which has perhaps figured in-sufficiently in the present chapter, and in the numerous assessments of a singular life-history still presumably in the making. Satow,[1] who in his successive manifestations remains axiomatically impersonal and objective, has said of the new summit diplomacy that it is 'a new style of negotiation and diplomacy and is likely to remain exceptional.' 'Under Dr Kissinger,' he asserts, 'an emergency technique becomes a method.'[2] By extension summit diplomacy could thus be a passing fashion and Dr Kissinger one of history's flukes. Alternatively, depending on how you see it, both could be a providential response to the exceptional human challenge presented by the insistent threat of nuclear war.

Satow goes on to say that the Kissinger innovation depends for its success on exceptional human qualities, backed up by total political, administrative and logistical support. It is questionable whether Kissinger, whose power-base was always in the White House, received from his own diplomatic machine all the help he needed, and which in particular a less powerful but more accommodating Secretary of State might have received in other days and circumstances. To a considerable extent his hyper-trophied White House back-up was substituting for an enfeebled

[1] Satow, Sir Ernest, *Guide to Diplomatic Practice*, 5th edition, edited by Lord Gore-Booth (Longman 1979)
[2] *Op. cit.*, chap. 43 : 8

State Department and, as we have already seen from his memoirs, was doing so inexpertly and frequently ineptly. There is a better way; and it is questionable how long Kissinger could have continued without the support of an effective State Department. There is little doubt that, despite his herculean propensity for single-handedness, he might have done much better for his country with such help.

That better way was illustrated prior to the Rhodesia/Zimbabwe negotiations of late 1979 in London. Referring to the British Foreign Secretary's presentation of the issue to his Prime Minister, the *Economist*[1] commented that he 'brought about over Rhodesia an even more remarkable discovery of the advantage of suppleness. Backed by a Foreign Office team who can now recite the details of the Rhodesian issue in their sleep – .' Here then is the difference between the career diplomat – which Lord Carrington has been in an 'acting' capacity – who is trained, indeed drilled, to use his professional resources to the fullest, and the summiteer-tycoon, who is not. It is also an early pointer to the integration of classic diplomatic method into the new techniques of summitry.

Cynics might, of course, see instead a take-over – 'the FO at its tricks again!' – not least when one eminent practitioner has assured me that, with every summit, the work-load of the professional diplomats is increased, with the result that, in the end, you need still more of them. So even in diplomacy it comes expensive to follow fashion.

Yet there are signs that, across the Atlantic, Dr Kissinger was in his day finding his own way to much the same conclusion. At various points in his memoirs he renders what seems more than a formal homage to the professional diplomat and his classic method. Thus many tributes have been paid at various times to the formidable Mr Dobrynin, for so many years the Soviet Union's ambassador in Washington, whose affable understanding of the country to which he was accredited was matched only by his unbending spokesmanship for his own. Ambassador Dobrynin's awareness of the limitations of Marxist-Leninist pragmatism must have impressed Kissinger, who remarks of him that he 'understood that a reputation for reliability is an important asset

[1] *The Economist*, 22 September 1979, p. 14

in foreign policy.'[1] Apart from this familiar truth – that the diplomat should not lie – Kissinger also recognizes that 'in foreign policy crude tricks are almost always self-defeating.'[2] He is referring to the Cienfuegos episode of 1970 in Cuba, an early Soviet essay in deception. Yet United States foreign policy is itself all the healthier for so frank an acknowledgement, at a moment when its own record is under public reappraisal, as are indeed some of the episodes attributed to the commentator himself.

In other ways, too, the Kissinger style harks back to a traditional diplomatic ancestry. For all the haste and hullabaloo that has always surrounded it, its working substance has in practice relied on the classic diplomatic usages of patience and secrecy. So-called détente was the end-product of a painstaking process that required at least nine summit meetings for its gestation, of which four took place between 1955 and 1967, well before the Kissinger era. The signature of a treaty may literally be the stroke of a pen – in 1972 SALT I at Moscow, in 1979 SALT II at Vienna. Yet it is not at a stroke of the pen that worlds are changed, but by the painstaking groundwork that precedes it.

Kissinger's use of traditional diplomatic secrecy in all this preparation has been much criticised as excessive. It may indeed be that his notorious addiction to 'back-channels', whether with SALT, the Middle East or Cambodia, corresponded to a certain inward secretiveness, different in kind from the discreet confidentiality of traditional diplomacy, and contrasting too pointedly with the external ostentation of his shuttle diplomacy. A favourite analogy for traditional diplomacy has always been the duck in its pond, placid to the eye but invisibly, below the plimsoll-line, feverishly active. Kissinger seems to have inverted the technique, the elaborate external flurry distracting the eye from the profoundly calm concentration of activity proceeding unseen below the surface.

Particularly in the United States, since the Watergate scandal, governmental secrecy has been under a cloud. The plain truth, that negotiation – like horse-racing, invention and industrial research – is impossible without secrecy, has been falsified by a largely emotive clamour for 'open government', by the controlled leakage and ever earlier disclosure of official secrets, and by

[1] *White House Years*, p. 140, Weidenfeld and Nicolson, 1979
[2] *Ibid*, p. 635

the new social acceptability of 'instant' and lucrative official memoirs. Yet Dag Hammerskjöld's 'quiet diplomacy' was much lauded in its time; and one of the early hopes of the United Nations had been what Hugh Seton-Watson calls 'serious secret diplomacy behind the scenes.'[1] Perhaps the difference lies in motive and environment. In a democracy official secrecy has come to be seen as a sin; under a tyranny it is practised as a virtue.

Another modification of an earlier diplomacy for which Dr Kissinger may be responsible is the transformation of the rather saccharine and unconvincing Eisenhower/Kruschev 'Spirit of Camp David' of 1959 into the less starry-eyed 'détente' of later years. Those who frequented the United Nations in those earlier days will remember how the 'Spirit of Camp David' was incessantly conjured up by Soviet orators or negotiators like a genie from a bottle, serving as a blocking device, an exhortation, or a code of behaviour and policy from which any hint of deviation was met with reproachful or indeed ominous reminders. In our later and less ingenuous days détente might well be formulated as the 1959 Spirit of Camp David, minus intervening Soviet expansionism, plus Dr Kissinger.

The 'plus' in the equation is well merited. Roger Morris, by no means an acolyte of Dr Kissinger, credits him with 'having helped the world to come to terms with the Russian and Chinese revolutions.'[2] Otherwise he sees the Kissinger achievement as flawed. No régime, or combination of régimes, has today the power to solve the most serious international problems. Morris therefore sees Kissinger's strategy as wholly superseded, dismissing it as 'the elaborate nineteenth-century European condominium he has tried to copy.'[3]

Yet his coming to terms of a sort with both Moscow and Peking is a reality and an achievement. It could well be that Kissinger's diplomatic testament to the world, non-Marxist and Marxist alike, will prove to be the growing openness to the West of the new China, an act of faith which is more than the Russian rulers have ever dared risk. The dimension of China's change of course is much as if in 1947 the Soviet Union had welcomed the Marshall Plan.

[1] *Neither War nor Peace* (p. 21), Methuen, 1960
[2] *Uncertain Greatness* (p. 298), Quartet 1977
[3] *Ibid.*, p. 298

The purpose of this chapter has not been to ascertain what kind of a man is Dr Kissinger, or how successful, but what so far has been his significance and contribution, negative or positive, to world diplomacy, in particular his effect on professional diplomacy. The two questions are not of course entirely separable, any more than results ever are separable from their causes. Bernard du Rosier in 1436 saw the aim of diplomacy as peace. It has increasingly seemed to me that Kissinger's aim was much the same, but subtly different, in that his first, or possibly even alternative target has always been stability. Behind the jaunty, increasingly assertive façade, the Kissinger within could well be a Faustian figure of sorts, seeking always to hold history steady by pinning down the fleeting moment that seems so fair. At least his compromise between the ideal and the possible has in it nothing of despair. He is no American Flying Dutchman, condemned to circle the world endlessly and forever, if with a more advanced technology than the original's tattered three-master.

This view of him has at least the merit of acknowledging – to abuse Goethe's hospitality once again – the two souls that dwell within Dr Kissinger's breast. If it is far too early to judge either the man or his impact on diplomacy, a principal reason – apart from the fact that his career and its implications are still with us – is that so much writing on him is heavily committed to a single preconception; Dr Kissinger has become a natural target for partisanship. There is even a successful novel of which the hero, if not quite Dr Kissinger in simulacrum, is at least the Washington milieu of slightly dotty omnipotence which for a while took hold of him. Joseph Heller's *Good as Gold* appears to me to seek truth through flippancy. As a result his hero-figure, an intellectual picaresque yet simultaneously a political Candide, is projected not only as larger than life – which the presumable model also is – but as something of a figure of fun, which the original ceased long ago to be to anyone.

A very different book, which I had hoped would help in forming an opinion, is *Sideshow* by William Shawcross, dealing with the atrocious destiny to which Cambodia has fallen victim, and the role in it of the USA's secret power-diplomacy. Whether Kissinger is the arch-culprit as portrayed is probably, by sheer unwritten and unfinished history alone, a premature conclusion for author and reader alike. Even more disturbing with so important and exhaustively researched a source of opinion is its avowed and passionate *parti-pris*. *Odium theologicum* can all too easily make one man's hero into another man's villain, with the truth falling disastrously between the two stools. Fear of the progressive take-over of a vulnerable strategic sector of the world's surface need not automatically turn its opponent into the hatchet-man of a converse tyranny. The ideological case remains unproven. Judgement in such cases, whether personal or political, can all too easily suffer from the complication remarked by a certain distinguished magistrate who reminisced that he had spent much of a long career adjudicating on collisions between two stationary automobiles.

If at this preliminary stage a single firm judgement on his international significance is possible, it would seem to be that Dr Kissinger has been one factor – though not the sole factor – in a certain current eclipse in public esteem of the professional diplomat – who may indeed find himself emerging from it by taking a leaf or two out of the Kissinger public relations handbook. If the latter-day summit has seemed something of a recurrent Potemkin village, it has taken more than a team of stage-hands to establish it as a genre. Likewise it will need more than a succession of false fronts, along with their stage-carpenters and scene-shifters, to maintain and in due course replace it.

In fact, it is not so much the function of the diplomat that the Kissinger phenomenon has changed; the professionals will continue to soldier on as assiduously as ever, though perhaps for a while less elegantly, or at any rate less resplendently, than hitherto. That after all is of our age, and of the redistribution of its resources, with or without Dr Kissinger. What he has probably modified far more substantially is the public and international role of the Foreign Minister. The voice that matters now is that of the Head of State or Government. Ministers of Foreign Affairs, whether strong or weak, are increasingly, since the Nixon/Ford/Kissinger era, seen as an extension, a 'pseudopod', of a President or Prime Minister, rather than the spokesman of a government and parliament. Autocracy is contagious. Those who host the summit, or join it, want either the master or his authentic voice.

By his short-circuits and back-channels Dr Kissinger has undoubtedly helped to make it more difficult to 'settle things' at ambassadorial level; but perhaps in the precarious and time-fused world of today fewer things than before can be settled – as against negotiated – at ambassadorial level. The danger is that, while Kissinger has played a major part in making summit diplomacy currently fashionable, few world leaders themselves possess his 'summit' skill. And none, on the present evidence, has his or her own Kissinger, who can make a whole world wonder 'that one small head could carry all he knew.'

So Dr Kissinger has made life harder for the Head of State or of Government who is not – or has not – his own Kissinger. At the same time he has made summits appear dangerously simpler than they are, through seeming to dispense with the solid infrastructure laboriously supplied by the working diplomat. In the end, by institutionalizing the summit, the Kissinger phenomenon will probably, and in the not so very long run, have rendered more indispensable than ever the man who produces the summiteer's brief – the professional diplomat, as before. Part of summit diplomacy seems to have been the response to a recent re-injection of autocracy into international relations. It would be ironic if, in due time, the resurgence of that epitome of oligarchy, His Excellency the Ambassador, were to proclaim the reversion to a more democratic norm.

Chapter III
Eurodiplomats

Meanwhile, in another part of the international forest, other Excellencies are plying their traditional trade in a novel environment, a new European Community. Yet however multilateral the apparatus, it is a reasonable guess that, for example, the application of British diplomacy to European affairs will, for a foreseeable future, be as closely bound as ever to the Anglo-French bilateral relationship.

This prospect had already been brought home to me in one simple lesson, long before its enhanced necessity was spot-lighted in 1968 by a Labour Government's improbable appointment to the British Embassy in Paris of a High Tory archetype, Christopher Soames. In that capacity his manifest function was to apply chosen linguistic, dynastic and personal aptitudes to the building of a causeway to the island fortress that was the late General de Gaulle.

Earlier, in 1963, I had been on, or at any rate not far from, a Swiss mountain-top when the General's brutal jilting of Mr Edward Heath in his courtship of the Common Market agitated even our phlegmatic Swiss hosts. A couple of years later I was on another mountain, this time in France itself, in a small and medieval French village near the Italian frontier. Our part-time post-mistress, who united into one truculent identity all the legendary characteristics of the French concierge, fonctionnaire and peasant-woman, had her own arbitrary way of handling our outgoing mail. Along with a tariff extracted from us, she handed it over to the postman who brought up our incoming mail, for eventual stamping by the main depot in the valley below. We had letters for England, Switzerland and Italy. Triumphantly this hirsute *tricoteuse* demanded nearly double for the English mail – 'Marché Commun, monsieur!' In vain we pointed out that Britain's status vis-à-vis the Community was no different from that of Switzerland. The off-shore island remained odd-man-out. 'Marché Commun, monsieur!' – take it or leave it.

This object lesson in the pragmatic selectivity of Gallic legalism was reiterated and brought home by the November 1979 meeting of the nine Community Heads of Government at Dublin Castle. At that very time I had just begun contemplating the pros and cons of this present chapter, in specific terms of the future that the EEC portended for professional diplomacy. It seemed to me that Mrs Thatcher's aim for Britain had been to establish what Dr Kissinger on such occasions likes to call a 'bottom line'. When her Community formula of approximate parity between financial intakes and outputs proved unacceptable, and in effect met with a Franco-German veto, an interesting and almost unanimous reflex ensued on the part of the British press and other media. In face of the impasse, all took it for granted that it would be followed at once by a 'diplomatic offensive', by 'intense diplomatic activity', or by whatever their particular editorial style chose to designate what was evidently to be the same process. In other words, diplomatic negotiation, over the coming two or three months, between officials at the appropriate technical level, was to precede yet a further summit.

That they were 'summits' at all was a proposition deprecated from a significant quarter, Mr Roy Jenkins, the President (British) of the Commission. In a worthy effort to remove steam from the Dublin pressure-cooker, he claimed in a radio interview that these meetings of Community Heads of Government had by now become 'institutionalized'. It was no longer therefore appropriate to refer to such admittedly high-level but regular and routine exchanges of view as 'summits'. Summits dealt rather with *ad hoc* emergencies and crisis episodes.

Whether Dublin – or what it had become – was or was not a summit by either of these definitions, it certainly seemed to me as an onlooker to corroborate one important summit criterion. The whole process of regularizing the British contribution to EEC finances seemed to justify, and be falling into line with, one of the more valuable of recent diplomatic maxims. Lord Home may not have invented it, but he certainly has endorsed it by both example and exhortation. I – though probably not he – like to think of it as 'the doctrine of the well-tuned summit' – that before every summit there should be the fullest diplomatic preparation, to the extent that it should not even be embarked upon unless its success is virtually certain and indeed, for preference *à la Macmillan*, its final communiqué included in the participants' baggage on arrival. Something of this philosophy had all along for example invested the 1979 Lancaster House Conference on Zimbabwe-Rhodesia, despite frequent indications to the contrary. Anthony Sampson of the *Observer* remarked at the time on the ability of the Foreign Secretary, Lord Carrington, behind all the pomp and glitter, 'to deploy exceptionally able young diplomats' in 'a kind of unconventional diplomacy' of which the Foreign Office had generally been considered incapable.

It might be alleged that Mrs Thatcher herself had failed to take such advance dispositions, to judge by the lack of tangible result at Dublin Castle. The appearance may not however have been at all what it seemed. The effect of Dublin, and no doubt the Prime Minister's real aim, was to bring into the open, to at any rate a British public hitherto unseeing, the intensity of Franco-German obduracy towards the problems of a partner currently self-wounded and economically weakened. The way was thus opened to a diplomatic process at which otherwise electoral opinion would probably, without such enlightenment, have looked askance. From this starting point an ensuing technical negotiation leading up to a definitive 'summit' would make positive sense, as against the initial 'dry run' at Dublin. It also poses the interesting question whether just such an alternation between 'quiet diplomacy' and the public ritual of the summit is not to be the pattern of the Euro-diplomat's, indeed the diplomat's, foreseeable future.

In the evolution of such a Euro-diplomacy the French have so far made the running. In two ways they have had a head-start. To begin with they were founder-members of the European Community; two of its guiding spirits and intellectual authors had been Frenchmen, Robert Schuman and Jean Monnet. On the basis of their pan-European vision their government, more pragmatically, had intended and sustained a position of moral ascendancy within the original Six, which had for example enabled General de Gaulle to impose his will by an interlude of non-cooperation in 1966. This same Gaullist temperament and aptitude, which is the second source of France's position of advantage in the Community, has its roots deep in the French culture, history and indeed psyche.

The French diplomat is, to begin with, the product of a power-ful centralized tradition in government and education which, inherited from Richelieu, Louis XIV, Fouquet, Colbert and their line, was not destroyed but enhanced by the Revolution in 1789 and the first Napoleon. I have occasionally asked colleagues and compatriots whether Britain's real Community trouble is not simply that the French as a people are that much 'smarter' than we. Invariably the answer has been a robust but qualified 'No – just better educated' – even in one case from a Wykehamist.

It has incidentally always impressed me that the words of French popular tunes are often remarkably erudite – so much so that they cannot really be translated into demotic English. They are far too intelligent, as compared with the mindless trivialities normally sung to our mid-Atlantic jazz and 'pop'. I always remember as quintessentially French one popular 'hit', about, of all things, the accordeon:

'Le piano du pauvre – Se noue autour du cou –
Sa chanson guimauve – Toscanini s'en fout – '

Or, in near-verbatim English:

'The poor man's piano – Is knotted round the neck –
To its song so marshmallow – Toscanini says "Heck!" – '

The imagination boggles that such intellectualism, poetry even, should trespass on a latter-day British vocal tradition which cul-minated in the ululations of the unhappy 'Sid Vicious', late martyr-king of the 'Sex Pistols', punk-rock, and the 'Seventies.

Whether or not Montmartre produces a superior 'lyric', the 'grandes écoles' certainly produce an officialdom of superior equipment. Whether, however, its parallel trend to a certain pro-fessional precocity, intellectual arrogance and political rigidity makes also for a good diplomat is another matter; perhaps at this stage of the Community's history, with national interests still being staked out, 'Inspecteurs de Finances' rather than diplomats are currently of a higher evolutionary priority. The 'inspecteur de finances', even as a fledgling, is a formidable species. I recall several such, one in particular – already in his youth a holy tartar around the Levant – who represented France with such eminence in the early years of the Community that, whenever back in Paris, he was reputed, like some Gallic Bostonian on speaking terms only with the Deity, to talk to no one less than his President or, at a pinch, the Prime Minister.

I eventually began to favour the possibility of some process of selective breeding which – admittedly perhaps in the hyperbole of recollection – produces a certain severity, even a corporeal typing, so lending a useful physical projection to an already intimidating intellectualism. Allied to a Cartesian dedication to the national interest, which makes their formal internationalism and Europeanism in Community activity and representation largely a matter of convenience and tactics, this product of the French forced-draught system of selection and training produces a formidable competitor – and indeed a formidable ally too, if once an Englishman can attain that status.

In fairness British diplomacy can produce its own stereotypes too for any French colleagues to enjoy in their turn. It was in fact a junior French ambassador at the United Nations who once volunteered to me delightedly, as one tall and slender young 'high-flyer' after another loped past, each with his Master's briefcase – 'I think all your British Private Secretaries are brothers. You must breed them!' Today he would have said 'clone them'; but at the time he just went on to add 'You, my robust friend, will never be anybody's Private Secretary – you have the wrong shape!' – though as far as sheer stature goes, I can think of at least two miniaturized exceptions to his rule renowned for their pocket-battleship fire-power. It was he too who once remarked abstractedly as, 'stately as two galleons', the wives of two of my colleagues swept by us – 'Why is it, *cher ami*, that so many of Her Majesty's ambassadresses are so much more regal than Her Majesty?'

Whether or not such stereotypes are just further products of an increasingly selective memory, objectively each Representation to the European Community can be said to have acquired its own style and approach. COREPER – the Committee of Permanent Representatives which meets twice weekly, at Head of Delegation and Deputy level alternatingly as a rule – is taken particularly seriously by France. Their Permanent Representative rates very highly with his own government. He and his staff are accorded great prestige by the Quai d'Orsay, who make sure that Commission matters always rank as 'foreign affairs', and that all fronts of Commission activity are covered in the first place by diplomats.

Though France has its SGCI – the Secretariat-General of the Interministerial Committee for matters of European Economic cooperation – it is axiomatically subordinate to, and overridden by, the Foreign Ministry. As as result of this integrated policy French officials at Brussels demonstrate exceptional self-confidence – as for that matter elsewhere. To know exactly where they stand is so great a strength to them that the French government has been able to keep its Representation comparatively small and compact in relation to the influence that it wields. Its central role 'reflects the French view that relations with the Communities are those of classic diplomacy.'[1]

Such traditionalism is not common to all Representations. The British comes nearer to the French than most, with a very senior career diplomat as the Permanent Representative, leading a staff largely also of career diplomats, interspersed with senior departmental advisers from Whitehall. Given however the British two-party system, and the doctrine of ministerial responsibility, the British Permanent Representative does not enjoy the same local autonomy as do some of his colleagues. Correspondingly, however, he runs a tighter diplomatic ship than, say, his German colleague, many of whose staff are seconded experts, even trainees, from assorted technical departments of the Federal Government. Their 'ambassador' leaves them to it, he and his diplomatic staff concentrating rather on the external affairs of the Communities.

There is thus no hard and fast distinction between what is 'domestic' and what is 'foreign' in a government's dealings with the Communities. What is foreign policy and what is domestic policy can easily be blurred. An agenda item – say mutton – can begin as 'domestic' and become 'foreign' as its significance grows, and as 'sheep-meat' evolves into lamb. Whether there can and will be a 'European' foreign policy, singly and as such, is another matter; but it has often occurred to me that the conjunction of six, nine, eleven, twelve, internal and domestic policies is already beginning to necessitate a kind of separate and internal 'inter-European diplomacy', to accommodate and reconcile continuing conflicts of national economic interest. Certainly one former British colleague, a habitué both of the Communities and of the roundabout of the Western-world capitals, commented to me on

[1] *National Government and the European Community* by Helen Wallace (p. 61), Chatham House, PEP, 1973

40

this speculation, that Community membership had not affected the nature of the British diplomat's task to anything like the extent he had expected. Another view came from a much lamented friend, the late Count Bentinck, Netherlands Ambassador in his time to the Court of St James's. Long ago he foresaw something like the Euro-diplomacy which I have been postulating, emerging inevitably from the early discovery that Brussels was not after all going to be quite like an inter-departmental committee transplanted from Whitehall to what was to be the quadrilobate labyrinth of the Berlaymont.

This blurring of the distinction between domestic and foreign policy, the merging of which was a prime aspiration of the Monnet epoch, has since been held firmly in check by the Council of Ministers and COREPER. Through them the voice of the national governments, originally resented as an intrusion on the authority of the Commission, has become an accepted part of Community proceedings. Here the departmental and domestic begins to impinge on the diplomatic. Seen in one sense, the workings of foreign governments – 'foreign affairs' – begin to have a wider domestic incidence, and so their interpreter back home – the Foreign Office – to have a correspondingly wider domestic involvement. Seen from the other end of the telescope, home departments in Whitehall look as if more involved overseas, in the Community, thus potentially cuckooing the diplomats out of their habitual negotiating nest into the more indifferent periphery of the Community's external policies alone. It is significant therefore that the Foreign Office keeps a close eye on this possibility, through not one but two fraternal departments, for long optimistically entiled 'European Integration (Internal) and (External) Departments'. These twin designations, voicing a pristine aspiration rather than existing reality, have now more functionally become 'European Community Department (Internal) and (External)'.

Behind this ambivalence of the 'domestic' and the 'foreign' lies a corresponding tug of professional interest and authority as between the diplomat and the technician. The chicken-and-egg question it poses is whether Community negotiation is best served by the traditional negotiating skills, reinforced by technical expertise from the home departments, or conversely by a staff of technical experts selected also for negotiating experience. Phrased in this way of course the alternative is based on a static premise, which in the real world can however be remarkably dynamic. Thus one and the same issue can be a 'diplomatic' question in certain circumstances, and be – or become – a technical one in others or, just as often, vice-versa. When an issue is politically live, perhaps indeed thorny – the Community budget, say, or what actually is now hideously termed 'sheep-meat' instead of mutton, whether dressed as lamb or not – then the operation is a diplomatic one, supported by technical experts. When, however, an issue is a strictly technical one – say the standardization of Value Added Tax – then the technical experts in the Brussels Representation may well initiate it.

Even so, they will always bring the FCO into the fray. They in their turn will quite possibly alert the European Secretariat in the Cabinet office, across the way in Downing Street, and perhaps the Treasury also, since a matter initially purely technical so often proves to have political implications, repercussions, even consequences. It is thus a characteristic of the Community that its affairs constantly shift between the two categories, between the political and the technical, the diplomatic and the domestic.

With a Permanent Representative who has usually had working experience of 'Number Ten' from both sides of Downing Street, and with a team so habituated to cabinet-level cross-checking, the FCO and the Cabinet Office are unlikely ever to be taken totally aback by events in Brussels. There is of course the endemic risk that an important department of state may have very much a policy of its own. My own experience, from other areas, is that one such is the Ministry of Agriculture, Fisheries and Food; their experts can be both single-minded and self-sufficient – evangelists indeed. To chaperone a veterinarian from the 'MAFF' – as I have – in the negotiation of British foot-and-mouth disease procedures with a River Plate exporter of beef, is to witness the legendary collision of the irresistible force with the immovable object. The thought of such encounters expanded in Brussels to a multilateral dimension is mind-boggling to any connoisseur in confrontation. A less frequent hazard could be that a particular individual negotiator is quite simply a bad negotiator, or that there might be a conflict of interests inside a particular technical team. These and similar reasons explain why the FCO so clearly prefer for Brussels a Representation maintaining the traditional role of diplomacy, and held firmly under their own aegis.

This interdepartmental working relationship perhaps sounds more tense than it is. In practice it is just a form of that 'positive tension' which I once heard the late and great American cardiologist, Dr Paul Dudley White, describe as a concomitant and indeed a condition of life. 'Where there is no stress,' he stated, 'there is only death.' Similarly if, under the impact of external events, the internal kaleidoscope of domestic governments can thus be jolted into fresh patterns and harmonies, it would seem reasonable that so too should the developing relationships of individual governments within the new Community. The British public has been bewildered, and disappointed, by the new patterns realized so far. Those of them who intuitively detest the Community philosophy see only an excess of integration, always, too, where it hurts Britain most, be it in mountains of superfluous butter, lakes of surplus wine, or pyramids of Golden Delicious apples which on close encounter are insipid and of a pallid green. Those conversely who long for a second Charlemagne's integration of culture, speech and interests cannot wait to see the Community as one united country, with for example the smaller Latin American nations receiving and sending one single ambassador from and to Brussels. Instead they see the FCO reserved, and the Quai d'Orsay strenuously averse, towards any suggestion of 'pooling', let alone of planned and progressive integration.

Yet ultimately it would all make sense, if the Community is truly to evolve. A start of sorts has even been made, in the shape of so-called COREU, a form of direct cypher linkage and distribution network for telegrams between the Foreign Ministries of the Community. Its importance should not however be overstated. COREU is not a function of integration, nor even yet a portent. Yet it is already a measure of a certain practical cooperation which, to one who comes afresh to Community affairs after some years away, shows itself as a novel fact of life, paradoxically however taken for granted already by its practitioners. Thus at the time of the so-called Tokyo Round in 1979, it seems that all ceremonial matters – formal signatures and the like – were integrated into single joint ceremonies with the Nine's representatives, rather than pursued individually, consecutively and laboriously. This eminently sensible procedure evolved itself virtually spontaneously, to everyone's satisfaction, particularly that of the Japanese hosts who were bearing the heavy burden of ceremony. The practice evolved indeed to the extent of joint briefings by the Japanese Government of the Community ambassadors, on matters of common concern such as trade with Japan's neighbours.

My impression is that in reality a considerable amount of inter-community machinery already functions, but at a preliminary, informal and 'shadow organization' level. Conversely nothing substantive exists at present by way of formal integration, given the jealous nationalisms of the components, not least the French. But the straws in the wind are there. Thus inside the FCO – and very sensibly – there is already a 'Political Cooperation Unit' – so demonstrating that, once the Anglo-Saxon addiction to contingency-planning asserts itself, it enjoys a dispensation from the orthodox diplomatic aversion to hypothetical questions. Not so however in the Berlaymont. Within the Commission there is no such thing as a potential or surrogate 'Community Foreign Ministry', although there are already Commission Delegates running Commission Offices even in capitals outside the Community countries, such as Washington and Canberra. Quite separately too there are constant *ad hoc* joint interventions of the Nine as a group, in various capitals where matters of common interest arise. A case in point was Tehran, when in 1979 the United States Embassy was occupied, its staff taken hostage, and the whole principle of diplomatic immunity jeopardized.

To the average Community functionary, or Representative, it probably seems by now an established, viable, indeed comparatively comfortable working organization. At the same time however, what to them as 'insiders' is an acceptably laborious degree of regular 'horse-trading' may instead lead the ordinary citizen of a Community nation to imagine that it is riven with dissension and bickering. Then again, seen wholly from the outside, to onlooker nations the Community seems already formidable and monolithic. Instances of achievement which for example the outsider can recognize better than the insider, than the involved, are the renegotiation of the Lomé Convention and the Tokyo Round dealing with the General Agreement on Tariffs and Trade (GATT), both within barely the one year. A next stage, already foreseen under the Treaty, is the harmonizing of Community positions in the face of the North/South world economic relationship. This again promises to be an area in which common action will be increasingly likely.

44

So the Community is growing in scope and dimension, despite the many and varied nuances of opinion which its branches shelter. Thus its weaker powers are more federal-minded, lending importance to the centralized bureaucracy of the Commission, whereas the larger and stronger powers take a more confederate view, focussed rather on the Council of Ministers. Of them the French Government is, as we have seen, the most implacably opposed to 'pooling', particularly to the consolidation of diplomatic representation around the world into 'Euro-missions'. Organizationally and financially such a development would certainly seem logical. Many 'Euro-diplomats' consider it already administratively feasible, and only politically and emotively impossible. Some of the new and more militant generation now emerging in the European Parliament believe to the contrary that before long there should and will be 'Euro-embassies' at all but the largest capitals. A favourite suggestion is that such missions should have nationally mixed staff, with successive ambassadors alternating from the different Community countries. One exemption foreseen would probably be the francophone countries of Africa, where the French roots have struck so deep that the absence of a specifically French ambassador would at present be unthinkable. For different cultural reasons, and despite all too familiar counter-indications, something of the same argument might in practice equally be alleged of the English-speaking African countries. In either case, the passage of time, along with the evolution of indigenous institutions, traditions and linguistic habits, might be presumed in due course to dilute, or at any rate refine, such persisting bilateralisms.

While the possibility or impossibility of such institutional pooling is being resolved or ignored, much of what we have seen evolving is therefore happening informally, by custom and almost spontaneously. COREPER itself, the Committee of the Permanent Representatives in Brussels of the member powers, was at the beginning viewed with suspicion by the Commission, as something extraneous, calculated to undermine its supra-national status. Yet even as it swelled to its present immensity of nearer seven than six thousand officials, the Commission grew to accept that the continuing conciliation process between member-states was best achieved not by them – the 'Eurocrats' – but by intergovernmental compromise, by diplomacy rather than by the intrusive mediation of the Commission.

After all, at the intergovernmental level the national officials, the 'Euro-diplomats', were getting to know each other rather well, and practice was beginning to make perfect. COREPER went on meeting constantly at its two levels; meanwhile the Committee of Political Representatives from the home capitals would meet, rather less frequently but still regularly, at Deputy Undersecretary/Director-General level. It is these officials on whom the logistics of the Community, the fog-bound airports and the traffic-jams, lie hardest – almost as hard as on the members of the peripatetic and increasingly self-assertive European Parliament. So it is that in the various Foreign Ministries of the Community there is now a new breed of very senior officials who, overnight bag always at the ready, carry the burden of top-level communication and liaison. Above them are only Ministers, their political masters, who have only the occasional European summit to claim them. Below them their young desk-men are entrenched at home, behind self-replenishing mountains of Community paper. It is therefore those between who commute with Brussels, and among whom a community of their own is being created by the very process of negotiating its divisions and differences.

This tension, the ambivalence between national interest and the growing *esprit de corps* of the Euro-diplomats, is elegantly conveyed in a revealing phrase of Helen Wallace's,[1] that in this elaborate game of Community diplomacy, 'negotiating skills are often more important than the content of policy'. The factors of the equation are all well known. Its resolution lies, and will continue to lie, in the technique of presenting and negotiating them. So perhaps the much vaunted and wholly benign '*copinage technocratique*', the 'camaraderie of expertise' of the Euro-diplomat, is simply a further evolution of the legendary freemasonry of the diplomat, of the 'chers collègues' down the ages – remarked on, frowned on often, but always a powerful element of conciliation and a factor for peace. At times Euro-diplomacy may indeed seem to be evolving into something not unlike that early vision of a Whitehall interdepartmental meeting, only mustered by air-bus rather than by street-omnibus. If so, the practical result cannot but be good for Europe. It should also be good for diplomacy if,

[1] *Op. cit.*, p. 68

with all the old skills still needed, the interplay of the old rivalries is sharpened by proximity and familiarity.

This built-in, continuing and I believe wholesome tension is also one of the features which saves the Community, and the Commission, from being the very boring organizations they might have become, now that the early rapture of Europeanism has subsided, the novelty lost its magic, and the shoe begun to pinch here and there. I have thus heard the cod-war and the Icelandic negotion of 1977 compared almost nostalgically with analogous negotiations since conducted via the Commission; after gunboats, dashing sea-captains and imperturbable ambassadors, all those shrimps, pout-boxes and mesh-sizes must come rather tame. Yet successive Commissioners, the expatriate functionaries making up each national contingent, and the Euro-diplomats working to them – all categories speak with enthusiasm and hope of their task and its future.

Ostensibly this simply should not be. At first sight theirs would seem less a labour of love and idealism than of contract, duty and the reward of a higher standard of living than most of the Community's member-governments have to offer. With its huge tomes of minute regulations, and these in their turn with their clauses in fine print, all corresponding to and directing a flow of trade rich beyond the dreams of individual avarice, the Community mystique should smack rather of banking and the law than of diplomacy. Logically and on material evidence it is hard to imagine any emotional appeal emerging from the Common Market headquarters in Brussels, save perhaps the kind of passion that stampedes rational men after the mirage of some frantic gold-rush. And even then the rainbow's end, the mother-lode finally fought over in the Community, is likely to be prosaically composed of butter-subsidies, green pounds, or illegally ostracized sheep-meat. I have concluded that those who work and thrive in Brussels must do so because for them the Community is a professionally exciting environment where intrinsically unexciting things are achieved in an exciting way. It is 'at the centre of the action'. So it reeks of power, which of all lures to ambition is the most seductive.

The role of the diplomat in Europe may well be to discipline and attenuate this power-imperative, so recurrently obtrusive in the early years of the European Community. The enduring function of the diplomat has always been not to seek and use power for himself, but to temper the impact on history of those who do. So if now he does evolve into a new sub-species of Euro-diplomat, what should become of him is already written large in the conflicting interests already forming him.

This Euro-diplomat will accordingly be prepared to defend as resolutely as ever his country's interests, within the Community and vis-à-vis its fellow-members. Equally he will defend those of the Community within the wider framework of international relationships and his country's other commitments, much as his British predecessors have done for the former Empire and now the Commonwealth. He must be a patriot and a European simultaneously, but with a controlled scale of emphasis. He should be able to interpret the Community's case impartially to his own government, and vice-versa, and not fear to be seen both as excessively 'European' by his home departments and as insufficiently so by his Community colleagues. To these latter he should be able to interpret his home departments with a spokesmanship so authentic that he can not only negotiate for his home officials but, if necessary stand in for them, even interchange with them. He should be able to move without strain from Downing Street to the Berlaymont and on to Washington, Lagos or Madrid, and his house and home accordingly. He should be able to state his country's case and the Community's elegantly and convincingly – and also mantain sincere personal friendships – in at least two European languages other than his own, preferably with two more competently, if not indeed fluently.

It may fairly be claimed that at any rate until very recently Britain's overseas representation was by all these standards outstanding, and not least for its linguistic excellence. Any current decline is largely a matter of educational and social climate, and so remediable. On such criteria the diplomat, as in general he has been, should have no difficulty in evolving into the Euro-diplomat, nor British diplomacy in particular in furnishing a fertile seed-bed for the new sub-species.

Chapter IV
'*Unfair to Vipers!*' - *The F.O.*

'That nest of vipers!' – with this broadside the Rt Hon Enoch Powell, Official Ulster Unionist MP for Down, South, inaugurated the FO's New Year in 1980. Still less enthusiastically he went on to liken them to a 'nursery of traitors' – which is another matter – throwing in a final analogy with the CIA and its erstwhile 'Dirty Tricks Department' for luck.

From the pre-war beginnings of my own recruitment to the Foreign Office I have been inured to the conspiratorial theory of its practices and alignment. When not deemed a 'Mein Kampf'-style tool of 'Freemasonry and The Jews', it was optionally presented as infiltrated instead by 'The Catholics' and, as time went on, by the homosexual community, the Trotskyite underground and, finally – who knows? – even by assorted 'Moles'. So the 'viper' epithet can be shrugged off as just one more such flight of fancy. Its probable explanation is that the bailiwick of the FO – who deal in foreign parts – identifies painfully to Mr Powell with the tiresome Irish Republican neighbours who loom over the garden-wall of his constituency. So presumably he views the FO not so much as on his side as on the other, forgetting a certain cruel tragedy which befell two of their number in Dublin, just down the road.

Even with all these allowances Mr Powell's analysis, with its 'Shut up!, he explained!' approach, seems a notch sterner than the routine criticisms I had grown used to. Thus I had not been perturbed when my old ally in Chapter I from the BBC in the Far East actually prognosticated the doom of diplomacy – 'the last bottle of diplomatic booze' – with the diplomat surviving only as a 'shop-minder between summits'. More often than not such liverish diagnoses are, paradoxically, themselves the aftermath of a surfeit of sincerely offered diplomatic hospitality. Nor did it surprise me to see grave error-by-omission ascribed to Sir Nicholas Henderson's memorable valedictory from Paris via the *Economist* of 2 June 1979, through his overlooking the alleged responsibility of Britain's own 'Anti-French' Diplomatic Service for her problems with Europe.

Such intermittent black legends of intestine partisanships and warring cliques are just another variant of the same old conspiratorial theory, as always re-activated by any latest shift in the focus of international political activity. Thus at the regular peaks of Middle Eastern tensions it is always 'the Foreign Office Arabists' who are adduced as 'weaving and unweaving their monstrous combinations'. Both General de Gaulle and President Giscard d'Estaing have in their time been associated with the corresponding 'anti-French' *canard* now brought out for Sir Nicholas. If I myself seem to contribute to it by my own mild parody of French colleagues of a chapter ago, I can only plead that, in acquiring the data for it, any 'anti-French' extrapolations from my activity and attitude resulted in a nomination for the Legion of Honour. When regretfully I had to decline it – 'My dog shall wear no other man's collar' (Queen Elizabeth I) – the French intermediary commiserated by remarking that, in practice, I was joining a small but far more select order, that of the meritorious 'regretters'. Our honorary status did not, he assured me, go unknown to France; and I have had occasion to experience his assurance in action. So it is that Englishmen, even diplomats, may occasionally feel at cross-purposes with Frenchmen, yet never lose their love for France.

Another critic seeks to substantiate the FO's remoteness from the real world by instancing the complacent titles peculiar to British diplomatic memoirs, bracketing Sir Ivone Kirkpatrick's *Inner Circle* with Sir David Kelly's *Ruling Few*. True, Kirkpatrick saw himself as the fortunate member of a charmed circle. Kelly's enduringly realistic title refers however to a very different and overseas élite. It applies to that effective seat of power in any foreign country to which the working diplomat must address himself and gain access – a very different coterie, immune to the class-war, identical in unbroken political significance and privilege if not in social and economic make-up, impervious to revolution and to the march of generations.

From these few out of many possible instances it wil be clear that criticism based on misapprehension, far from breeding paranoia in the diplomat, immunizes him against it. Accepting popular criticism as an occupational hazard, he is used to it, and owns, or acquires, a skin not so much thick as resilient. Indeed he must. He never knows when he may need it; for apart from still newer hazards, his is a profession in which, in an instant, that which is ceremonial can become pompous, and the solemn absurd. Where however he tends to be and must be hypersensitive is when anatomizing his own Service and his colleagues. He is probably – on the one hand – rather fond of them both personally, and equally – on the other – could not bear injuring them in that institutional capacity which the diplomat, however humanly individual, carries around with him as does a snail its shell.

'On-the-one-hand/On-the-other!' That prudent ambidextral image, as of some slowed-down Hindu deity, is so traditional to diplomacy that Britain even celebrated her accession to Europe by a numismatic elaboration of it. She struck a fifty-pence commemorative coin displaying a manual circuit, endlessly joining nine national hands, in what a well-known satirical weekly would define as an ongoing hand-gripping situation! Yet it is a reality that, with personal affections obtruding 'on the one hand', therefore 'on the other hand' any forward look at the British component of diplomacy must bring in its own institutional caveats. Since such forecasting necessarily has recourse to retrospection, inevitably it must subject itself to precise inhibitions – professional, legal, even social and conventional.

There is, of course, the much disputed Official Secrets Act. Reputable voices would deny it any further extension of scope. Having in my own experience seen far more of the havoc its flouting can inflict on the public weal than its over-zealous application, I have always assumed its intent to be honourable. When for example the factors of patriotism, and of the national well-being and security come in, then even the 'thirty-year rule' for official documentation must be a nominal and minimal self-discipline; at this point discretion should be 'for ever', no matter what the law. Then there is a further and civilized convention, that for fifteen years members of the Diplomatic Service – and presumably others – do not abuse the confidentiality of officially acquired information by using it to portray their colleagues, or the quality of their advice and performance. I see this understanding as simply the formalization of what should be, but is not always, a normal convention – likewise 'for ever' – to the effect that no one should use 'insider-information' maliciously or sensationally. It is a discourtesy to peddle gossip – even at times for a Pepys, a Boswell, an Evelyn, or a member of the Inner Cabinet.

With these reservations, I like to believe that from the objectivity – the hindsight even – of professional retirement, I am better able than from the fray to reckon how the British diplomat will fit into the new pattern of diplomacy. The qualities of the new man are nascent in the old, along with those of his successor-organization; it has never been a wise updating totally to sever the new from its traditional roots, since affection and loyalty cannot be created full-blown from scratch. Significantly enough, the Foreign Office was long and affably known to its habitués as 'The Old Firm'. The custom seems however to have faded, perhaps because of changed attitudes, perhaps, too, since another entity, the American CIA – the Central Intelligence Agency – became more publicly tagged as 'The Firm'.

This near-plagiarism, or at any rate overlap of names, came close to costing me dear, even irreparably so, during the months when I was held captive by the Tupamaro urban guerrillas in Uruguay. On only two occasions was I reasonably sure that my captors were genuinely allowing me a message through, to assure my wife of my continuing existence. One of substance did reach her. I included in it a cheerful phrase to the effect that she could count unreservedly on 'The Old Firm'. By this of course she needed no telling that I meant the Foreign Office; but unwittingly – and happily only briefly – my harmless shorthand was taken by the Tupamaro censorship as confirming their worst suspicions about my true function; they were better equipped than I in the newest television jargon, including 'The Company' and 'The Firm' as synonyms for the CIA. Fortunately my disconcernment, and amusement too, when my hosts challenged me as a multinational intelligence operative, were taken as confirming my formal status as just an ordinary British diplomat, if perhaps a little too breezy about his parent body's tradition.

Not all the successive Secretaries of State whom I recall have seemed to me totally to embody this tradition. In any event, their assorted personalities and idiosyncracies, however anecdotally rewarding, are in the main immaterial to my theme of the future shape of the diplomatic profession, with perhaps one single exception – their individual atitude to, and proclivity for, leaving their desk to travel abroad.

Here I must confess that, despite much investigation, I have failed to disentangle how far it is the element of personal *Wanderlust* or official obligation that determines the mobility of our leaders, both in the Foreign Office and across the road at Number Ten Downing Street. As a generalization, however, those most professionally static among them seem also to have been temperamentally the most equable. One of my own favourite categorizations of people is into those who are 'one man' and those who are not. Ernest Bevin, Michael Stewart, Alec Home – all these of their line were unmistakably 'one man'. All three, I suspect, also liked to keep their absences from their desk to a minimum, though by Lord Home's time there was evidently little they could do about it – apart form anything else with the sheer problem of 'returning calls'.

In this changed world, Foreign Secretaries and Prime Ministers have had travel thrust upon them. By my rough reckoning, however, one overseas trip a month per Foreign Secretary was about the average through the Brown, Stewart, Home, Callaghan and Crosland eras, with the then Mr George Brown rather exceeding the score, Michael Stewart almost halving it, and Doctor David Owen afterwards, between 1977 and 1979, nearly doubling it. Meantime their respective Prime Ministers held their own excursions down to a steady half that of their Foreign Secretaries.

During his tenure Dr Owen evidently sought travel out, as well as having it thrust upon him. One cause was, no doubt, his engrossment in matters African, frequently involving an oblique approach to the Dark Continent, with for example a detour via Washington and the United Nations in New York. Statistically a more normal and contemporary logistical yardstick might be the first six months in office of his successor, Lord Carrington. It could be argued that the new Secretary of State had in reality far more freedom and leisure to travel than his predecessors, sitting as he did in the House of Lords, and with a Deputy Foreign Secretary to take care of the usual parliamentary commitments of his office, such as Question-Time and policy debates. Yet listing his movements during that first half-year, it is difficult to see which of his journeys, had he been sitting, and required, in the Commons, he might have delegated to, say, a Minister of State.

53

Nor, conversely, do any of his trips bear the stamp of spontaneous tourism for its own sake, let alone of officiousness or self-aggrandisement; each of his journeys justifies itself as necessary in its context.

In that first half-year of office I calculate that Lord Carrington made twenty-three overseas journeys – an average of almost one a week, though he did have something of a rest between Lusaka in early August 1979, and the UN in late September. Six of those trips were *ex officio*, 'recurrent unavoidables' – the half-yearly NATO ministerial meeting, the Council of the EEC Foreign Ministers, etc. etc. The rest were all of an 'extraordinary' character, imposed by the nature of the new diplomacy – *ad hoc* meetings with foreign governments, direct discussions with other foreign governments, direct discussions with other Foreign Ministers, state visits accompanying the Prime Minister or, in one case, the Queen. Most were day-return trips, or overnight only. Two alone were prolonged, each of a week or more. In general however Lord Carrington was a lucky man when he slept in his own bed and country for an entire week at a stretch.

From such a timetable it is revealing, and interesting to see, that the Secretary of State for Foreign Affairs himself is by no means totally insulated from the discomforts and inconveniences of the new diplomacy. True, there is VIP treatment, intended – quite rightly – to safeguard the top negotiator's time for rest, preparation, and the execution of his assignment. Much is done for him. He probably never even sees his passport, flight-ticket, a customs-form, or a laundry-list. He may, being of Cabinet rank, have the privilege and comfort of his wife's company. When 'on tour' he, his staff and the escorting press-corps enjoy all the amenities of a commodious four-jet VC10 aircraft, discreetly converted by the Royal Air Force into a 'Flying Foreign Office', with perhaps less of the splendour of the US1 presidential Boeing but, by all accounts, rather more in the way of ease and atmosphere. But he must still cope with jet-lag, time-zones, and a shattered circadian rhythm. With all the cosseting, and however resilient he may be, a Foreign Secretary on tour is exposed to the same basic tensions and preoccupations as the humblest junior officer ever airborne.

It is just as well. He should know that in a changing Service its servitudes loom larger than its grandeurs. It is impossible for his troops to isolate what may seem to be temporary and personal occupational worries – inconvenient postings, separation, promotion blocks, premature retirement – from the ground-swells of the larger world. It is these major changes in function which, more often than not, are the deep-seated causes of anxiety, underlying all the departmental budgeting and economic electioneering. Of these trends the increasingly well-organized 'Diplomatic Wives' – and not only the British – are the most vigilant monitors.

If the role and status of the diplomat around the world are going to change, to evolve perhaps into something rather different, the first to feel it, probably to know it, will be his wife. The diplomat's wife seldom becomes demoralized; but she does worry. She has a nose for trouble, even though immediate hazard – amounting often to imminent physical danger – usually leaves her commendably self-possessed. But long-term uncertainty, that emotional tooth-ache, tends to compound in her a special permanent vulnerability. Its essence, a vestigial blight of exile and Empire shared by all overseas wives, and now often by those of the Third World, derives mainly from the pain of separation – from country, home and, above all, children. The transition from sail and steam to subsonic and supersonic helps only relatively. No matter how alleviated by the formerly inconceivable provision of concessionary holiday fares, nothing will ever convey the stoical anguish of the exiled mother, watching that twice-yearly charter-flight hoist itself from some tropical runway, bearing back to school – or, surely, to the nightmare of some unimaginable aeronautical catastrophe – the small, subdued, slightly sweating tweed-jacketed figure she loves best of its kind in the world. Diplomats and their families have coped for centuries with what the multi-national corporations, or their psychiatrists, have just invented as the 'Executive Gypsy Syndrome'.

But now there are newer anxieties. The goal-posts have been moved since she and her husband joined the game, as its style and even its rules have been modified. The pitch is bigger. The team suffers increasingly from the anonymity of size. If the scope of international diplomacy has widened, the Service too has grown with it. So too, with increased governmental intervention in the affairs of individuals and nations, has the ministerial component of British diplomacy, in many ways at the expense of the career diplomat.

True, the Permanent Under-Secretary of the Foreign and Commonwealth Office now has a Deputy Permanent Under-Secretary to help him out; for a while he even had two. Yet a generation ago nothing and nobody stood between the Permanent Under-Secretary and his Secretary of State. No mere Parliamentary Under-Secretary would have tried; he simply did not carry the guns. Even when Ministers of State were invented to spread the load, it would have been a brave one, or a fool-hardy Private Secretary, who sought to interpose a Minister of State, let alone several, between the Head of the Foreign Office – Lord Strang was a case in point – and his political master. So today the ambitious wife – there are such in all walks – must often ask herself whether the glittering star at which her husband so constantly has aimed has not sunk against a changed horizon. However, her husband, if he is less motivated than she – this too can happen – may adduce a compensating reassurance. His ever more peripatetic Foreign Secretary, and the increasing cohort of junior Foreign Office Ministers, are going to need ever more professional help and guidance, thanks to the ferociously intensive briefing needed for their enlarged and incessantly changing spectrum of negotiating themes.

This proliferation, and international mobilization, of Foreign Office Ministers from the political side may well therefore open the field to more and more gifted junior diplomats. It could, however, correspondingly encroach on the area of policy-forming, so leaving fewer and less responsible top posts for them to fill as, in the fullness of time, they blossom into outstanding seniors. Already the FO has more than fulfilled its norm in producing the percentage staff-cuts required by the latest national emergency. Fifteen overseas posts were closed in one year. Euphemistically styled schemes expediting premature retirement are fought off, rally, and return to the charge. Room at the top, exiguous on any pyramid, can only diminish further as it is eroded by all these outside frictions into a pinnacle.

The reasons are all common knowledge, and accepted philosophically by the Diplomatic Service as well as the public. They know that Britain's place in the world – still a surprisingly good one, if capable of being made much better – has been affected by her loss of military and economic power. They accept that summitry has diminished the role of the ambassador, to which they all aspire, in favour of negotiation at ministerial level. The ambassador's own work will accordingly be less 'political', and have an increasingly economic and commercial bias – if indeed that distinction retains any validity; it is for example interesting to see how much the work of, say, the ambassador in Washington entails continuing negotiation on such self-sustaining themes. Civil aviation and aerospace policy, bilateral and multilateral trade, economic summitry – all these create a daily agenda ostensibly not so momentous and dramatic as strategic arms limitation, Rhodesia or the Middle East, yet the real stuff of which useful careers are made.

There is however one adverse factor against which the average ambassador will have to draw on all his own internal resources. It has to do with that same anonymity of size, a certain impersonality, which has pervaded the Service, leaving only a handful of very senior or very resourceful ambassadors, the tapestry of whose working lives has not been dimmed and faded by it. It has to do also with the sense of belonging, another manifestation of what was called *esprit de corps*; and it may not be under-rated. As an instance, the governments to which an ambassador is accredited overseas assume that he, like their own ambassadors, is on terms of personal acquaintance and informality with his Foreign Secretary, and indeed Head of State; if successful in his mission, he will usually achieve the same relationship with them too. When, inevitably, they find out that with the complexities of British society today this picture is erroneous, the ambassador's stature and impact are diminished, unless his personality and local 'legend' more than compensate – as fortunately is still quite often the case.

Conversely, when for example the Secretary of State for Foreign Affairs is reported as descending from his aircraft in, say, Ankara, and giving the ambassador a warm greeting, and his wife a kiss on the cheek, the ambassador's local credibility is correspondingly and enormously enhanced. Not enough attention and sensitivity have lately been devoted by officialdom to significant detail of this kind, partly perhaps owing to social and administrative changes in the Service. For post-war expansion, and the end of the old, club-like ethos, have not yet developed instead a new Old School Tie as has, say, the the French Ecole d'Administration Publique, whose post-war alumni are all mandarins together. A present day British ambassador is lucky if he ever eats informally with his Secretary of State, or even with his junior Ministers. He is even

57

luckier, and all the better kitted for his new posting if, as well as by the invaluably gazetted 'kissing hands' at the Palace, he is able to substantiate acquaintance with the Head of State whose person he embodies abroad, by the testimony of a signed personal photograph for desk, study or drawing-room.

Such signs of confidence count. So too, negatively, has the considerable withdrawal of traditional 'honours' from the nation's overseas representatives. Applied with particular dedication by the first Wilson government, it was continued by its successors of all complexions. By now of course many of the diplomats in the game have joined it since those particular intangible goal-posts were shifted, and so subscribe philosophically to the new unspoken rule. But many pre-Wilson survivors still do not. So the withdrawal of what used to be an authentic professional motivation, and not just a nominal and automatic 'perk', has created a real sense that the Diplomatic Service has been diminished in public esteem and comprehension, and its members in professional recognition, or what is now termed 'comparability'.

Nor is it just a question of those aggrieved wives who, it was sometimes unkindly said, had always hoped to be a lady at the last. Even their less insecure predecessors, titled and bemedalled, subjects of so many an Edwardian vignette, were never really the risible Osbert Lancaster clichés of stereotype. Nor were they figures of fun, simply because their hope and expectation was to withdraw from public life with the *nunc dimittis* of a husband's 'K', rather than the more quantifiable testimonials of today. It was indeed a perceptive immigrant writer who sympathized with those who haunt 'that limbo between the CBE and the knighthood'.

The cutback in diplomatic honours has worked out as a particularly selective disavowal of the career. Honours still do pertain and count in Britain – recently in strange and inexplicable nooks and crannies of the national life. Yet recognition – the esteem of his countrymen and of those to whom he was on their behalf accredited abroad – these have always been a principal reward and incentive to a profession in which disinterestedness and intangible recognition have to be, or should be, a way of life. It is, after all, ironic that Philby, Britain's 'one-off' arch-traitor, was promoted General – and with some ostentation – by the government which had suborned him in his teens – a category of accolade to which he could doubtfully have aspired in his ostensible capacity at home. British governments would do well to repose an extra dose of overt confidence in those selected to embody them abroad, as indeed they did until recently. If to be hand-picked smacks of the contemporary heresy of élitism, and to be seen to be hand-picked even more so, then so be it. A country which to the contrary were to choose its overseas spokesmen for their mediocrity, and by the random shake of the bingo-bag, and ignore their aptitudes, would have only itself to blame.

Even more than negative indifference, the withdrawal of a sense of mattering, it is an awareness of positive discrimination that alerts a Service whose natural position in the world is always an exposed one. Very strikingly all-round staff cuts, reductions of function shared with the rest of the public sector, do not alarm the diplomat. Admittedly, and rightly, with the 'Think-Tank' they hollered before they were hurt, loud and clear. Its selective and active hostility provoked a defensive reaction which some commentators have found diverting, others merely hypersensitive. In reality the *odium theologicum* of its fluently documented flying-squad, for what it evidently had anticipated to be a bastion of élitism, was not funny at all, and wasted a great opportunity battering down a door already open. For though averse to control by the Civil Service Department, the rising generation inside the Diplomatic Service are noticeably adjusted to the concept of a smaller, more stream-lined Service. What produces the perceptible and uncharacteristic tension behind the traditional, if today less stylized urbanity of the young British diplomat and his wife, is nothing more than a moral uncertainty, analogous in some ways to that of a young Jesuit, weighing the pros and cons of his possible laicisation.

At an earlier stage of social transformation Ernest Bevin, a Labour minister, inspired total confidence in the apolitical Diplomatic Service of which he took charge. Lately, at a similar time, there has been no evidence that his distant Labour successor, Dr David Owen – whom I do not know – can claim the same achievement. During his tenure of office as Secretary of State for Foreign Affairs his 'image' was one of chronic irritation with his diplomats, an aversion which could only have added to the increasingly oppressive sense that they and their work no longer mattered. Many of them have especially felt a loss of recognition as against that very British industry for which they do permanent battle overseas. So more and more middle-ranking diplomats have the uneasy suspicion that they may, any minute now, be 'laicised', and need to seek a second career in the private sector. Any devaluation of their professional expertise, not least in trade promotion overseas, jeopardizes therefore an accepted escape-route from planned redundancy in the public sector. In reality, of course, the protean, 'multiple-specialist' nature of his business and formation means that any good diplomat can usually make a formidable businessman, as many secondments and early retirements exemplify.

Another and basically well-intentioned proposal – so-called 'interchange', or mutual secondments and transfers between the Home and Diplomatic Services – has yet again had wives even more concerned than their husbands. They foresaw the 'flyers' of the Home Civil Service picking and choosing the plums among the Diplomatic Service's most attractive postings, and elbowing their career diplomat husbands out to remote, desert places and dull, dead-end functions. They also take a wifely and sceptical view of the growing incidence of diplomacy-by-conference; often it necessitates 'temporary' marital separations of months at a stretch, vulnerable to conversion into more permanent ones, presuming the available wiles of secretarial ladies, deploying the particular seductiveness of that which is *in situ*. Less imaginatively, and all too realistically, wives more than anyone must watch the diplomatic career drawn into an increasing world violence which no longer acknowledges the concept and safeguards of diplomatic immunity. Though a separate theme of its own, violence as a new hazard to the diplomat and his family is yet another factor shaping the future of his profession, and yet another goal-post, or moral boundary-line, which has shifted under his eyes.

All these are real concerns which I believe merit more than nominal or administrative attention. They call for leadership and visible personal involvement from Secretaries of State, and for greater understanding, frankness and identification from administrations. Technically the Foreign Office has never enjoyed so much, so comprehensive and so efficient 'welfare' in its history. There are entire departments, sections and offices to deal with the 'sociology', as it were, of its members' personal problems. Yet never, I believe, has it been so detached, and so lacking in human warmth. From time to time I come into brief contact with young officials who are what I hope I was thirty or more years ago. From them emanates a warm-hearted and cheerful courtesy amounting, I find, almost to a sort of affection. Yet the place in which they work, the rather battered old Palazzo, which should be 'like home' despite its architectural grandiosities, remains cold and impersonal. The denizens of its corridors walk them too fast and too preoccupied. Behind all the FO's first-name convention, the light that bathes them from above has the warmth not of the sun but of the fluorescent tube.

My wife is as it happens an expert in the keener hazards of professional separation. While I was kidnapped by urban guerrillas, and she usually presumed she was a widow, she had sensibly suggested, for the comfort and reassurance of other wives conceivably exposed to comparable circumstances, an instant roster of Foreign Office wives who would daily get in touch with them and keep an eye on their well-being. When first she pointed out this special loneliness of a wife desperately awaiting news of a husband missing or endangered overseas, the immensely 'senior wife' present interjected 'But wives at home aren't expected to be social!'

There is no reason why compassion cannot be institutionalized via a willing human intermediary. Some such injection is therefore due, into a Service some of whose magnates cannot see, and have personally denied to me, that Service morale is under pressure at all. That the Diplomatic Service and its individual members are not demoralized, despite a most unpropitious international and domestic climate, is to their immense credit. Only a tiny minority would, for example, contemplate recourse to the strike weapon in any circumstance. But their tenaciously enduring morale needs to be fostered, and neither put out of mind nor taken for granted. Their excellent Diplomatic Service Association, functioning gallantly at the administrative level, needs to be recognized and developed at the personal level, encouraged by a warmer and more individual relationship between its members and their masters, both professional and political.

When the rest of the public service and the nation are tightening the belt, it is not the Diplomatic Service that is going to clamour for 'special case' status, or to falsify economy here by offsetting expenditure elsewhere. Unlike other 'industries' in the throes of transformation, the current needs of diplomacy involve no major social cost. Even so, they lie just as much in the area where wisdom, the prospect of stability, consideration, even compassion are most required. Just how much successive governments have failed to stand by their overseas representatives, and how dim the lustre of their head-office at home has become, is evident from so vituperative a testimonial from the important if particularly vehement statesman heading this chapter. A total communication-gap may be presumed when a legislator so closely conversant with the machinery of government can choose as his scapegoat those who do not decide foreign policy, but execute it, those whose task is not what is done, but how.

I can think of no sadder commentary on the need for the re-evocation of the old Foreign Office *esprit de corps* than the rather poignant reflection of one retired but still active ambassador. Less lucky than me perhaps in this respect, his experience is nevertheless far from unique. 'The day you retire,' he mused, 'it's as if you'd never belonged.'

Chapter V
Parachutism or Progress?

The preceding chapter suggests that any problems besetting the British diplomat, as his profession enters its newest phase, are largely the product of his times – intangible, even hypothetical. What does he do, however, about their more substantial manifestations? Does it matter, for example, if large and vigorous cuckoos from without are intermittently deposited in his family nest? Are these intrusions – in the *lingua franca* of diplomacy commonly known as parachutists – on the increase? Do they mean that the negotiating function is being diverted from the professional diplomat to the professional politician? Is diplomatic representation reverting to the up-dated equivalent of the eighteenth century and earlier, when the envoy himself was some great lord, with a scrivener of humble function and bearing to lend him expert support?

A certain Latin American *caudillo* is reputed to have decreed that, as from a given tomorrow morning, his turbulent country was to be a traditional peace-loving democracy. Something of the same may have happened to the Diplomatic Service, with the designation as a 'tradition' of a gently increasing number of top ambassadorial appointments allocated to political nominees. The British representation to the United States is the oldest and most accepted case in this category. Distinguished lay ambassadors there whom I have known go back as far as Lord Halifax, with his famous acknowledgement of an aggressively neutralist egg thrown in his face before Pearl Harbor – 'How lucky you are to have them to throw!' It aroused American sympathies for a Britain at war well before the USA was involved, displaying a precocious sense of public relations which any career ambassador a generation later could have envied, yet speaking also with the unfeignable voice of total sincerity.

This episode could be taken as embodying the whole special

status of the Washington embassy. The career Diplomatic Service seems to be reconciled to it, their misgivings mollified by a virtual alternation of the appointment between such outside designates, each bringing their particular qualification, and the most senior and successful career ambassador available at the time. Thus Lord Harlech's special attribute was primarily his close personal friendship with President Kennedy; if he was an unusually young top ambassador, the Head of State to whom he was accredited was an unusually young President too. Similarly Lord Cromer's most outstanding qualification was no doubt his most timely banking expertise. It could be said that all of these appointments were political only in the most generalized sense; all were men who would have made their mark at any task they took up, if provided with the expert technical and local support which, for that matter, a career ambassador appointed to a large and difficult post also expects and requires.

A less orthodox exception to the Foreign Office rule of a career diplomacy, with its ambassadors normally recruited only from within the Diplomatic Service, was the appointment in 1968 of the comparatively young Christopher Soames to the British Embassy in Paris. As Sir Winston Churchill's son-in-law, the loss of his parliamentary seat in 1966 must have been a blow not only to himself but to those Conservatives who saw side-tracked in him the best equipped of the new generation of potential Tory leaders. By training and temperament an intensely political figure, his award of a choice alternative to the political office dashed momentarily from his grasp seemed, coming from a Labour government, so elaborately apolitical as almost to justify the speculation what its political significance really was. However, the Paris Embassy, too, had its own 'tradition' of special exemption from the rule of career incumbency; the Duff Coopers not so long before had embodied it with *éclat*.

So eyebrows only, and no hackles, were raised in career circles sufficiently 'papabile' to register disappointment at the temporary loss to the service of a major plum. In the event this philosophical acceptance was vindicated by the 'Affaire Soames', when President de Gaulle's lunchtime reflections on Anglo-French relations echoed so promptly and loudly in Bonn that another ambassador's career might well have been shattered. Only Christopher Soames, it was felt, could have survived the 'Soames Affair'. Equally of course, without him there would have been no 'Soames Affair'; only he could have been close enough to the remarkable General to find himself in a position from which, in turn, only he could extricate himself. So just as personal factors had enormously amplified the potency of Lord Harlech's mission to the Camelot of President Kennedy, so too the Soames appointment earned a special dividend in the approach of Britain to the European Community, in which afterwards Lord Soames, as he since became, played a forceful role as Vice-President of the Commission.

Where however not only hackles but voices too were raised was at a less 'traditional' non-career appointment, as Permanent British Delegate to the United Nations in 1974, in replacement of a Diplomatic Service officer only recently installed. Raised not, it must emphatically be added, by the ostensible victim, whose amiable stoicism when apparently 'limogé' only added further to the subsequent achievements for which he was anyhow destined. Sir Donald Maitland's spartan professionalism soon reaped its due reward, his apparent eclipse lasting less than two years.

Before New York he had been seconded from the Foreign Office to 'Number Ten' as press secretary to the Conservative Prime Minister, Mr Heath, and was then appointed by his government, in the event so ephemerally, to the New York post. In other countries the move could have been taken as a political reward, but in the British Diplomatic Service it was an unremarkable and appropriate sequel to a successful series of sensitive postings. What was not normal was that, within months of what should be and usually is a long-term appointment, Donald Maitland should have been recalled, after the Labour victory at the February 1974 General Election, and superseded by a Labour parliamentarian who had lost his seat, Mr Ivor Richard.

The ambassadorial appointments of many governments – and for some reason especially that to the United Nations in New York – can rate equally as dust-bin or pork-barrel, exile or accolade, political punishment or reward. Since the British Foreign Office, with an essentially professional career-structure, has never followed such procedures in its diplomatic appointments, the question at once arose among the diplomatic fraternity just what Mr Richard could do that any good career ambassador could not? In the event, he seems to have done it competently, on the direct evidence of radio and television. So for that matter did subsequently his career successor too. Even so, the appointment seemed to take political encroachment on the career a stage further, and to raise several questions.

Any possible reflection on his predecessor, or inconvenience caused by this upheaval to him and his family, have since been dealt with by events, and by the personality of the diplomat concerned. It might also be claimed that the United Nations is *sui generis*, by the nature of things a 'special case', with its annual importation of political figures into the General Assembly Delegation, and with the precedent of an earlier non-career Permanent Head; Lord Caradon, of the West-Country Roundhead Foot family, already a distinguished public servant in retirement, had been sent to New York with deliberately enhanced status as Minister in the government of the day.

Even so, these latest appearances were open to much interpretation. It was a fair assumption, corroborated ultimately by events, that Mr Richard's mission would not outlast a change of government. And the British diplomat's secret nightmare has always been a Diplomatic Service hitched to a party-wagon, with the career official just as co-extensive with the party-man as any Soviet Russian *apparatchik* – save that in the British two-party case such affiliation could mean a total ambassadorial reshuffle with every General Election.

It is also pertinent to remark that, in the autumn of the year 1979, with Mr Richard barely back from the United Nations after the next General Election, international events were such as to stimulate much commentary on that body's proceedings. He was accordingly in demand, on the radio for example, for his assessment of them. As it happens I have also meanwhile found myself listening – and with some misgiving – to interviews on radio and television with the ambassadors in London of various foreign powers, eliciting their governments' version of controversial events involving their country. Is not such a virtual apologia, going over the head of the receiving government, a direct appeal to its public? At what point therefore does a degree of accessibility, latterly a public-relations norm for diplomatic representatives, become propaganda, a by-passing of the host government, and so effectively an interference in its internal affairs?

Clearly a public figure, freshly returned from some crisis-spot abroad, and therefore highly knowledgeable, is ideal fodder for a broadcast interview. Recourse to the expertise of an ambassador, whether foreign or one's own, may well therefore come to be a valuable new source of coverage for the news media. All these innovations are still, however, relatively experimental, and they may conceal their traps. Certainly returned ambassadors, fresh home from a posting in which they have acquired 'insider-information', have not as a rule employed it to provide a public commentary on the circumstances of their recent post. If this were to become normal practice the confidentiality of their previous activity there could come under question, the future discretion and credibility of their successor be put in doubt, and the 'usual channels' with their own government seem, or be, short-circuited. For this reason the career ambassador does not usually figure publicly as an authority on the current affairs of the country where he has lately been *en poste*. But which practice is right today – the old or the new?

Mr Richard's tenure of office at the United Nations coincided with another and, in its national context, more orthodoxly political appointment. The mission of Mr Andrew Young, the American negro leader who was United States Ambassador at the United Nations till August 1979, may well prove to have had an important negative influence on the future of diplomacy. Though Mr Richard paid a warm tribute to him on his resignation, Andrew Young had used his political position very differently; and it may be taken as a classic demonstration, if not a hideous warning, of what can become of political appointments to diplomatic missions. His importance to President Carter lay evidently in the electoral appeal to the negro vote of a gifted, articulate, mercurial and successful fellow-negro. In international affairs he himself, quite understandably, gave corresponding priority to racial issues. In the process he associated Great Britain, and her Foreign Secretary, Dr David Owen, with a particular and radical approach to Southern African affairs. The Conservative government elected in May 1979 promptly disowned it. Meanwhile Mr Young had alienated Britain's sympathies by publicly accusing her of institutionalizing racism on a gigantic scale, indeed of 'almost inventing it'. On his own domestic front this personable but all too predictably outspoken ambassador had, *inter alia*, compared a much delayed judicial execution in his own country to the summary killings then proceeding in Iran, and had outraged patriotic sentiment by applauding the Cuban troops in Angola for 'bringing stability' to that country. He had also implied that persecuted Soviet dissidents were paralleled by 'political prisoners' in the USA. The last straw for an exasperated State Department – and White House – was when he attended an 'unauthorized' meeting with the unrecognized Palestine Liberation Organization; his resignation was accepted with alacrity.

The Andrew Young saga is relevant to most of what is happening to professional diplomacy today. The final and abrupt termination of his mission, after so many blithely repeated apologies, was inevitable not so much because – of apparently his own initiative – he might have committed his government beyond their intention, i.e. have perpetrated a 'sponsion' (v. Chapter X). In addition however, while not conceding that he had actually lied to his government about the episode, he did admit that he had not told them the whole truth. To a career diplomat any such prevarication is an unthinkable breach of professional ethic, duty and loyalty. To Mr Young, with the leverage of the negro vote to support him, it was evidently a mere political liberty which he could risk taking. Mr Young therefore never was a diplomat while in the execution of his mission – a gifted politician, even perhaps to some a statesman, by his venturing onto the Palestinian high-wire, but by no manner of means a diplomat. The principal significance of his diplomatic career may well indeed have been to exemplify just what a diplomat is not, and to personify the hazards of installing as such a professional politician.

A less cerebral and more appealing version of the same phenomenon – almost by Alan Drury out of Molière – was recently portrayed in the Foreign Service Journal of the United States State Department. According to it a certain up-dated and real-life Monsieur Jourdain, appointed ambassador 'somewhere east of Suez', for political services rendered, publicly and repeatedly demonstrated blank ignorance of elementary international data, ranging from the identity of President Giscard d'Estaing, via the partition of Korea, to the difference between India and Pakistan. Officials and notables of the host country evidently enjoyed his successive malapropisms as much as his own staff did not.

British diplomacy has so far been spared such mortifications. Some time ago however there was a more than usually laconic correspondence in *The Times* on 'the career diplomat'. The question how he differed from other kinds, such as 'amateur, part-time and nepotist', was answered by a former British ambassador, of both professional and literary eminence. Sir Nicholas Cheetham supplied as a British definition of the species 'One who, after passing a difficult examination, has spent his working life in HM Diplomatic Service.' As a good diplomat would, he himself considered it more charitable to refrain from exemplifying the other kinds. Along with Sir Nicholas, all of the rising generation too of British diplomats quite naturally share this aversion to any form of induced embolism in the anatomy of their profession. What is impressive however is that it should also be shared, and even more vehemently, by those still functioning at the summit of their profession, who by their eminence have no further vested interest in excluding the outsider, or 'parachutist'. I cannot think of one who does not ultimately consider political appointments, even of the best material and to the most 'traditionally' justifiable postings, both injurious to long-term Service recruitment and exacting of an immediate penalty in morale. The Service accepts them courteously and hospitably, as it should, and indeed as public servants must. Essentially it makes do with them, but would on the whole rather not.

So much so that I tried out on one or two of them a small experiment in devil's advocacy, seeking to rationalize an increase in politically inspired appointments in terms of the present social and political reality. Once again I returned to the invaluable David Kelly, with his *Ruling Few*[1], the power-nexus to which the diplomat abroad must axiomatically apply himself. In the past, I contended, the oligarchic connotation of diplomacy meant that the ambassador, when he spoke to the 'Ruling Few' at his post abroad, did so with the voice of an equivalent 'Ruling Few' at home. As recently as a couple of generations ago the ambassador was close to, part of, a bipartisan consensus, of aims if not always of political means, a 'Ruling Few' which we would today call the 'Establishment' of its time. Now we have no consensus, I suggested; and a different 'Establishment', composed of industrialists, economists, parliamentarians, broadcasting personalities, trades unionists, leading columnists – all with a powerfully political identification themselves.

[1] Op. cit.

Indeed, I postulated, given the potency and polarization of our two-party system, it could almost be said that today we have two roughly alternating Establishments. It might now therefore be more realistic, and efficient, to accept that, if an ambassador is to function with real authority, he should probably be nominated from the current Establishment. Coming from that which is in power, he would speak for it, and to it, with the voice of authenticity. On this basis, I suggested, there would seem to be no logical reason why the ambassadorial Letters of Credence signed by the Sovereign, and which once resulted from an accident of birth and a system of education, and later from an apolitical selection process, should not be prompted today by an arbitrary and politically inspired initial on a new Secretary of State's minute, or even by a nod from the democratically elected legislature, as personified in the latest Prime Minister of the day.

Needless to say, my revolutionary hypothesis – that henceforth only political appointments would really work out – was brushed aside on a wave of outspoken comparison with other countries, in which those diplomats with professional training endure permanently secondary status vis-à-vis the majority of their Heads of Mission, who are generally brought in from without, and for political reasons. What no serving British diplomat ever mentions however – though it may be at the back of his mind – is any analogy with Britain's own and never-to-be-forgotten 'Affaire Jay'; her Diplomatic Service have been commendably – some would say excessively – laconic and conscientious in the discretion of their reaction to an innovation so remarkable and so potentially explosive to the structure of their Service. As a result consideration of it must rest largely on the not ungenerous press coverage dedicated to the episode, expanded by a retrospective effort in thought-transference, empathy, and imaginative shoe-swapping with today's working diplomats and tomorrow's Heads of Mission.

What then would I have done, or felt if, twenty or more years younger, I had learnt out of the blue that our most senior ambassador, a successful former 'high-flyer', highly esteemed as a model for emulation by all right-minded and ambitious juniors, had suddenly been ousted. Nor had he been declared *persona non grata* by the United States Government for some unspeakable offence, but rather, to add insult to injury, declared *persona* 'fuddy-duddy' by inspired rumour promptly laughed out of court.

Furthermore Sir Peter Ramsbotham's replacement was to be – as it happened – the Prime Minister's son-in-law, Mr Peter Jay, a personable and brilliant young economist and television personality. Had he been a career diplomat of the same age and attributes, he would have already been rated a 'flyer' and earmarked for great things, and already due for his own department in the Foreign Office, or for a desk overseas as Head of Chancery to someone like Sir Peter Ramsbotham. Like Sir Donald Maitland at bay before him, Sir Peter Ramsbotham did not bat an eyelid either. Even had I ever spoken to him about it he would not have offered any comment, any more than would have Sir Donald Maitland in his time; though I know both, I know their likely responses even better.

So we can restrict ourselves to considering the evidence of the public domain alone. On the one side a very successful career ambassador, in his fifties, incumbent, not yet due for transfer, not identified either politically with his home government or personally with any particular régime or coterie in his host-country. On the other a comparatively young man, young certainly for his forties; as dynastically Socialist as, say, Christopher Soames is Tory; computer-dated to appeal to the youthful and exuberant image and entourage of the Carter régime; a recognized economic writer; a skilled television practitioner, already a star in fact, with his own top-rated current-affairs programme; handsome, articulate, front-cover-rated by Time Magazine. A close friend of the similarly youthful, photogenic and star-rated Labour Foreign Secretary who technically nominated him, he was obviously potential public-service material anyhow, needing only a decade or so of political activity or professional achievement to lend him major substance. By that time, with Washington come round and available again as a political plum, Peter Jay might well have been the natural candidate for the post. In 1977 however his comparative youth still required the underlying *gravitas* which the British public – and most receiving governments – even today see as an essential component of senior statesmanship, however attractive the overall personality. This disqualification would normally have excluded him from any such candidature almost as effectively as his other fatal handicap, that of having the Prime Minister of the day as his father-in-law.

71

That it was not so fatal, and that he was nevertheless nominated, has been attributed to a nocturnal 'eureka' of lateral thinking on the part of his friend and future Foreign Secretary, Doctor Owen. Racking his brains over the quandary – *prima facie* unnecessary one might have thought – of replacing Sir Peter Ramsbotham as British Ambassador in Washington, he is reported as having awoken from sleep with a cry of 'I've got it!' Thereafter his remaining though formidable task was to convince candidate and Prime Minister, both, one may suppose, dubious and hesitant at first. Certainly this order of events is more acceptable a version than would be that of a Prime Minister, similarly inspired, nocturnally convincing a reluctant Foreign Secretary and son-in-law of the international merits of such an initiative.

In this interpretation Mr Jay was awarded this resonant and precocious recognition of his talents irrespective of, despite even, his family relationship with his Head of Government, and his close friendship with his future Foreign Secretary, and entirely on his professional merits, which are outstanding and uncontested. So however are those of at least some hundred British executive 'flyers' of his generation, as indeed are those of at least a dozen or so alternatives – male and female – from within the Diplomatic Service itself. The nub of the question is therefore whether Mr Jay was automatically and irresistibly short-listed and selected, through having the Prime Minister as a father-in-law, and a friend as the future employer who could take public responsibility for this appointment.

On the basis that that which has fins, scales, gills and swims is a fish, and unless there are undisclosable considerations of vital national significance, this appointment cannot but seem to be the joint product of party-political motivation and conscious nepotism. The risk that both these factors presented was such that they should have outweighed all the candidate's merits, and nipped the appointment in the bud, since it could hardly be vetoed once publicly launched. Instead its maintenance and justification have displayed a placid imperturbability, an insistence on the coincidental, which has shocked into lasting taciturnity a loyally speechless Diplomatic Service, and left the newspaper-reading public, in the USA as well as Britain, with a lingering after-taste not commonly associated with the British administrative and diplomatic tradition. The intimate decisions taken for and against this nomination by the various participants must be assumed to involve their own highly personal mixtures of patriotic obligation, self-interest and self-respect. It is not the purpose of this chapter, nor within its material competence, to seek to disentangle them. Once again the question is simply whether yet another personal but public episode may not have influenced the future of the diplomatic profession. My own conclusion is that the manner of Mr Jay's appointment came close to debasing the British relation to the whole institution. So too, in the fullness of time, would have been his own rumoured and retaliatory replacement by a former British Prime Minister from the other party. By a salutary and happy rebound however, his eventual succession, unorthodox as it was in an opposite way, may have done much to restore the representational position to health.

For his successor, Sir Nicholas Henderson, is the career-diplomat *par excellence*, or was. He was invited out of retirement by the new government for the Washington appointment, and reinstated as an ambassador almost before his returning feet had touched again his native soil. British diplomats normally retire at sixty; and in the prevailing climate of retrenchment by 'natural wastage', any extension of tenure would be unfavourably publicized as frustrating normal policy. After the non-standard Mr Jay a conventional career appointment – in Sir Nicholas's words a 'square' – was anyhow due, by what had become standard rotation. Yet no ordinary 'Buggins' turn' could have succeeded so flamboyant a predecessor as Peter Jay. Sir Nicholas had, fortunately, acquired along the way his own decorous flamboyance; though it was probably unfair of the diplomatic correspondents to have contrasted it with a 'dearth of suitable and available top-level diplomatic and political talent' in the Foreign Office.

Perhaps for United States consumption it is anyhow felt that the pre-packaged talent of the career-man has to be supplemented by what is multinationally known as a 'gimmick' or 'angle'. Sir Nicholas's 'angle' had been amply provided for him by the leakage of his farewell despatch from Paris of 31 March 1979. In addition to the instant celebrity accorded by headlines of any kind, his text had furnished a public demonstration of a professional competence, clarity and brutal frankness normally reserved for an uninhibited Foreign Office and Whitehall circulation. Thus his strictures on British productivity, as compared with the countries in which he had served, would not normally have become known to, and cannot have endeared him to, the extreme wing of British trade-unionism

Yet even they must have benefited from such a revelation of the perception, realism and factual expertise which go into the considerable best of the Foreign Office's much maligned 'flood of paper'. And if Mr Jay had offered Washington an admixture of personal glamour and academic intellectualism, Sir Nicholas, who had more than held his own against the Duff Cooper/Soames legend of the Paris embassy, evidently had his own more mellow version of the same on disposal. He was also to find in Washington, as had been recorded before in Paris, that non-career predecessors do not always adhere to convention. One unwritten but highly civilized rule is that the outgoing ambassador always leaves the field clear to his successor by getting out from under his feet. Above all, he does not embarrass him by locally accepting gainful employment where lately he was enjoying extra-territoriality.

Amid the general relief – this time faintly audible even from the devoted Foreign Office – at so unexceptionable an appointment as that of Sir Nicholas Henderson, one small misgiving was also audible, and that from the same quarter. Was Sir Nicholas's after all really a career appointment, after that of the laical Mr Jay? Or was he, though like Lords Harlech and Soames to be accepted rather than tolerated, still only some sort of an 'honorary' career colleague? Had Sir Nicholas technically left the career on retirement at sixty, and so was he now just another non-career ambassador trawled in for appointment to Washington? Or had he been reinstated as a career ambassador? In that case the Foreign Office would have reverted to an older dispensation, by which careers can optionally be extended to the age of sixty-five, as with their rivals, the Home Civil Service. This latter solution would be bad news for those officers impatiently preferring the prospective demolition of promotional log-jams to a protracted queuing for dead men's shoes, but equally good news to reluctant candidates for standard retirement at sixty.

For myself, I believe that the Gordian knot of Mr Jay's replacement was cut with more elegance and efficiency than had been the case with the disposal of his predecessor and his own appointment. Whatever the ambiguity of Sir Nicholas's administrative and acturial status, his appointment demonstrated unequivocally that the British Diplomatic Service still breeds its men for all seasons. I also hope that the outcome may be relevant to the future organization of Britain's Diplomatic Service; acceptance of my second interpretation above would after all significantly reduce the present inflexibility of diplomatic retirement procedures. Its early ratification, by one or two further voluntary postponements beyond sixty of a frequently unnecessary and probably unwelcome retirement, would add greatly to the rewards and incentives of a successful career.

With that one exception, professional diplomacy will be all the healthier if its working canons are tampered with as little as possible, both as regards retirement and, especially, resignation. Resignation with subsequent reinstatement has been a rare though occasionally distinguished phenomenon in the British diplomatic profession, as in the case of Sir Con O'Neill, who managed it three times. In general however it seems to promote restlessness in the practitioner, and malaise in an ever vigilant Service, to whose vast majority taking the rough with the smooth is a professional maxim, and almost a law of life. The non-resignation principle stood me in good stead personally, when confronted with one of the newer hazards of diplomacy, interrogation by an urban guerrilla inquisitor. After a long chain of sophistries, intended to identify me with the conditions against which he was rebelling, he finished by triumphantly pronouncing my guilt as self-evident; I had not resigned when my government persisted in recognizing so allegedly corrupt and tyrannical a régime. Even were it so, I explained, diplomats like soldiers just did not resign precisely when their duty became tiresome or unpalatable.

Nor did they resign when confronted with specialized tasks for which the non-career envoy is often instanced as better equipped. Instead they learn how to handle them. Relations with the news media are a case in point – even, too, after-dinner oratory, and television. In consequence there has been no particularly noticeable difference of public-relations attainment between for example successive career and non-career incumbents at the United Nations Delegation in New York, nor of export-driving achievement in Washington DC. Things have indeed changed since, in 1960, Sir Willam Hayter concluded that, while Washington might be an exception, elsewhere public appearances might be left to visiting politicians, 'who will do it better'[1].

Today instead we sometimes see the role of the resident diplomat abroad usurped perhaps, reinforced perhaps, by an 'Envoy Subsonic' flown in on special mission, or as a public-relations operation. The visitor may equally well be a political figure or a colleague of particular expertise from the Foreign Office. In such circumstances – South Africa, Namibia, Zimbabwe-Rhodesia – a Sir John Graham, a Sir John Thomson, a Sir Anthony Duff can alternate with a Lord Cledwyn Hughes as travelling emissary; we can even have a Mark Heath or his successor, who alternates with no one at all as ambassador accredited to Chad, flying out from his habitual desk in the Downing Street Palazzo as and when required. Such devices, products of economy, expediency and even efficiency, are not however in the same category as a different style of proxy diplomacy, that conducted by political dynasty.

A mainly American practice, along with such roving ambassadorial appointments as that of Muhammed Ali the boxing champion, it originated possibly with the late Mrs Eleanor Roosevelt, and was readopted by Mrs Ladybird Johnson. It was subsequently taken up with particular enthusiasm by President Carter. His son Chip had already in his twenties participated in various special missions, including one to the austere but appropriately dynastic kingdom of Saudi Arabia. His aged mother served as Special Envoy for a state funeral in India, and his wife was delegated Special Ambassador to the inauguration of a new and, finally, civilian government in Ecuador. A ubiquitous and impassive small daughter also clings like a leech to her parents on numerous public occasions, whiling away the occasional black-tie dinner by reading a picture-book, thus doubtless achieving the ambition of many a plenipotentiary before her; one wonders whether the young lady is not being groomed for some new departure in what some of her compatriots would probably endorse as 'pee-wee diplomacy'.

In most countries however the presence of family at summit meetings or on major official occasions is meant either to relax the statesman or to humanize his public image. So for that matter does the ambassadress accompanying her husband on tour, yet also often unostentatiously performing her own parallel represen-

[1] *The Diplomacy of Great Powers* (p. 733), Hamish Hamilton, 1960

76

tational role in such areas as, say, women's activities and community matters. Otherwise formal family delegation carried to excess can create a presumption of 'elective monarchy' incongruous in an egalitarian tradition and environment, and unlikely to thrive, or even to survive.

Of survival it has been said that the bird is evolution's device for the perpetuation of the egg. Diplomacy too must sometimes appear to be the diplomat's invention for the perpetuation of his profession – hence the legendary diplomat riposting to the condescension of the generals that they would have no wars to fight were it not for him. In reality of course the diplomat's business is what by the very familiarity of his organizational label tends to be overlooked. His is a 'Diplomatic Service', and he is a servant of the people and their government.

Bernard du Rosier, in his *Short Treatise on Ambassadors* of 1436, is generally regarded as synthesizing the medieval view of diplomacy – that at its heart lies the pursuit and maintenance of peace, which the envoy abandons or exceeds only at peril of dire loss of immunity. This medieval concept seems to have become once again strangely contemporary. And the human element entrusted with so precious and precarious a burden calls for a very special selection and answerability. The normal healthy factor of ambition must be bridled with an almost vocational dedication, canalized rigorously towards professional fulfillment, and only incidentally to personal achievement. For this reason the occasional politicization of diplomacy has seemed to me to raise new and disturbing possibilities. The two faces of ambition can be confused, indeed be fused, by the surrender of a wholly professional objectivity. Possibly the hardest task for those diplomats saddled with career-planning in their Service must be to separate and distinguish between the two imperatives, and assess their respective proportions. Supplying the counselling, and the other raw materials of foreign policy, to those in government who will make that foreign policy, calls for wisdom and dedication rather than appetite.

Yet the ambivalence of motive cannot delay its assertiveness. Ambition shows early. Gifted and aggressive recruits to diplomacy have been known discreetly and decorously to fight tooth-and-nail for that notorious open-sesame, a first appointment as Private Secretary to a political master. Such postings were once described by an expert as 'a good start, but a not exacting job, which involves sending quantities of flowers to the wives of visiting Foreign Ministers'[1]. Yet that self-same effortless start can be not only spring-board, but lure and drug also. This must have been one of many considerations when the Foreign Office – who do not care for rat-races, much less any recurrent suggestion of 'jobs for the boys' – invented instead what I have already mentioned as 'career-planning'. Even so, any human contrivance operating over the long term risks acquiring a certain fixity, and needs constant monitoring against it, especially if any element of the closed-circuit and the politically identified creeps in.

The British diplomat, like any other public servant, is subject to very meticulous restrictions on his participation in party-political activity while still a member of the Diplomatic Service. Equally he should remain aloof from party-political associations relating to his career and future. Once only, and that since my retirement, have I had the uneasy sensation of sitting in on some sort of a network which might, with perfect propriety, frustrate these principles. In a small and purely informal gathering a particular senior statesman and a most distinguished journalist were suddenly, and admittedly to my fascination, discussing – one might almost have said disposing – the next round of top appointments in the Diplomatic Service. Among others they debated the future allocation of the principal European embassies. They did so, it must be said, in strict Labour Party terms, though it required no shift of setting and little of imagination to reverse the party criteria. Each man voiced his pros and cons; one or two candidates were taken in their stride as certainties, needing no time wasted in discussion. Events proved that their assessment could not be faulted. They got every top appointment right for the next few years.

The entire analysis was conducted on a basis of close personal knowledge. First names alone were used, not with the spurious intimacy of the television panel or the executive dining-suite, but with every evidence of familiar and continual acquaintance. To me, as a one-time lobbyist – though detesting the label – the conversation sounded like anything but casual gossip, and uncommonly like a combined exercise in lobbying and handicapping. As a lifelong professional apolitical, it unsettled me. A moment came

[1] Patrick O'Donovan, the *Observer*

when I too was drawn into the discussion. I used it to explain – perhaps too dryly – that I had no comment to offer. I had made a point during all my years of service to abstain from demonstrating any party political position, both personally and in the nuances of my official reporting. So much so that neither my wife nor my son had known till I retired which way I cast my vote – though admittedly they had the point of reference that, while overseas, my electoral proxy was vested in an elderly and devout great-aunt.

I had the impression that my contribution cast a certain chill over the enthusiastic form-studying. Had I still been in the Service, I somehow sensed, it would have done me no good at all. Certainly, I contemplated, I had opened no avenues for myself in my retirement. Since however I planned to spend it in ways remote from party considerations – or for that matter by this time from the City – it was indifferent to me that my aversion to bandwagons should now be official, or at any rate overt.

Yet many times since I have wondered whether, in many a similar setting, some colleague perhaps needing that last nudge for maximum professional achievement, may not have been informally invited to cast his lot one way or another – or perhaps just the one way. For the mathematical probability is that it would not be the Tory way. There are enough ex-Foreign Office Conservative MPs, or MEPs, to testify that a diplomat with an active Conservative motivation can always leave diplomacy in the hope of becoming a Douglas Hurd or a Ray Whitney, to name but two. Conversely Lord George-Brown's memoirs do not disguise the highly personal nature of some of his diplomatic appointments; one in particular he traces back to a future ambassador's wife having publicly taken a partisan stance in his defence and presence. Similarly the widow of another ambassador has asserted to the media that her husband, like herself, had approached each new post as a committed Socialist.

My personal antipathy to such express political commitments by the traditionally unaligned found a Whitehall echo when, in September 1979, the *Economist* suggested that the 'mandarins' themselves might soon be mending fences with a potential successor to the Thatcher government. A spokesman of a generation even earlier than mine demonstrated its still less situational and cynical attitude, by writing to voice his blank and terse incredulity.

This recent whiff of what might be termed unilateral politicization has been strong enough to account for the familiar legend – which may not be wholly tongue-in-cheek – that under a Labour government the ambitious FO man takes care to make known his allegiance to them. He does so in the full knowledge that when the Conservatives are back in power, he will not be penalized or his promotion affected. The impact of non-career appointments can, as we have seen, similarly add fuel to the suspicion of politicization. Even if only a suspicion, or a fad, it justifies a certain nostalgia for the days when a Socialist Foreign Secretary, Ernest Bevin, marvelled at the total absence of any strain on the loyalty of those who, in no time at all, he was to see as 'my boys', when overnight they were switched from a patrician to a supposedly proletarian leadership.

When I consulted one eminent serving colleague on the existence of such a newer trend he laughed, and added to his affirmative that it was common knowledge that two-thirds of the Foreign Office and Service voted Labour nowadays. As indeed they have every right and obligation, if from conviction. The wrong is only if they make it known, which more than one colleague has confirmed is indeed now commonplace. The Diplomatic Service will be all the healthier when the convention is restored that domestic party-politics, as formerly sex and religion, remain excluded from the diplomat's conversational impedimenta, let alone his career equipment. The desirability of such a self-discipline is further enhanced by the decline of consensus government in Britain, which increasingly is transforming the creative party-political nuances of old into the ideological incompatibilities of today.

Or so it seems to me. Yet there is a point of view which would deny that the diplomat has any sacred right to live in his own tight and unchanging little island, or to run his own philosophically closed shop, no matter how fashionable that institution may be in other craft organizations. Other fellow-countrymen, duly elected by the nation, may think otherwise for him. One of our recent legislators – he must have a fixation against the bureaucracy – alternates between scarifying Civil Service beneficiaries of top pensions beyond the dreams of most of us, and urging a 'democracy in public government' which would entitle incoming Ministers to swap their senior civil servants – and no doubt ambassadors – in accordance with their political choosing. Preferment or not, the day parliament gives him his way, and says so, it must be so; the diplomat too must run his profession as the society he serves dictates, or votes, though he need not officiously strive to anticipate its wishes. Since history evolves he too must evolve. Like society itself, he cannot become static, and still live.

But history has also taught him that her principles do not change. It is his duty to safeguard them. If to do so he must stand apart – as in modern times he always has – from the dynamic and commitment of politics, so then in their turn the politicians must respect the impartiality of diplomacy. It is their privilege, but their responsibility too, that in diplomacy it is always the politician who has the last word, and the diplomat who obeys it.

Chapter VI
Diplomacy and The Moles

It is impossible to consider the future of the diplomatic profession, especially in its British manifestation, without the names of Burgess, Maclean and Philby still casting their long shadow. The more recently prominent name of Blunt falls into a separate slot; his activity, whatever it was, did not impinge on the practice of diplomacy. That of the other three did, and has damaged the institution probably as much as their treason must be presumed to have harmed the country of their birth.

Philby of course was never a diplomat, though he served abroad as an official of the secret intelligence organization. His true connection with British diplomacy was, as events proved, one of manipulation and communication – a puppeteer, himself a puppet. Burgess was a diplomat of sorts; he figured authentically on the diplomatic list in Washington, and served in the Foreign Office in London. Yet in essence he was more one of those fringe-characters that haunt the diplomatic community everywhere. They usually but not always occupy a function of a sort, but a vague one. They tend to be 'in it for the champagne', and to be accepted kindly but not seriously, as harmless parodies playing at diplomacy, licensed clowns more diplomatic than the diplomats, revelling in the trappings without any contact with the substance. Burgess was one of these, but gone badly wrong. Even at face-value he was a squalid version of the pseudo-diplomat; yet behind his sordid façade he was carrying out a real and dangerous parallel function.

Donald Maclean however was a genuine diplomat, and could have been a great one. If the waste of talents is a mortal sin, it was his, and of those who split his personality and addled his mind. He and his second-stage masters may have believed the contrary – that the abuse worked, that indeed never was talent used to more spectacular effect. Yet a powerful and ordered intelligence, given substance by a fine education and a professional training, could have made his life's achievement not just one further twist applied to already convoluted events, but the consistent legacy to his country of a great career and, in the end no doubt, some lasting contribution to scholarship.

The bibliography, and speculation, which have grown around this apparently ill-assorted trio, have by now clearly identified the principal milestones on their respective paths from Cambridge to Moscow. Philby, Burgess and Maclean went up to Cambridge, as her alumni say, in 1929, 1930 and 1931 respectively. All were recruited there, by the Soviet Union, as what Philby describes as intelligence probationers, via an assortment of Soviet and fellow-travelling British intermediaries. By wartime he had found his way into the British Secret Intelligence Service, Burgess – via a similar route – into the Foreign Office, into which Maclean too was steered by his mentors, but through the conventional examination route open to him by his academic and personal qualifications. During the war and after, Philby's road was taking him even higher up the slopes of the intelligence organization, Burgess's at least keeping him in contact with it, and Maclean's had already led to a headship of department in the Foreign Office.

The outward appearance of effortless success in their clandestine mission is misleading in all three cases. It had cost each one of them dear. By 1950 all three must have represented a problem to their shadow-employers. It was a bad year for each of them. Philby, the coolest, was under suspicion to the United States authorities at least, and was taking heavily to drink. Burgess, also in Washington, was attracting attention by his scandalous lifestyle, also but not only for its alcoholic manifestations. In Cairo, Maclean had been excused repeated berserk episodes of an alcoholic violence which, even if condoned as the product of nervous strain, were by their recurrence in London beginning to disqualify him as a representative of his country.

In 1951 the three-fold edifice of subterfuge collapsed, or was dismantled, overnight. On Friday 25 May 1951, Burgess and Maclean fled together in circumstances that still reverberate in the popular literature of espionage. The most depressing Monday of my own life followed hard on that strange Friday. By a series of coincidences I was in charge of Donald Maclean's department that day. On the Tuesday morning early my 'phone rang at home in Albert Court, just behind the Albert Hall. A distant voice on a crackling line enquired 'Hullo? Hullo? Donald Maclean here.' 'Where on earth are you speaking from?' I demanded. The crackling stopped and, clear as a bell, the voice said 'From Thurloe Square, of course! Where d'you think?' Some time later, when the story had broken and the press had had their day, my friend and neighbour Donald Maclean – the other one, in the bloodstock business – remarked that he now realized what a bad day he had chosen to ring me up, and on a bad line at that.

And that shall also be all of that. But not of what they, and especially that other more notorious Donald Maclean in particular, have done to the profession which he had looked like adorning so elegantly. Despite the sensationalist headlines the British public were not so much shocked as amused by the collapse of the stout FO party; they have always enjoyed a double-act, from Rosencrantz and Guildenstern to Laurel and Hardy. Even the visiting Soviet statesmen Kruschev and Bulganin in 1956 became 'Krutch-and-Bulge' instantly on arrival. Anyone who, in those years after 1951, was called upon to mention that his destination was the Foreign Office, will remember the taxi-driver's raised eyebrows, and the instant 'Aha! Berjiss and Mack-leen!'

The identification, and the story, have never quite been allowed to die down. As if fed in by some celestial and systematic prompter, reminder has succeeded reminder – in 1953 the spiriting away from the Bernese Oberland of an ostensibly rusticating Mrs Maclean; in 1956 the stage 'unveiling' of her husband and Burgess in Moscow; in 1963 the 'beaming-up' of Philby to the Soviet Union, his award of Soviet citizenship, the death of Burgess, all these in one year; Philby's matrimonial adventures; in 1968 the publication of his autobiography; in 1979 his promotion to General; the competing candidatures to his succession as Fourth and Fifth Man, if not an even lengthier lineage. Until Andrew Boyle's *The Climate of Treason* (Hutchinson, 1979), this was publicly the end of the affair; the trio of names remained a closed triangle.

Meanwhile the brief scar left on public opinion has faded. Only a minority of individuals still ache under the sorrow and the outrage, and of them only a few, with their special motives, voice it so savagely and pointedly as has Mr Enoch Powell, quoted in Chapter IV. A colleague, lately on a tour of industry between one senior ambassadorial appointment and the next, has assured me that never more than today was in his experience the British Diplomatic Service's help and and advice so sought, esteemed and acknowledged by business, banking and legislature. So any damage done to external reputation and standing of the diplomat by the events of a generation ago, and their continuing repercussion, seems to have been repaired. But the injury is not there. It lies deeper.

Donald Maclean's crime against his country was committed as a spy, not as a diplomat. His treason did not manifest itself, by such accounts as are available, by his falsifying his reporting and advice to his government, and so adversely influencing foreign policy. He simply used his position of confidence to purloin and pass on vital information to his spy-masters, to their considerable advantage. What he did was treason; however much manipulated as an undergraduate, he was old enough to know where he was going, and eventually what he was doing – the betrayal of his own country in the service of another and, in due time, of a solemn, formal and binding oath. His rationale may have been ideological, even at first idealistic; equally well, of course, he, Burgess and Philby may have made a mere cynical and ambitious calculation of the international political and military odds. The result was the same – a switch of loyalty, legally indefensible, morally still less so.

Donald Maclean's offence was all the greater, both as the inheritor of a professional and personal tradition and as a man of great intellectual potential – as both diplomat and scholar. Where Philby can evidently have the lives of his fellow-men laid directly at his door, Maclean, who apparently cannot, has certainly added greatly to the moral confusion of his time, to its relativism and its acceptance of an arid situational ethic. Despite the revelation of the dark and disorderly side of his nature, Maclean has, by the public and enduring fact of its once bright and conventionally professional side, lent respectability to ideological treason.

Not the least entertaining passage in Lord Trevelyan's entertaining book *Diplomatic Channels*[1] is his account of the western 'amateur spy' spirited to a safe haven in the Communist world, condescended to by the professionals, brought in from the cold, put out to grass. The bridge-playing purgatory in which the de-

[1] Macmillan, 1973

scription sets their exile is ironically evocative of the desolate cantonments he himself has since described in his own youthful Indian reminiscences; one Collector's bungalow seems, in its transplanted suburbanism, dismally like another defector's dacha. The element of difference which Lord Trevelyan's consciously light-hearted version bypasses is that the latter-day expatriates in their more northerly dachas are men who have done immense international harm; their boredom, wife-swappings and hangovers have been bought with the coinage of life and death.

To equate the confusion between right and wrong, to which the Maclean trio have so massively contributed, with the harm they have done to the technical intelligence function, is neither so absurd nor so immoral as may be contended. One effect of their activity has been to impart a certain unilateral 'protest' quality to the western view of espionage. Once again a dual standard is encouraged, a lending of intellectual respectability to the Communist version, from which western intelligence comes out very much the loser. 'Their' intelligence is acceptable. 'Ours' is not. Admittedly over recent years the United States Central Intelligence Agency has not perhaps, in its wider aberrations, been its own best friend. Yet 'Intelligence' is an honourable and indispensable profession. It is neither noble nor ignoble, merely useful; and any country which neglects it is guilty of a grave imprudence. Maclean, Burgess, and Philby, who illustrate the manufacture of traitors rather than the recruitment of agents, have, by blurring the frontier between treason and intelligence, turned the objective reality of intelligence into subjective disrepute. By rendering it less acceptable to our open society, they have contaminated the role of diplomacy, obscuring the crucial distinction between diplomacy and espionage.

It would be foolish to deny that the defence of the west, and the security of the North Atlantic Treaty powers, have been greatly harmed by this discrediting of the intelligence function. The mistakes, indiscretions and abuses of the CIA were obviously going to be intolerable to an open society when it came to know of them. But after discipline and correction, its work should and must go on. That work, and the work of other less vulnerable intelligence organizations around the world, will have found its rehabilitation and fresh start handicapped, not so much by the self-inflicted disrepute of the 'dirty-tricks' indictment, as by the obfuscating of its status and location in the moral structure of its society and times. By helping to 'glamorize' to a whole generation the abstraction of spying and treason, while discrediting intelligence as a legitimate function of state, Maclean and his collaborators have correspondingly helped massively to 'deglamorize' a principal instrument of national defence. For when a Donald Maclean abandons all his principles for their opposite, inevitably there are those who will conclude that he must have a point, and so therefore must his new idol. The adversary has thus been strengthened, and the defence equivalently weakened.

In addition, by all this new mass-exposure, that which quite properly requires twilight has been flood-lit. Legitimate anonymity has been posted on bill-boards. Names have been named. Never has the reality of intelligence been so repudiated, and its fantasy so relished. Here I entirely agree with Lord Trevelyan, when he goes on to deplore the sanctimonious attitude of certain ambassadors to the intelligence-gathering function, however uninvolved they are in it.

That such an intellectual prudery is fairly widespread is far from contradicting the contention that the defection of Burgess, Maclean and Philby caused at the time more titillation than consternation among the general public, and left a scar, if any, that soon faded. Yet again, its aftermath registered at a more intangible and moral level, the subliminal operating on the subconscious. Especially in the world of literature and entertainment, in its orientation of our society, the legacy of the trio is plainly visible. The spy-story has become a popular obsession. A respectable if stereotyped genre since Erskine Childers and John Buchan, it has acquired a new dimension from the 'case of the missing diplomats'. An aura of authenticity and an injection of contemporary ideology have legitimized what once was fiction, and have turned a pastime into a national spy-mania. Fortified also by an importation of fashionable violence, spy-fiction has assumed an obsessive and morbid quality which frequently trespasses into the masochistic and unwholesome. John le Carré defends himself against it intransigently in his 'Smiley' novels, by building his house of words on a foundation of rigid morality, of implacable right and wrong, as does Graham Greene less unambiguously in his analogous writings. In the cinema and on television these moral absolutes show as more diffuse, with the 'sympathetic spy' often tending to oust the 'respectable spy-hunter' in human appeal.

The spy and the 'bent' diplomat in entertainment are at one and the same time a product of cross-fertilization with reality, and a device of immunization against it. The Maclean episode seems itself to have initiated a certain shamelessness in the newer devices of international perfidy – a public washing and instant drip-drying of dirty linen that would have been unthinkable not so long ago. The international atmosphere was entirely changed when a respected and ostensibly conventional diplomat so spectacularly betrayed his country; till then certain atrocious things had long been done unavowedly and surreptitiously only. What was too evil for His Excellency to concern himself with professionally must also not be seen to involve his government in any way either. Today secret and shameful things – the stuff of the most lurid and meretricious film scenarios – can happen publicly, unashamedly, inexplicably and, furthermore, be accepted with a shrug. Exiles die mysteriously, by rare poisons administered in bizarre and tortuous ways, and are soon forgotten by the world at large. Fugitives are kidnapped, and bundled back illegally to the torture from which they fled, drugged and parcelled – literally like a package. All these atavisms, up-dated reversions to the more byzantine phases in the history of international relations, are manifestations of a new decline in international morality. The Burgess/Maclean/Philby sequence represented a major publicity operation in the business of immunizing western man against moral outrage. Its actors share heavily in responsibility for the process of conditioning which has made such a retrogression possible, and for the blunting of public sensitivity and conscience which has facilitated its wider acceptance.

If a counter-thesis to this proposition were desired, it might be found, paradoxically enough, by expanding on an observation made in one of the most ethically motivated approaches to the 'missing diplomats' saga. In his *The Climate of Treason* Andrew Boyle spends much of his preface and opening chapters emphasizing that the probing feeler of treason was particularly searching of, and effective on, the sons of the proconsular 'imperialist' type of the inter-war generation. The old British Empire was disintegrating. Nothing was more adolescently normal than a revulsion against it, and a sense of guilt for it, among some of those whose fathers had been pillars of that same Empire, serving an idol that to their sons now seemed to have had feet of clay. Conceding such a reflex, it predicates only one short step further from foreseeing the collapse of Empire, to rejoicing in it, and seeking to expedite it with the help of any available agency.

Yet again an instant morality of sorts can be alleged here for treason. It is however a specious and pragmatic one, which does not stand up to the scrutiny of conscience. For if – as the Spaniards say – God writes straight on crooked lines, so the devil may be presumed to write crooked on straight lines. A genuine moral inspiration picked up, and then applied to an evil purpose, will accordingly lose its morality. Thus the urban guerrilla – or equally the death-squad 'patriot' – who invades an intensive-care unit to finish off a dying victim, ceases thereby to be an honest soldier. Equally an official vowed to the promotion of his country's world-wide interest, but who clandestinely substitutes for it that of a stranger, is no longer a diplomatic agent, but an agent of the other kind. Once more it is Maclean, the diplomat turned spy, who has injured the whole function of diplomacy as a world-wide institution – as indeed the modest absolute of sorts which it has always been, in its own ancient way.

As my ambassadorial friend mentioned a few pages ago pointed out to me, he finds that those compatriots whom he is there to serve have more than recovered from any crisis of confidence towards his Service which the Maclean episode may have engendered. The fact speaks well for the stamina and resilience of his Service and profession. For, seen from within, it would be idle to deny that the family humiliation of Maclean's betrayal was a brutal and personal affront to the self-respect and professional pride of the British diplomat; many today must consciously or subconsciously have spent the years between seeking, in whatever way they could, to redress it.

It also seems possible that, looking at Maclean, his colleagues of other nations too thereafter looked in on themselves – and on their profession and their own Service – with a new misgiving. 'This can't be happening to me!' is one of the most painful of human disenchantments, especially when it does. And in Maclean's case the incredulity was intensified by his undisputed early rating as a 'golden boy', the 'high-flyer' *par excellence*. Among those who have had the candour to eschew hindsight, and to acknowledge without retrospective qualification his professional stature, Lord Gore-Booth flatly describes Maclean's work as 'impeccable'[1]. To those therefore unaware of his deterioration in the last years and months, the toppling of such an epitome of professionalism came as an unbelievable shock – the kind of experience which can be lived down, but never forgotten.

British public opinion, as I have maintained, had little difficulty in living that shock down doubtless it had accepted it as a mere nine-day wonder, and thus without the moral agonizing that, in retrospect, I have attributed to the diplomatic profession. But morale is different from, though bound to, morality. And I incline to the belief that British national morale too was more subtly affected than was realized at the time. Britain today is a more cynical country than she was a hundred, fifty, even twenty years ago. And if in the last generation, since World War II, there has been a 'destabilization' of British society and of the British ethic as recorded at Waterloo and the Somme, then a *trahison des clercs* of such dimensions must have been one major factor in it. That some deny it is a demonstration of insensibility which is itself a testimony to that very destabilization. I had lately to ask myself if I was listening to realism, morality or demoralization, when I heard a most personable and intelligent young man briskly commenting on these things to an audience of millions over the television. He was ruminating over a Graham Greene film in which there was 'a traitor about'. 'Ah well,' he went on – 'In the Foreign Office when isn't there a traitor about?'

Some writer once commented that for the spymasters the years must have names, just as they do for the Chinese, past and present, with their successive 'Rats' and 'Dragons'. 1945 would thus be the Year of Gouzenko, 1951 the Year of Burgess and Maclean, 1963 the Year of Philby – and so *ad infinitum*. These therefore are all names which have left their imprint, however negative, on history, just as the old movie-stars are recorded in cement along the side-walks of Hollywood Boulevard. In an age of anti-heroes, it is an irony of fate that so spectacular a prototype should have emerged from the ranks of a profession in which the externally ceremonial has always belied the anonymity and self-effacement within.

[1] *With Great Truth and Respect* (p. 144), Constable, 1974

After Andrew Boyle's re-opening of the case, Robin Cecil, a former diplomatic colleague far more knowledgeable than I in these matters, has publicly urged[1] that a full official statement be made, to dissipate surviving ambiguity and innuendo. The easy-going disposition of our open and kindly society has always been to 'let sleeping dogs lie'. Now, ironically – in the new jargon – it is the 'sleepers' in their turn who are left to lie. To lie hard, or to lie mendaciously however? To bring ourselves up-to-date we can always go back to our ancestor Sir Henry Wotton, in Chapter I.

[1] *The Times*, 25 January 1980

Chapter VII
Diplomacy Without Immunity

Front-Line Diplomat was the title given in 1959 to his memoirs by the late Sir Geoffrey Thompson[1], who retired from the Diplomatic Service almost a generation ago. He had been effectively my chief for a brief special assignment in Rio de Janeiro. Though he had the reputation of operating on a short fuse, I not only respected him but became fond of him, especially when I found that his temperament was the product of a permanently unhealed leg-wound from World War I. Though he had gone straight from the army into diplomacy, like William Strang, the title he gave his book had to do with the posts he had held, and their nature, rather than with his time in the trenches.

I thought of him – as I quite often do – when one day I was lunching with an up-and-coming young broadcaster. He was commenting on the changes in my old profession. What had always been considered an elegant, diverting, and safe occupation had suddenly revealed itself as hazardous and exposed. 'You diplomats,' he went on, 'really are in the front line nowadays.' In a way of course we always had been; Congress danced only briefly, and that was long ago.

As suggested in earlier chapters, diplomatic immunity was invented to protect the envoy from those hazards which any stranger in a strange land may expect to encounter, but particularly so when acting for his ruler, and probably carrying his confidential instructions. The hazards of ruder times had by convention been attenuated down the centuries, from ear-cropping and occasional ritual murder until today not even a parking-ticket can technically threaten the envoy. The diplomat's mission, and person, because of his special status, had become safe, from both governments and individuals alike. Suddenly however, and re-

[1] Hutchinson 1959

cently, the convention has been turned upside-down. It is precisely because of his special status that he is now unsafe.

The general safety of the diplomat from personal violence has always been an extension of his official immunity His privileged status has only functioned by right in those areas of his life where there was a law from which to be exempted. Beyond that his exemption was a courtesy. Thus the ambassador could not in law be sued by his tailor, which did not however make him immune from the attentions of a passing burglar or a jealous husband. Yet in general the aura of immunity and high office was of itself a total protection of sorts of pracice – invisible, intangible, yet effective; the very thought of a kidnapped ambassador would till lately have been a contradiction in terms. So would that of occupied embassy premises, whether the intruders were there in pursuance of a revolution or *coup d'état*, or at the behest of the local authorities, disguised as *vox populi*.

For centuries this immunity was no more than a marvellously efficient illusion, projected by the mirrors of moral persuasion and the mutual self-interest of rulers. It did not even exist on paper as an international institution until 1961 when, after years of painstaking labour by the International Law Commission of the United Nations, the Vienna Convention on Diplomatic Relations was finally signed. It is adhered to by virtually all the world's nations, though there are times when one would not think so; never has immunity been more ruthlessly abused than since it was codified.

Nor have subsequent codifications helped in practice. In 1973 the United Nations 'Convention on the Prevention and Punishment of Crimes against Internationally Protected Persons, including Diplomatic Agents' still referred to murder and kidnapping, in suitably solemn and generalized tones, as 'crimes punishable by appropriate penalties which take into account their grave nature.' Not until 1977 did it receive the necessary numbers of accessions and ratifications to come into force, for whatever that is currently worth. In the same year the 'European Convention on the Suppression of Terrorism' was signed by member-states of the Council of Europe. While it, too, spoke with a stern voice, categorizing as mere ordinary criminality such politically motivated offences as kidnapping and hijacking, it left loopholes aplenty open. States could thus argue prolongedly about the extradition of, for example, the Baader-Meinhoff defence lawyer Klaus Croissant.

Down the centuries until 1961, diplomatic immunity had rested and functioned on a hodge-podge of differing national laws and standards. Behind them, however, was always one abiding criterion – the inviolability of the envoy's person. We have seen that even so it was, under the theologically centred medieval concept expressed in Bernard du Rosier's *Short Treatise* of 1436, an inviolability severely qualified by moral considerations. The moment the envoy exceeded the bounds of 'the public good', and for example transgressed the recognized moral code in his aims or methods, he was open to the gravest penalties. Yet by the time of Machiavelli a century later, the opposite view was preached. The envoy was positively expected to abuse his immunities in the pursuit of his ruler's interests, to an extent not to be seen again till the extravagances perpetrated by the various intelligence services of the late twentieth century.

Meanwhile diplomacy was being salvaged from this first phase of discredit both by the efforts of good men and by the effects of history – and surprisingly quickly too. While Machiavelli was codifying expediency, Thomas More was between 1510 and 1530 empirically evolving, on a series of missions for the king who was shortly to behead him, an essentially 'respectable' technique of diplomacy, which exploited all Machiavelli's subtlety without any of his moral turpitude. Paradoxically enough, the self-same theological polarization which cost More his head, was the principal factor in establishing the real-life need for law-and-order – out of which diplomatic immunity was to grow, and yet again with surprising rapidity.

For the Reformation had to all intents divided Europe latitudinally, into a Protestant north confronting a Catholic south. As diplomacy plodded on with its time-honoured craft of maintaining contact between adversaries, despite all their differences and hatreds – once again that new-fangled 'interface' in its most ancient of guises – the envoys themselves were human enough to worship in their own way under their own roof. 'Portingale' and, later, Sardinian envoys were as obnoxiously papist in Britain as the English ambassador in Madrid was unyieldingly Anglican. Each insisted on the untrammelled use of his own embassy chapel, which the indignant populace of each country, in a

fine reverse ecumenism, just as devotedly stormed and desecra-
ted. After a number of *causes célèbres* the tacit acceptance, that
even an ambassador may be left to pray in peace, grew into the
broader concept of the secular inviolability of diplomatic premises, as generally accepted today.

For a while it was even broader than modern international law
acknowledges, once again thanks to the endeavours of decent
men. In 1588 Pierre Ayrault, a French lawyer, produced a revised
edition of his book *L'Ordre*, which attracted the attention of the
diplomats of his day by its new version of immunity. Under the
name of 'extraterritoriality' it persisted until quite recently, in
such manifestations as the 'Capitulations' still surviving in the
Egypt of my youth, hang-overs from the days of the Ottoman
Empire. Ayrault's thesis had been significantly reinforced half a
century after its appearance by the powerful endorsement of
Grotius, in his *Law of War and Peace* of 1625. Grotius held it to
be essential that foreign envoys should be safeguarded against
harassment in the performance of their duties; evidently he was
firmly set against what today would be called 'dirty tricks' –
though in the event of any reciprocal perfidy on the envoy's part
he too, he stipulated, should be shipped back to his master against
an assurance of proper punishment. In justification, or ration-
alization, of this immunity, he twice proposed what in each case
he termed 'a certain fiction'. The first was, precisely, extraterritoriality, the second the identification of the envoy with the
person of his ruler.

Both these 'fictions' have impinged on my own life with a
strangeness which surpasses most recognized fiction. In the Near
East, when my son was due to be born, we had a neighbour whose
wife remains to this day a dear friend of my own wife, as her
husband, if living, would still have been mine. Their first preg-
nancies had synchronized conveniently, so our neighbour was
far-sightedly determined that her baby might as well be born a
dual-national, the second nationality to be British. Being of a
strongly Ottoman tradition, the 'Capitulations' of the old days
were still very much alive to her, but their exact extent somewhat
fluid in her young memory. At all events, she was convinced that
my wife's bed in the local lying-in hospital was British territory;
and she wanted her baby to be born in it too, side-by-side with
her friend. It took much persuasion to convince her that inter-

national law was not actually with her, let alone logistics and hygiene

On the other occasion I remembered my Grotius well enough to allege immunity of premises without actually claiming extra-territoriality. At the time I was sojourning in what its landlords had designated a 'People's Prison'. Nomenclature is something to be accepted philosophically, even on a 'sticks-and-stones' basis, and especially when there is little that one can do about it; in any case the designation was evidently an 'article of faith' – a commodity which I myself rate highly – and of great token significance to my hosts. When however some officious new-broom of theirs decided to nail an arbitrary number-plate on to my cage-door, and to address me as 'Numero Diez', I demurred. I did not go so far as to suggest that wherever a British ambassador set his foot – in my case a bare one at the time – was British territory. I did however insist that wherever an ambassador was in the country to which he was duly accredited, it became for the purpose of his official actions the British Embassy; and I was with them on account of my office. Logically therefore our habitat could not simultaneously be a People's Prison, complete with cell-numbers. The head-warder accepted the reasoning with good grace, even good humour. The number was removed, and my nomenclature normalized to 'amigo'. So I am grateful to Ayrault and Grotius, even though on reflection my extension of their dogma may not have been wholly watertight under the Vienna Convention of 1961.

Grotius's second 'fiction' – the envoy as a projection of his ruler's person – also came in useful though, being largely obsolete, I thought it might do with some suitably artistic restoration. One team of these youthful turnkeys chose on occasion to be deeply and personally offensive about my own 'ruler', expressing an ideological spleen as familiar within the privileged zone of parliament as in my 'People's Prison' overseas. My invoking the Grotius doctrine, rebutting their language as a personal affront to myself, did have a certain effect, but only partial. I therefore took my case a stage further, with the assertion that the British monarch was the single repository of our national patriotism, combining in the one institution and person the threefold veneration devoted, in their own case, to the national flag, the national 'Hymn', or anthem, and the national hero, a quite admirable founding-father, for whom I have the most genuine esteem. I respected their symbols; they should respect my articles of faith. This mutual position was accepted; so an at least partial success can be attributed to my up-ending of Grotius, thanks to which the immunity of the envoy reverberated briefly upon the person and dignity of the monarch away back home.

Owing particularly to the sixteenth-century evolution of diplomatic theory, and the greater formalization of practical international relationships that grew out of the Treaty of Westphalia in 1648, the observance of diplomatic immunity became standard throughout Europe. Frequent aberrations – usually associated with ambassadorial debts and unpaid tradesmen's bills – expedited rather than retarded it, by the very arguments and precedents they initiated. In most countries it was accepted as a kind of international common-law, without statutory embodiment. One surprising exception was Great Britain, when in 1708 Peter the Great's ambassador was arrested and flung into a debtor's prison. Who knows if he was not some kind of precocious technological spy? But with underpaid, even unpaid, oligarchic ambassadors struggling to live up to their rulers' expectations, this kind of episode was still a commonplace around Europe, though it was normally rectified by prompt release and a profuse apology. The particular fury and outrage of Czar Peter however looked like precipitating disastrous repercussions on Britain's current war with France. Queen Anne accordingly despatched a Special Embassy to Moscow to apologize ceremonially to the Czar; the injured Russian ambassador was suitably compensated, and a comprehensive law was rushed through that same year to ensure against a repetition.

The Act for Preserving the Privileges of Ambassadors – otherwise known as the Act of Anne – was till 1961 one of the very few instances of diplomatic immunity becoming written law. It applied to the person of the ambassador, and of his staff and entire household; yet even so the inviolability of his premises was not clarified in law for a further century. In practice of course it was generally accepted that these personal immunities extended to the envoy's premises too. Their sweep was in fact so broad that few countries today would go so far as they did then. For nations are always reluctant to give force of law to accepted conventions which, in effect, legalize a certain criminality, and create a category of privileged person who is openly above the law of the land. That Britain did so, and so long ago, is as much a measure of her early sense of law-and-order as of her discomfiture vis-à-vis Czar Peter. The episode at least provided her with legal definitions of immunity, for long almost unique among the nations, and which still underpin her application of diplomatic immunity, even today.

The fact that 'aberrations' had become unacceptable by statute and conviction did not mean that they ceased over the following centuries. They were usually, however, the exceptions that proved the rule, and of a comparatively minor and personal nature only. The average diplomat of today simply does not use his immunities to dodge his debts. Consequently a mere 'phone-call to the local Foreign Ministry is sufficient, for example, to silence a dishonest tradesman threatening, say, the invalidation of a diplomatic client's credit-status by a fabricated prosecution for debt. A foreign notable is at first sight fair game for this or any similar and latest form of nuisance-suit 'squeeze', a possibility increasingly frequent in countries geared to the extensive use of credit-cards. Potentially ruinous to the average citizen, it could equally impair the whole credibility of a foreign representative in the community to which he is appointed, were it not for such protection.

So with time such minor and personal invocations of immunity have come to be dealt with as a matter of administrative routine. If a genuine need exists for protection against legal harassment, the local Protocol Department of the Foreign Ministry takes over. If however some diplomatic official habitually relies on his immunity to break the law – by speeding, drunken driving, violence etc. – then equally a 'phone-call from the Protocol Department to his ambassador will normally settle the matter by internal discipline. For in the background looms the implication that an incorrigible offender may always be declared *persona non grata* and be whisked off home in disgrace.

The real 'aberrations' are of a more serious quality, and regrettably have lately tended to become more common. To the most candid of souls it is obvious that, at times, governments themselves are behind a particular assault on an embassy, evidently pricing the ensuant profession of regret, and the transaction of due compensation, as a fair investment as against the propaganda point scored. Historically it seems possible that the calculated assault on diplomatic premises, today increasingly frequent where there is a strong central authority, is a perfectly logical development. It may well have grown out of a Machiavellian inspiration, applying to today precedents taken from times and places where the central authority was, unlike today, too helpless to offer conventional protection.

An early yet in many ways strangely modern precedent goes back to the beginning of the recent history of Iran. Russian expansionism in Asia led to a constant ebb-and-flow of military activity on the Russian/Turkish/Persian frontiers. In 1827 a Persian counter-thrust into the Caucasus boomeranged, resulting in the Russian occupation of Tabriz and, in 1828, the comparatively punitive Treaty of Turkomanchai. It imposed a rectification of frontiers, also 'Capitulations' – special privileges for foreigners – which as time went on were to be extended to other Europeans, and were not abolished until 1928. An indemnity was also imposed of thirty million silver roubles – some three million pounds. An instalment was due in August of that same year, otherwise the Russians were entitled to annex Azerbaidjan. The Persians had made no fiscal provision for the payment, but were bailed out by the British Minister, a Scot, who cannily advanced the sum due, in return for the cancellation of two awkward clauses in Britain's own Definitive Treaty of 1814 with Persia.

Later in that autumn of 1828 the restoration of peace between Russia and Persia was celebrated by the despatch to Tehran of a Special Ambassador from the Czar. Monsieur Grebaiodov was received with the customary festivities and courtesies. Unfortunately he brought with him a further demand, for the surrender of two Armenian ladies, presumably Christian, held in Tehran. The Shah accepted. In the background however was a dissenting voice. 'Mujtahid' can mean many things – the struggler, the diligent one, even the sacred warrior – but always behind it is the hint of the 'jehad' – the Holy War. And the Chief Mujtahid of Persia was a dignitary who even today, a century and a half later, seems strangely familiar, if perhaps under another hierarchical designation. The Chief Mujtahid promptly authorized the faithful to 'rescue' the two ladies from the 'infidels'. At once the bazaar shut down – always an ominous sign. Riots developed, and the mob stormed the Russian Legation, burning it to the ground, and murdering the Special Ambassador and the whole of his staff.

The Shah, appalled, made profuse apologies to the Czar, exiled the Chief Mujtahid, and punished the immediately guilty, whose sole immunities presumably rested on the success or otherwise of their enterprise. As for the Czar, who by now was skirmishing with Turkey elsewhere on his steadily advancing Asian frontier, he was quite satisfied to leave it at that, even marking down the outstanding war-indemnity by one tenth. If, as they say, the Almighty does not pay His debts in money, neither evidently does He expect the princes of His unpredictable world to put a fixed cash valuation on their own envoys either.

'Little local difficulties' of this order – which at the receiving end seem, of course, to loom fairly large – usually tended to be spontaneous, or products of fanaticism, and to be disowned, but promptly indemnified, by the authorities. Gradually however a new pattern has set in, with the old-style primitivism put at the disposal of a new political sophistication. Shortly before World War II a colleague of mine was savagely murdered in a remote consulate in northern Iraq – where later I myself was to dedicate much foreboding to the same macabre isolation. He had been hacked to pieces by a bloodthirsty, fanatical and dubiously spontaneous mob, the national government reacting with authentic outrage, and making such material amends as were possible to the widow and family. The flaw in the spontaneity of the demonstration in question had by now however an external origin, with Nazi overtones; its remote-control author, whom to this day I have little doubt I knew well, is nowadays frequently heard of as thriving, in civic virtue and respected and prosperous old age, somewhere in Western Europe.

Official recourse to the violent demonstration as a precision instrument of 'armed propaganda' is for its exponent conveniently difficult to distinguish from the spontaneous expression of crude nationalistic feeling. Many recent assaults on embassies lie in the penumbra between acts of organized official hostility and the anonymity of authentic mob violence. Into this category, so far as I can remember and see, fall the assaults on the British missions in Bagdad in 1958, in Jakarta in 1963, and in Peking in 1967. Particularly, however, in the case of China, it is difficult to judge how much there the excesses of the Red Guard and the Cultural Revolution were governmentally or factionally inspired, were merely tolerated, or indeed were just watched helplessly.

Certainly with the Soviet Union such manifestations must always be presumed to have a governmental complexion, whether those mounted on occasion by young Africans studying in the USSR, or those against the British Embassy at the time of the Suez crisis, by Russian students. On that fifth of November 1956, when the British Embassy in Moscow spent their Guy Fawkes Day serving as the guy themselves, I recall asking myself, from far away, how in a totalitarian and heavily rationed state could the students lay their hands on such limitless supplies of ink-bottles to hurl at the embassy walls? Who, too, was restraining the normally ubiquitous security forces? They would scarcely have failed to materialize had a less xenophobic student manifestation been prising up the cobble-stones for some less delinquent or exotic set of windows.

It has often seemed to me that the stoning of the British Embassy in Moscow that day in 1956 was the archetypal demonstration of what the world was to see frequently thereafter – the vicarious deployment of a parallel force, when a hostile government does not wish to commit itself overtly. With this technique there can be a negative infringement of diplomatic immunity by the withholding of police or army protection, not therefore from loss of control, but from the totality of absolute control, and quite deliberately at that.

A precedent of sorts does on reflection exist, for the time when the sound of breaking plate-glass rings out, while a stone-faced police force stands by with its arms folded. That precedent is the notorious Kristallnacht of Hitler's Germany, in November 1938, save that the windows then shattered were not those of an embassy but of a doomed and helpless minority. Nor was there any question of Hitler's government, having scored its point, making ritual amends; there was no tongue-in-cheek penitence in the sequel to the 'Week of Broken Glass'.

In one sense the British Embassy in Moscow, on that occasion in 1956, had no problems. Their immediate procedure was clear. Their experience of violence had not arisen from internal strife or a change of government. In such a case as theirs the first duty of an ambassador, when he, his staff or his premises are subjected to official violence, or to the withholding of normal official protection, is to make an instant and strenuous protest; it is usually paralleled by his home Foreign Ministry summoning the ambassador of the offending government for a matching protest. In the less cut-and-dried circumstances of 'the field' however, a technical problem can arise, of increasing probability nowadays. Violence, and the breakdown of law and order, are often the concomitant of the overthrow of a government and, quite possibly, the handiwork, accidental or deliberate, of a successor government which has not yet been recognized. How, therefore, is the envoy to make representations, on behalf say of his endangered national community, or to register an immediate protest against the violation of his own immunity, when any exchange of communications can be taken as implying recognition of a new *de facto* government? His own government may not wish to recognize it; and for that matter who knows if it will still be there tomorrow, or Box have embarrassingly replaced Cox all over again? The solution is that of personal initiative – as indeed it frequently is, in contradiction of the legend of today's ambassador as a glorified postman.

For no ambassador is going to waste time, or risk lives, waiting for a telegram authorizing him to lodge a formal protest. He will make personal and informal representations, and to whatever authority he can reach – to the devil himself if necessary, as at times he must often have felt that he was doing; he may need to be a very brave man in such emergencies. For apart from other imponderables, recognition is a two-way ritual. Just as his own government have not yet recognized the new authority – who may just be a man with a gun – so that *de facto* government may, on a whim, choose not to recognize him either, or his diplomatic immunity, and with summary results too. Such are the more uncertain moments of a supposedly pacific profession.

Fortunately the loss of physical and personal immunity which they involve is still comparatively rare, even by today's more casual standards of international conduct. The more common abuse of immunity, that of assault on diplomatic premises, falls usually into three types. These are, first, attacks on, and occupation of, a foreign embassy by some local revolutionary movement; second, the counter-attack on the occupied premises, without the authority of the ambassador, by the national security force and, third, a hybrid of both. All three forms of violation of diplomatic immunity can be instanced from the first weeks of 1980, in El

Salvador, Guatemala and Iran respectively, with the Iranian Embassy in London offering a further permutation later.

It is difficult for the average newspaper-reader and television-watcher to put themselves inside the skin of the participants, and to form a true impression of what happens on such occasions. Perhaps with the help of so-called 'faction', fictionalized documentary, and emotionally overcharged current affairs programmes, the public subconsciously discounts these mortality-filled news bulletin versions as something unreal, with corpses rising to their feet and normality continuing as usual just off-camera, to be resumed thereafter by the players. For present purposes therefore a useful if occasionally hazardous method may serve, in the form of an imagined reconstruction based on a composite of realities. So let us call on the Mancunian Embassy to the Republic of Poldavia:

It is a sunny December morning, and the Poldavian summer is already hot and muggy. But though the entrance-hall-cum-waiting-room is fairly crowded, the air-conditioning is functioning well; it is not too hot, and the customers are reading trade journals and time-lagged newspapers good humouredly. The ambassador has not yet arrived. At the foot of the broad entrance-steps a young man is selling pistachios, and a student is propping his elbows on the handlebars of a parked moped; he is gazing into the eyes of the girl-student straddling it, and singing to her very softly the Poldavian version of 'I've got you under my skin'. A trained observer would have noticed that the expression of their eyes did not correspond to the sentiment being enacted.

A large, shiny, black limousine – as stipulated by the Mancunian Treasury – pulls up at the foot of the steps; it is followed by a small station-wagon containing two large men. The ambassador has arrived. He walks briskly through the main door, followed by his escort, who repair thankfully to the staff-room, the drinking-fountain, and safety till the return-trip home to the residence. The student outside uncoils himself from the moped, and follows the cortege into the embassy at his leisure, noticed indifferently by the office-messenger on duty in the hall. The girl-student pedals her moped into life, and rides off round the corner.

The young man follows the ambassador to the lift-door; the

chancery is on the fourth floor. 'May I see you for a moment, ambassador?' he enquires politely. By this time the office-messenger is tugging officiously at the student's elbow. 'You can't see ambassadors like that! You must make an appointment – maybe see the consul – .' The ambassador interrupts him – 'That's all right – What d'you want to see me about?' he enquires, pleasantly, a little distantly, but in a surprisingly effective version of the local language. 'To present a petition,' the boy answers. 'We are the Students' Patriotic League of the 29th of February. There are more of us right here – .' And indeed a dozen or so of the morning's customers have risen from their chairs and fallen in behind him.

The ambassador is well-trained. When he finds that they will present their petition to no one but himself he resists the temptation to send them on their way. He remarks however that delegations of more than one tend to become round-table conferences. So he will see two of them, and no more, in his office upstairs. But they will have to wait a few minutes. However, at the same moment he notices that he is having to raise his voice; there are noises-off. The girl-student has come back, on foot now, from around the corner, at the head of a couple of hundred other jean-clad youngsters.

The student inside signals with his hand. His girl-friend calls to her reinforcements to follow her up the steps. Meanwhile the messenger, alarmed, has summoned the ambassador's body-guards, and rung the Head of Chancery upstairs. The bigger escort strides to the door, holds up his left hand, palm forward, to the demonstrators and, disastrously, reaches into his side-pocket, for a handkerchief to mop his anxious brow. Thereupon the pistachio-man also reaches into his basket, pulls a machine-pistol from under his pistachios, and instantly shoots the guard in the head. He rolls dead down the steps. Bad reconnaissance – they should have known he went unarmed.

Half a dozen people from inside have been quick enough to make a dash for it to the delivery-door at the rear, in the moment of paralysis that follows. The rest, jammed in a bottle-neck as they make for the main door, are swept aside by the mob of students that suddenly floods the entrance-hall and, moments later, every office in the building. The main door is shut behind them, and only opened to admit more students.

'How many?' the leader asks the young woman. 'Forty-three staff and twenty-one visitors.' 'Turn Poldavian women visitors and female staff loose,' he orders. 'And get me Poldav-TV on the 'phone.' Within minutes the nation, several wives – including the Ambassadress – the security authorities, and the Foreign Ministry – in that order – have realized that some thirty-odd assorted foreigners and Poldavians are held hostage in the Mancunian Embassy, the ambassador included. For their release the Poldavian Government is to concede five million poldmarks, the release of the imprisoned survivors of the Heroic Action of the Twenty-ninth of February 1984, a safe-conduct to Zia Airport – henceforth to be known as Guevara Airport – and a guarantee that the diplomatic immunity of the Mancunian Embassy will meanwhile be respected.

Within minutes all the security forces – police, army and Metropolitan Guard alike – are all assembled outside the Embassy of Mancunia; by this time the lady formerly on the moped is prominently posted just inside the embassy door, calling authoritatively outwards through a loud-hailer held in her left hand. She is screened by a stout, elderly and very alarmed Mancunian business visitor, steered a pace ahead of her by his constant awareness of a heavy automatic pistol in her right hand. One of the numerous pressmen, edging among the furiously arguing senior military in search of an exclusive, finds an unexpected one. It later wins him an international award, and also provides a valuable research line for a variety of psychiatric and security specialists. He is the only one to notice that this rather beautiful girl doing all the talking is marred by a peculiar icy hardness of expression, which he tracks down to an abnormal fixity of gaze amounting to a total physical immobility of the eyeball. He designates it 'the eye of the terrorist'. It eventually turns out that she is a well-known psychopath, an expert assassin with a record computerized in a dozen cities and countries, and brilliantly endowed with the chill logic that, in madness, does duty for reason.

From behind her human screen she warns the now besieging force not to become an assault-force, and to make no hostile move. She emphasizes her point, having noticed one officer slowly raising his machine-pistol. Instantly she shoots not him, but the elderly businessman, under the left shoulder-blade; and he too rolls down the steps. 'You,' she announces in a reasonable voice, 'have just killed this man. I had no wish to do so. You made me. In the same way any further hostile action, or denial of our just demands, will result in the destruction of the imperialist embassy and the execution of all their lackeys and capitalist clients presently inside. The comrades,' she adds as an after-thought, 'have hand-grenades and fire-bombs.' She backs in at the open door, and calmly sets about organizing the commissariat for a long stay; most of the comrades have brought reserves of food, and they already knew that the embassy had a canteen.

Inevitably many of the officers outside have attended a variety of training courses, in various countries, for army and police personnel confronted with terrorist action. Just as inevitably, there are far too many separate security forces in Poldavia, their lack of mutual liaison being exceeded only by their inter-service rivalries. One particularly strong-minded colonel, who has made a special study of the commando-style Mogadishu operation of October 1977, imposes his will on the group. He orders his men to place under arrest the young counsellor from the Foreign Ministry, who is already denouncing his plan as madness, and demanding that the Foreign Minister, the President even, be consulted. 'For the President, I speak. We move in.' – that is all the satisfaction he receives from the colonel.

And indeed they do move in, with surprising efficiency. The students by now are spread all over the building. Of the group holding the entrance-lobby only the original student and his girl-friend, being from the Movement's Political Command, have read the same text-books as the soldiers, and so know all about assault tactics and stun-grenades. Where the rest panic they keep their heads. They fire back from defensive positions. The girl makes a mental note of the ambassador's fox-hole, to deal with him before it is too late. Unfortunately for them all she hits instead one of the comrades – a change from her usually deadly accuracy. He is holding both hands high over his head, in panic and surrender. In one of them is a hand-grenade. As her wild shot hits him he drops it. He, and in a chain reaction his neighbours, are blown to pieces, with him his fire-bomb and, in a sheet of flame, those of the other comrades. The ambassador, who has suddenly seen his chance, propels himself horizontally along the floor, under the worst of the blaze, out through the door, where he too rolls down the steps, in a ball of flame which the particularly sharp-eyed journalist wraps around and douses, with the aggressive colonel's purely decorative great-coat.

A few hours later a furious Mancunian Foreign Minister has administered to the Poldavian ambassador an itemized protest at the intolerable infringement of Mancunia's diplomatic immunity, thanks to his government's failure to provide due and requested protection to the Mancunian embassy in the first place, and thereafter by their uninvited irruption into the embassy premises, precisely as the Mancunian ambassador was negotiating a peaceful solution with his intruders.

The embassy itself is a smouldering shell, with a score of assorted civilian and armed forces bodies buried under the rubble. The aggressive colonel has made sure that the woman-student, though wounded, has been taken alive for interrogation – by him personally. Half a dozen surviving embassy staff and visitors were lucky enough to be winched off the roof, by the US Air Attaché's helicopter, just before it caved in. One of them was, very fortunately, the First Secretary. He is going to be very busy, and also come in very handy, as Chargé d'Affaires for quite a while yet. The Heroes of the Action of the Twenty-ninth of February have meanwhile been fervently analysing the acoustics of assorted weaponry from the depths of the main penitentiary, but will be there for many years more.

Meanwhile the ambassador 'lies for his country', heavily bandaged in a hospital bed, and wonders what on earth they will do with him next.

Of late years something of this sort has happened repeatedly. In April 1975 six German terrorists with a known psychiatric background occupied the German Embassy in Stockholm. They murdered two of the German diplomats found on the premises, when their demands – for the freeing of twenty-six convicted members of the Baader-Meinhoff Group in Germany – were rejected. They blew up the embassy as the Swedish security forces, in agreement with the German government, prepared to assault it. Later that same year a mixed Palestinian and Baader-Meinhoff group invaded the OPEC headquarters in Vienna, which many would accept as a rather special embassy of sorts. Among the hostages taken – after the murder of a humble Austrian policeman – were several large fish indeed. On some of them even the most hardened Sardinian shepherd-cum-kidnapper would have been hard-pressed to fix a ceiling-price. For who can quantify the value to society of a Sheikh Yamani, Oil Minister of Saudi Arabia? The assailants' demands – transport to safety and a reputedly astronomic ransom – were granted. The previous year a Japanese terrorist operation took over the French Embassy in The Hague, their demands too being met. The list is endless.

Guatemala figures in various ways at its top. The first of the diplomatic kidnappings – both culminating in murder – took place there in 1968 and 1969, when the United States Ambassador, Mr John Mein, and then the German Ambassador, Count Karl von Spreti, were shot by their assailants, one during, the other after their kidnapping. The Guatemalan Government take a hard but tenable legal line against any concession to terrorists which would contravene the national law; so Count von Spreti's death cannot technically be held against them. The same cannot however be said for them in the case of the Spanish Ambassador to Guatemala, Senor Máximo Cajal.

On 31 January 1980 he had a very narrow escape with his life, some elements of which inspired my 'model' episode set in 'Poldavia'. His embassy was taken over by a Guatemalan peasant protest-group, and all in it held hostage, with the aim of exacting social reforms from the Guatemalan government. The ambassador evidently hoped to negotiate his way out of the occupation, and insisted that there should be no police intervention. Against his specific orders the Guatemalan police stormed the embassy, which was destroyed by fire-bombs carried by the initial invaders. Most of them, and several of the Spanish staff, including the First Secretary, were killed. The Spanish government very properly broke off diplomatic relations with the Guatemalan government. For the local police to have entered, let alone violently assaulted, the embassy premises, and against the express wish of the ambassador, was a deliberate and inexcusable breach of their inviolability.

During 1979 and 1980 a series of similar occupations and hostage-takings succeeded each other in neighbouring El Salvador, as a direct product of that country's profound social and political unrest. On successive occasions the Costa Rican, French, Venezuelan, Panamanian and Spanish embassies were the victims of onslaughts, occupations, sit-ins and hostage-takings, some of them repeatedly. In none of these cases however was there any suggestion either of governmental complicity in the assaults, or of excess zeal by officially infringing the immunity of the mission. To the contrary, the Salvadorean government was evidently concerned to avoid over-reaction against the various dissident groups cooperating in this incessant use of the local diplomatic representation as a stalking-horse. On each occasion therefore they acted with rigorous propriety. They avoided drastic action, expressed regret at the inadequacy of the protection afforded the embassies, and accepted responsibility for material damage done.

A similar if more external correctness was shown by the Libyan government to the French government when, in February 1980, the French embassy in Tripoli and the Consulate in Benghazi were stormed, sacked and burned by the traditional 'angry mobs'. The Libyan government, itself no advertisement for internal laissez-faire, was already notoriously displeased at France's apparent support of Tunisia against certain Saharan activities of their own. Ostensibly however any breach of the French embassy's diplomatic immunity had been a 'spontaneous' popular Libyan reaction; only a negative participation could be alleged against the Libyan government, by its presumably deliberate withholding of the protection officially requested by the French embassy, in anticipation of these manifestations.

The occupation of the United States Embassy in Tehran on the fourth of November 1979 has already been instanced as a 'hybrid' form of the violation of diplomatic immunity. Perhaps the word 'mutant' would place it more clearly in its relation to the type of vicarious, remote-controlled infringement just described which, for example, Libya has inflicted upon France. In Iran the United States embassy was invaded, occupied and taken over by armed students, as a protest gesture when the deposed Shah was reported in the United States for medical treatment which, the assailants assumed, was a form of camouflaged political asylum. Iran was in a virtual state of anomie, if not yet anarchy, with an assortment of power-centres all vaguely accepting however the ultimate theocratic authority of their religious leader, the Ayatalla Khomeini. Though the armed students holding eventually forty-seven hostages prisoner enjoyed total autonomy inside the occupied embassy, they also enjoyed the approval from without of the Ayatalla who, far from seeking to dislodge them, endorsed their conduct.

The take-over of the embassy, and the use of diplomatic personnel, captured by 'private enterprise', as bargaining counters in an official attempt to secure the extradition to Iran of the former head-of-state was, of course, in direct contravention of international law, as expressed in the Vienna Convention of 1961 of which Iran was a signatory. The violation of immune diplomatic premises was aggravated by its simultaneous and multiple infringement of personal immunity, which amounted in practice to a mass kidnapping of the embassy staff. Less publicized, but legally probably even more outrageous, was the detaining in the Iranian Foreign Ministry of the United States Chargé d'Affaires. That a Head of Mission should be deprived of his liberty by and in the very Foreign Ministry on which he was calling at the time, and which has the prime obligation to guarantee his immunities, is prima facie inconceivable by all diplomatic convention and accepted international law, and will require much explanation.

It is to be hoped therefore that, like most mutations, the latest Iranian interpretation of diplomatic immunity will prove to be a non-viable abnormality. For each development in the Tehran story has a topsy-turvy, Alice-in-Wonderland quality, from the assault on a foreign embassy by a non-official, parallel, paramilitary force, its subsequent occupation condoned by such central authority as exists, via the detention of the Head of Mission in the very chancellery responsible for implementing his immunity, to the continuing detention of his staff in their own embassy, and the untenable proposition of placing diplomatic personnel on trial in the country to which they are accredited. It will be many years before this knot is fully and finally unravelled, its ominous precedents neutralized, and the offence and suffering inflicted duly repaired.

As a further peak of international inconsequentiality, the selfsame Iranian government which has flouted established immunities beyond the tolerance even of the United Nations, has itself complained to the Security Council that its own immunity has been violated. The defendant was the Canadian Government, which had clandestinely spirited out of Iran half-a-dozen United States diplomats who had escaped capture by the armed students, and gone to ground with friends in Tehran. That they had, by the issue of false documents, been spared wholly improper and illegal arrest by the receiving country was thereupon alleged by it to be a breach of international law. Meanwhile the rest of the world applauded this spirited humanitarian gesture.

As already indicated, events in Iran were to reverberate spectacularly in that country's own embassy in London. In the early spring of 1980 six young men, apparently Arabs, rented an assortment of comfortable rooms in western London. They had money to burn, and for a month or two lived the life of prosperous Middle Eastern tourists, enjoying themselves unobtrusively, if in ways perhaps not always consistent with their native mores and faith, and building up an ample store of luxury shopping to take back home.

On the morning of Wednesday the 30th of April they left their rooms empty. Minutes later, a mile or so away, heavily armed, they had overpowered the single policeman from the diplomatic protection unit who was guarding the front entrance of the Iranian Embassy, in an elegant Victorian terrace set back from Kensington Gore, opposite London's Hyde Park. Shortly afterwards they telephoned the World Service of the British Broadcasting Corporation, announcing that for specified political reasons they were holding under threat of death a score of non-British occupants of the embassy offices, as well as the admirable and providentially sent Police Constable Trevor Lock and three other British hostages. Over the next day or two they released one of the British nationals and a Pakistani, both of whom were sick, and an Iranian lady-secretary who was pregnant.

The by now increasingly familiar procedures of the Scotland Yard Anti-Terrorist Squad and other specialized groups were swiftly concentrated on the scene, as were likewise the attention and apparatus of the world's news-media. Yet the expected cycle of the hostages' days and their captors' moods, as theoretically established by the pundits and psychiatrists, was falsified by certain variables which had crept into what can never be a wholly predictable sequence of events.

Thus the occupation of the Iranian Embassy in London was inevitably – and dangerously – compared, linked, even specifically associated, with the parallel episode still proceeding in the United

States Embassy in Tehran. Nor were the London intruders native British militants publicizing some British cause, or bargaining for imprisoned British comrades. They were 'imports', themselves Iranians, though of the dissident Arab minority seeking secession for Khuzistan – Arabistan in their terminology – as also the release of some scores of comrades held in the gaols of the new Iran of the Islamic revolution. Furthermore, they soon aroused and cemented the suspicion of political involvement with the Arab world, by demanding the intervention of certain Arab ambassadors. Just as the Iranian Government had had recourse to the diplomatic channel while itself ignoring all diplomatic convention, with the same unconscious irony these six massively armed young intruders found it normal to appeal to, and thereby in practice justify, the same pacific institution which they were simultaneously violating. Once again therefore we see, extended now into the area of international relations, that 'revolution with guarantees' which is the essence of political terrorism, using the very liberties characteristic of its victim to destroy it.

As the days went by the familiar undulance of rising and diminishing hope and reassurance repeated itself inside the embassy and among its millions of invigilators. Honest brokers from without were summoned to parley; the imprisoned 'bobby' within was brought to a window to talk to his colleagues without; takeaway meals appeared sporadically from a nearby Persian restaurant. Over a weekend of strenuous diplomatic activity it became evident however, and not least to the intruders, that what was by now their main stipulation, a guarantee of safe-conduct out of Britain, would not be forthcoming. The Iranian Government too had regretfully relinquished its hostages to the best endeavours of the receiving country and the mercy of Providence. Though astronomical ransom demands and multiple exchanges of prisoners were thus now out of the question, the invaders of the embassy had nevertheless already achieved what is always the most essential and unquantifiable result, the world-wide publicizing of their cause. Yet they knew that they were cornered, themselves the captives. From this point therefore tension could be expected to mount into hysteria, and almost certainly into a readiness, even a thirst, for martyrdom. It manifested itself first in one of the hostages, a young Iranian diplomat who, affronted by his captors' denigration of his national leader, the Ayatollah

Khomeini, offered himself as a victim. They obliged, and promptly shot him dead, making it clear that the remainder would be picked off successively pending arrangements for their safe-conduct.

The British police, though they have provision for recourse to weaponry when necessary, clearly and wisely prefer to leave to specialized elements of the armed forces the type of violent para-military intervention which urban terrorism must from time to time be expected to invite. The shots announcing the first murder inside the embattled embassy were the signal for Britain's crack commando unit, the SAS, or Special Air Service, who were already standing by, to move into action. On the evening of Monday the 5th of May the externals at least of this dramatic operation were witnessed by the world – 'live by satellite'. The unseen precision and speed of the storming operation inside the embassy were such that the gunmen had time to kill one only of their score of hostages, before five of their own six were themselves instantly shot dead.

The human cost of the rescue had therefore been minimal, though the material cost must have been enormous. To the paralysis for several days of an important section of the capital and its police force must be added the virtual reduction to ashes of the entire embassy building. The intruders had been lavishly equipped with arms and explosives for the threatened holocaust which is always a main component of a hostage-taking. I myself was first alerted to the violent climax of the whole episode by the unmistakable thump of high-explosive through the window at which I was writing, and a pillar of smoke blowing across my skyline of Victorian chimney-pots.

The successful reduction, by the controlled and expert violence of the professionals, of random and impersonal violence directed against the innocent, typifies the correctness with which this assault on society, and on the immunity of one of its institutions, was confronted at all levels. Despite the irrationality then dominating so many sectors of the sending government's society, Iran too responded properly, and with traditional procedures, to this novel threat. Britain, the receiving country, had likewise meticulously observed its obligation to afford the embassy the maximum protection possible without encroaching on its immunities. Only with the eventual permission of the sending government were the premises of the embassy entered, and that with a manifest humanitarian purpose and, very shortly, achievement.

From my own experience at, as they say, the 'receiving end' it was, I hope, a salutary lesson for the world to see how, for a while and in a variety of manifestations, irrationality could suddenly impose itself on the normally sedate face of London. Noisy and ugly demonstrations, by conflicting national and sectarian groups, proceeded for some time outside the occupied mission. Student groups of all derivations dropped any semblance of academic motivation. In their various home countries, too, tendentious political fantasies were propagated and publicized as to the origins, aspirations and sponsors of the embassy occupation. Some of the lady hostages even manifested symptoms of the well-known 'Stockholm syndrome', by which so-called 'rapport', and the personal charm and human identity of their captor, blind the captive to his lethal potential and purpose. Most ominous of all however – though perhaps only to one at home with the history and mythology of the Middle East – the millenial dragon's teeth of the legendary 'Assassins' seemed to be sprouting again in an incongruous late twentieth-century harvest.

In the arid Syrian mountains of the Ismailis – a thousand years ago, or it might just as well be today – the 'Old Man Of The Mountains' would enlist his most likely recruits, as often as not spirited away by kidnap into his uncharacteristically well-watered mountain fastness. Piled with a steady regime of what today we would call cannabis, the hasheesh-takers – 'hashshasheen', and so by derivation 'assassins' – were conditioned into the certainty that – with its entranced abundance of fountains, lawns, nightingales, orange-groves and, of course, houris – they had been transported to and were sojourning in the 'earthly paradise' of Arab legend. Bemused by this illusion, the candidates were sent forth, each with his murderous assignment and a 'booster-charge' of hasheesh, in lieu of today's psychological indoctrination. The target was habitually one of the 'Old Man's' political enemies as, among others, many a crusading knight was belatedly to learn. Included in the bill-of-goods was an assurance of the assassin's permanent reintegration, alive or via martyrdom, into the paradise they so briefly had enjoyed.

The cruel analogy of this lethal confidence-trick is sinister or pathetic as you choose, with in today's rendering a political

assignment half-fulfilled, much material destruction, a few innocent dead, and a half-dozen riddled corpses in a London mortuary,
to return no more again to the brief earthly paradise of Harrods
of Knightsbridge and the pubs of the Earls Court Road. Yet by
confronting this madness with unceremonious legalism and much
personal discipline, a small but potentially fateful breach in the
dyke of civilization was held.

The common factor between all the foregoing instances of the
precariousness of diplomatic immunity is their occurrence in a
setting of social and political disorder, of violence, and of revolution. All too apply primarily to the immunity of the diplomat's
premises. But the person of the diplomat is infinitely more vulnerable than his premises; and if that particular immunity is violated
in totality, not all the apologies and indemnities in the world can
reinstate it. In any case, the immunity of life and limb which is
currently in jeopardy is threatened by governments only negatively and incidentally, as the occasional byproduct of the withholding of immunity from premises. The direst threat to the
person of the diplomat comes from what I have termed 'private
enterprise', from 'parallel power'. It is unofficial, though far from
amateur; those seeking the person or the life of the envoy today
are highly professional – till lately far more so than those chosen
to combat them, and certainly infinitely freer from moral inhibition.

Most of the physical hazards to which diplomacy exposed its
practitioners in the past have been virtually eliminated by air-
conditioning, refrigeration and antibiotics. There is also a better
understanding of the role, in difficult climates, of food and,
especially, drink; all climates away from home, of course, are
'difficult', even for the diplomat. In any event immunization
against disease was always a more chancy proposition than the
abstract legalisms of professional immunity, the provisions of
which have never pretended to safeguard the diplomat against
run-of-the-mill mortality. Diplomatic immunity can only do so
much. There was one terrible night in the Cairo embassy when
an official dinner had to go on even so, despite the whispered news
that the cook had just slid under the kitchen table to die of
cholera; there is no Vienna Convention against that.

Today's latest threat to the diplomat's professional immunity
comes from without – from the assassin and the kidnapper. There

is nothing new in murdering people not for what they have done, but for what they are and for what they symbolize; Sarajevo in 1914 is a monument to the practice. In the past diplomats had in effect a certain immunity against it because, though representatives, they were not seen as symbols. His Excellency was not so much a person as an institution, for once deriving some advantage from being a lay-figure, a cardboard cut-out rather than a human being. Freak assassinations, such as that of Sir Lee Stack, the Sirdar of the Sudan in 1924, had a specific and colonial connotation rather than diplomatic.

Terror itself – admonitory murder – is as old as man; the very phrase 'Kill one, terrify a thousand' goes back to Sun Choo, a Chinese general who was a contemporary of Confucius. What has updated it, so that it extends now to the traditionally immune person of the envoy, is an alliance of science and ideology. Pavlov's conditioned reflex is harnessed to the cause of the social revolution, to the toppling of governments and societies by the powerful leverage of the vicarious. By this token, he who speaks for one people to another shall also suffer for them, and so feed back to them the message of pain and indignity, determining their will by some form of distant cybernetic. As it was put to me by one of my terrorist captors on just such an occasion – 'You are being punished as the notional symbol of institutional neocolonialism.' Admittedly the message itself was marred by its human medium, in some strange way pathetic with its ideological pomposity and atrocious terminology. Yet it indicates that guiltless human beings are now at constant risk, not from any personal odium or offence, but for what they symbolize. Two British ambassadors were most brutally murdered within a couple of years, along with other lives less illustrious but just as precious, merely to demonstrate that an internationally recognized symbol is wholly vulnerable to a minority purpose with a trans-national capability, and with access to modern technology and training.

In those two tragic cases the question of kidnapping did not arise. Both Christopher Ewart-Biggs in 1976 and Richard Sykes in 1979 were in effect ambushed, with no other intention than their instant, violent and total physical destruction, one by culvert-bomb, the other by gunfire. The aim was therefore one of propaganda alone. The kidnapping of diplomats had had a different aim at its peak which, by the late seventies, it had already passed;

during the five years until 1973 some twenty-five instances are recorded. Certainly the kidnappings had shared the same essentially psychological purpose as the later assassinations; one definition of all terrorism, and indeed guerrilla action, is precisely 'armed propaganda'. In addition however they incorporated the further element of ransom. Since time immemorial 'civilian' kidnapping has in practice always been for profit. In the case of the terrorist however, the acquisitive purpose is not, or should not be, personal, but directed to the accumulation of a war-chest; the arming, feeding, housing and deploying of such a movement all come expensive. Another aim of kidnapping for a trade-off is the bartering of the hostage, or hostages, for members of the terrorist movement previously captured and imprisoned by the target government.

At first diplomatic kidnapping succeeded, both as 'armed propaganda' and as a funding technique. Thus around the turn of the decade, up to the early 'seventies, the American, German and Swiss ambassadors in Brazil were kidnapped in succession, and ransomed against a progressively more exorbitant permutation of cash and concession, such as exchanged prisoners. It was this phase which clearly conveyed that the escalation, both of the practice and of its steadily raised 'ante', simply had to stop. If money is always negotiable, but principle never, a time nevertheless comes when the two curves of the graph cross, and the ransom concession becomes intolerable. Current doctrine, with its kidnap insurance component, is that this point may never be reached with 'ordinary', non-diplomatic, purely profit-making kidnapping, though my own conviction is that it inevitably must with time. But by the early 'seventies the diplomatic community, of both sending and receiving governments, was beginning and ready to accept that the undertaking of a host-government to protect the immunity of accredited diplomats could not extend to yielding to terrorism, and discrediting its own national law. A number of demonstrations of obduracy towards the kidnappers – some with fatal results for the victim – conveyed the 'no deal' message that the diplomat was an unrewarding target for the political kidnapper. The wave abated.

It was then realized that the diplomat's premises were just as vulnerably symbolic as he himself, with the incidental propaganda bonus that a well-timed assault, in office hours or on a ceremonial occasion, might also entrap a random sample of the public, or other uninvolved 'outsiders', with all their additional emotional and public-relations impact. The Iranian Embassy incident of May 1980 in London was a case in point. Even more so in this respect was the multiple ambassadorial hostage-taking at an Independence Day reception in the Dominican Embassy in Bogotá, the capital of Colombia. Here, on 27 Feburary 1980, a score of diplomats were seized and held hostage by a Colombian revolutionary group for two months. The Colombian Government negotiated, but was adamant in its refusal to exchange the hostages for imprisoned members of the dissident group; its tradition as a 'nation of lawyers' would have seen this as a breach of its own law. In return however for the liberty of the hostages a ransom of sort was paid, and the expatriation intact of the intruders granted, a partial concession which, in the echoing underworld of international terrorism, may well have invited a repetition of the technique, there or elsewhere.

So the risk still continues. Protection by host-governments, and precautions by the diplomats themselves, were intensified to, and remain at, a high, costly and tiresome level. Thereby, in a sense, yet another immunity of the diplomat has been forfeited – immunity from restriction of movement. There are of course those countries in which the movements of diplomats are officially and habitually circumscribed as a matter of course, attracting reluctant retaliation from governments so penalized. In many formerly unaffected countries today the same diplomatic constraint has been imposed unofficially, by the latently persistent risk of kidnapping.

Under international law the position remains unsatisfactory. Self-evidently diplomatic immunity, the safety of the envoy, means nothing whatsoever to clandestine revolutionary movements. But once a movement becomes a government, then it should. Events in Iran in 1979 and 1980 have already demonstrated that the 1961 Vienna Convention can be flouted with impunity, and without any effective and unanimous international reaction. In its turn the United Nations Convention of 1973 gives only a qualified extension of the protection due to the diplomat in an age of terrorism; it was long and dilatory in ratification, and loopholes will inevitably be found in it to evade the punishment or extradition of an offender. The European Convention of 1977, while similarly vulnerable to evasion, at least embodies a satisfactory exclusion of certain key offences from the 'political' category, which otherwise becomes a routine sanctuary in the case of crimes against diplomats. Yet the whiff of 'Realpolitik' clings to all three Conventions. Despite them, the personal and physical immunities of the diplomat remain uncertain, and diminished by events.

I am the fortunate owner of a copy of a minor masterpiece of light verse, written most of a lifetime ago by a distinguished figure from what Geoffrey Moorhouse evocatively calls the 'hyphenated litany of bygone ambassadorial names[1], the late Sir Hughe Knatchbull-Hugessen. It describes at some length the kidnapping – surely apocryphal – of a British ambassador to the Old China, by bandits from across the Great Wall. The ransom negotiations are as protracted as is the correspondence with Whitehall. The Treasury, in the absence of precedents in those more innocent days, are shown as being in a quandary. For the purposes of ransom how were they to fix a valuation on the increasingly alarmed and uncomfortable captive? An ambassador was neither work of art, objet de vertu, nor genuine antique, while ancient monuments came under the First Commissioner of Works. In the event the Treasury settled for the sum of half-a-crown – twelve-and-a-half new pence today. It was never paid, because for unexplained reasons the bandits – who all along seem to an experienced eye far less professional than was, for all his insoutiance, the ambassador – took flight. He, a more portly Spring-Heeled Jack, 'with one leap' was over the Wall, and back into safety.

Today we can still enjoy this harmless fun, but as a parody of fact rather than a fantasy of imagination. The reality is no longer funny at all. Of the numerous check-lists of terrorism available the most detailed and formidable that I know figures in Dobson and Payne's *The Weapons of Terror*[2]. It records one hundred and forty-seven major incidents of such violence in the decade from 1968, a high proportion of which have a diplomatic connotation. As well as by this atrocious multiplication of statistical episode, General Sun Choo's sardonic dictum of long ago has now been revalidated, and enormously amplified, by the new ubiquity of television and the instantaneity of the satellite; instead of a thousand, ten million simultaneous spectators can watch a man made dead 'live', or contemplate in person the kidnap victim,

[1] *The Diplomats*, p. 47, Jonathan Cape, 1977
[2] Macmillan 1979

crouched beneath the by now traditional lop-sided and five-pointed star.

Another disagreeable innovation, which exposes the diplomat still further to this new and unofficial deprivation of immunity, is what might be termed the menace of erroneous denunciation. We have already seen how the American CIA's own failings have been exacerbated by the fashionable blurring of the distinction between the diplomat, the spy and the subversive. It now appears that respectable career members of the US Foreign Service are being gratuitously put at risk around the world, having been quite wrongly denounced as 'Company-men' in the writings of a renegade from that Service.

As a compensation of sorts – one which no diplomat would enjoy – it is arguable that the spotlight of kidnapping has moved latterly from him to the businessman overseas. The adoption of stringent precautions by sending and receiving governments, together with the no longer merely tacit assumption that they will not bargain with a kidnapper, has had a so-called 'knock-on' effect. Its effects have been particularly noticeable in Latin America. The chosen target for ransoming is now, more likely than not, the executive of a wealthy multinational corporation, or even the random crowd who happen to be in an embassy selected for occupation. In the latter case, as we have seen, the diplomat is still, of course, at high risk; statistically and actuarially his chances of being 'where the action is' are higher than average.

And if perhaps less likely than before to be violently bundled from his official limousine into captivity, there is a correspondingly greater probability that he may become the victim of the ultimate 'armed propaganda', unadorned and unremunerative, his death its own justification to the murderer. Terrorism contends that there is no such thing as an innocent bystander. By extension it sees all human symbols as self-condemned. The assassination-list shows that they come in all kinds; 'He was killed because he was a British soldier', says an IRA instance from peace-time Germany. Like all such, the diplomat, his wife, his family, must accept that for an indefinite future he too must live, and perhaps die, at risk.

It is tragic too when by some sort of a schizophrenia, controlled or not, governments themselves harness diplomacy to the kind of aberration considered in this chapter. The British Government, as no doubt other governments too, have found it advisable and timely to remind their local diplomatic corps that the immunities of the diplomatic bag do not extend to unimpaired freedom of movement for the appliances of destruction. And it is a sad fact that one abuse of the institution of immunity can all too easily be identified with another, and contempt for its forms spread to its substance. Such an association of ideas by the public was noticeable when a number of Libyan nationals, not diplomats but political refugees of a sort, were successively assassinated in the streets of London and other European capitals, after an open official threat by their President that they should return home to confront his justice, or face 'execution' wherever they might hide abroad. Such a threat clearly placed his diplomatic representation in an ambiguous posture vis-à-vis the law of the receiving nation.

Meanwhile Libyan embassies in various countries had arbitrarily assumed the novel designation of 'People's Bureau', with no ambassador or formal staff. This lack of accreditation places their diplomatic status and immunities, under the Vienna Convention of 1961, into a form of suspended animation. So anomalous a status thus prevents the receiving government from invoking the normal swift sanction of declaring *persona non grata*, and expelling, any diplomat exceeding his function. At best this unilateral metamorphosis of established practice can only destroy itself, if ever it leads to the anarchy of its multilateral adoption; and so it should perhaps be regarded as no more than a temporary and irrational desire to shock the international bourgeoisie. At its worst however it has a disturbing affinity on the international scale with the terrorist's exploitation at the internal political level of the 'revolution with guarantees' already adumbrated. The coincidence of exported violence with administrative inconformity is no foundation for stable and friendly relations.

It is a disquieting thought that, by a kind of diplomatic Gresham's Law, contamination tends to spread from the part to the whole, corrupting and deadening our received moral criteria. The repudiation, as if they were mere taboos, of millennially and arduously evolved immunities, by unrepresentative and violent minorities, has already infected governments. Sooner rather than later, they themselves will pay dear for their new ambivalence towards the law of nations. Meanwhile the diplomat must watch with regret as, resurrected after many years, the spectre of Niccoló Machiavelli walks the corridors of the world's chancelleries once more.

Part Two

YESTERDAY, AND TOMORROW

Chapter VIII
Diplomacy in the Dark

Yet diplomacy is not just as old as Machiavelli. It is indeed older than the diplomats themselves, as the Cro-Magnons of my first Chapter recall. The professional – the career ambassador – only came into the business as states evolved, and as their relations began to require care-and-maintenance instead of the occasional major overhaul.

This evolution was particularly marked during the resurrection of Europe from the Dark Ages via the Middle Ages into our modern scientific and technological age. It was a secondary evolution, a progress that had happened there once before, to early man, till checked and reversed by the collapse of Greece and Rome. Once again it is a characteristic aside from Harold Nicolson that reminds us of our time-scale; as early as 432 BC, according to Thucydides, a recognizable diplomatic conference was summoned by the Spartans.

In our terms it seems to have been less a summit than a technical conference. Its participants – though already they did have vocational imunities – were evidently not so much professionals as 'wise men'. It has often seemed to me that, from the earliest days of the 'elders of the tribe' the ageing process has had its compensations, both for the individual 'senior citizen' and for the community that must either support or scrap him. As his physical contribution to the tribe waned, so his accumulated knowledge-ability took its place, while correspondingly his human wish to justify his continuing worth fitted in neatly with his group's need to see its members pay their way. By Thucydides' time these imperatives had no doubt been nicely institutionalized into an esteem for tenure, for the kind of elder statesmanship traditionally authenticated by a venerable aspect and a druidical manner.

But the wheel of civilization turned comparatively soon, helped by an extra heave from the sturdy shoulders of the Goths and Vandals down from the North. By the time Europe re-emerged from the Dark Ages, the negotiator's task had degenerated. The laurel-wreathed elder statesman of classical days – now styled 'nuncius', legate, procurator, even orator – was again little more than his still remoter predecessor, the iron-lunged herald, who from his cliff-top stentorianly bellowed his chieftain's terms to the enemy in the valley below.

Such was once more the situation from which diplomacy was recovering by, say, the fourteenth century AD. It is a period when the Anglo-French connection was still close, even in terms of origin and consanguinity; when one ruler can call another 'cousin' and mean it, then diplomacy as inter-state apparatus becomes almost a tautology. Yet even when warfare is internecine, and feuding virtually a family affair, conciliation is still necessary. Edward III, and all those of the Hundred Years War who seemed to luxuriate in conflict, by their own works best demonstrated the dire necessity of conciliation. A couple of centuries later it was the young Henry VIII who finally conceded and formalized that necessity.

In between, European man's emergence from the Dark Ages was, paradoxically, amounting in practice to a retrogression. It's product was an ebullient primitivism, on all the evidence far worse than the generally obscure and stagnant centuries preceding it. Compared with it Charlemagne's was an age of gold, even the Merovingian, let alone the almost or totally forgotten civilizations of Greece and Rome, and of geographically still remoter organized human communities inconceivable to medieval man.

A glimpse into the pre-Renaissance Anglo-Saxon nightmare was afforded me long ago by an excellent science-fiction story built round a popular variant of the time-machine theme, known to addicts as the 'time-probe'. This ingenious device seems even fictionally to have worked quite unpredictably, as well as so rapaciously of energy as to be unsuitable for application to our real-life circumstances, and therefore unlikely to be manufactured just yet. But it made a good story, of which one special scene remains fixed in my memory.

Instead of the rotund prelate, the berobed king or armoured nobleman, or even the sturdy and rubicund yeoman whom the modern scientists had confidently expected to retrieve from, and interrogate on, their past history, their catch seemed to them scarcely human. Barely articulate, gaunt, pock-marked, his teeth rotting stumps, his clothes filthy rags, this lamentable majority specimen of humanity manifested every conceivable clinical symptom from vestigial rickets to incipient bubonic plague.

Even those who prefer the verdict of serious historical analysis to that of second-hand science-fiction will be unlikely to dispute this dismal picture. The century of the Hundred Years War seems in fact to have been just about as bleak and atrocious as human history can offer. From Italy to the Low Countries and to the anonymous sculptors of our own great cathedrals and village churches, the art of the time dwelt on the charnel-house, large coffin-worms, and the general uncertainty of existence. The horrors of the Black Death were only the last straw in a century when war ebbed and flowed across Western Europe, when pillage and brutality became a way of life, when the British bowmen of Crécy and Poitiers left behind them a carnage equal in its own scale to that of the Somme, and when even peace was so precarious as regularly to necessitate the exchange of the participants' nearest and dearest as a pledge against treachery. Treaties such as that of Brétigny in 1360 stipulated no less than forty such eminent hostages.

That treaty's preliminaries seem to have been as prolonged and laborious as any professional diplomat would wish or contrive; today's London-Paris shuttle of an hour or two could alone take two or more weeks then. Yet however professional the result, the exponents seem to have been simple 'commissioners', *ad hoc* appointees for what amounted to hastily assembled parleys, rather than what we would consider authentic conferences preparatory to important treaties. This 'instant diplomacy' was entrusted to men who enjoyed the royal confidence through their experience, education, and habituation to the exercise of power. Unsurprisingly there was a preponderance of eminent clerics, who tended to enjoy all three of these advantages, also of royal dukes, though these are on record as tending to be literally a rather expensive luxury. Perhaps for this reason less exalted names begin to feature among the successive negotiators. So as well as cardinals with familiar names like Talleyrand, names of a different familiarity begin to emerge – a young military historian named Froissart, a rising civil servant, Geoffrey Chaucer, on his own road to eminence both as an envoy of the English court and as a poet of its still half-formed language.

These were the blossoms that were beginning to bud from the rich ordure of this cadaveric century. It was a Danse Macabre that could not go on. The advent of the Tudors, the stabilization of city life round an increasingly prosperous and enlightened bourgeoisie, a settlement with France in 1492 at Etaples – all these were harbingers, if not of peace and the earthly paradise, yet of a new decorum, a less anarchic pattern to the life of nations, and of men.

Henry VIII deserves to be remembered better for his sensing of this change in the rhythm of the European heartbeat, and not only for his serial polygamies, as in his own heart even he probably saw them. Cardinal Wolsey may take the credit for the balance-of-power principle which was the Tudor heritage to British foreign policy. Yet it was his master, in the brilliance of his imaginative and intuitive youth, who sought a more spectacular way to end the interminable brutishness of what at the beginning had been almost an Anglo-Norman civil war.

Henry VIII is another historical phenomenon for which my memory cherishes a fictional mnemonic. This time, though, the analogy is not with science-fiction, but with a story, as I recall, of the early Somerset Maugham, dealing with a character known as 'Red'. In an unattractive antipodean tavern a traveller, back from the South Sea Isles, is regaling the bar-tender with a not wholly mawkish account of a second-hand Polynesian love-story. He had met on his island-hopping a handsome, grizzled chieftainess who had told him of her lost girlhood love, a titian-haired Adonis cast ashore on her island long ago. Their idyllic passion was interrupted for ever – and, pathetically, his unborn child, her only keepsake, lost through shock – when he was shanghaied aboard a passing blackbirder. The story-teller's audience – the bald, gross, drink-sodden barkeep – listens, thoughtfully strokes the ginger bristles of his thick forearm, squints up out of his red-rimmed little blue eyes. 'Y'know,' he smirks, 'they tell me I was quite a nice-looking laddy once. And they called me Red out there.'

Each time that I hear 'Greensleeves', or see the familiar Holbein, or the great suit of armour, I think – I hope without retrospective lèse-majesté – of Red. The last years' monstrous bladder of disease and, no doubt, remorse, had as barely more than a boy had the vision and the sensibility to see that the French and the British simply might not carry on like this. They were too akin, still too like each other, always too close, to go on destroying each other senselessly.

That they should live in perfect amity was perhaps too much to hope. But at least they should live as civilized neighbours, and according to a code. A start could be made by teaching them that instead of sharing battle they could share sport. The Field of the Cloth of Gold was in its way a premature, perhaps rather more honest manifestation, of the United States late-twentieth-century theme of 'Make love, not war'. There are those who say of that particular slogan that it was a drop-out euphemism, rationalizing personal survival in terms of sexual permissiveness. Henry at least, and for all his later excesses, was in his time sincerely concerned with exposing the Anglo-French aristocracies to the sublimating virtues of hawking, hunting, jousting and part-song, in the lavish and care-free setting evoked by Shakespeare in the opening scene of his Henry VIII from which I have quoted in Chapter II.

The Protocol and Conference Department of the Foreign and Commonwealth Office are reputed to have performed their own prodigies of logistics and catering in their time too, not least when several international junketings have overlapped in Britain, as in 1977, the *annus mirabilis* of four London summits in barely as many weeks. So, too, in 1520 Henry VIII had to juggle competing occasions, honouring first the newly elected Emperor Charles V, in England briefly on his way from the Low Countries to Spain, then at once Francis I, just across the English Channel. He and Wolsey synchronized between them a contemporary version of Chequers, Lancaster House, Leeds Castle, the Government Hospitality Fund and Protocol and Conference Department all in one: –

'That the Emperor's visit ... did not de-rail the other operation is another measure of Wolsey's capacity for organization and of the competence of early Tudor administration. Over five thousand persons made up the suites of Henry and his queen. Hundreds of pounds' worth of velvet, sarcenet, satin, cloth of gold and doublets, bonnets, shirts and boots were supplied for them. They had to be gathered at Dover, shipped over the water, given lodgings at Calais and then Guines. Hundreds of tents and pavilions were sent over, together with enough food for men and beasts, and mountains of plate, cutlery and glass. Six thousand men were busy preparing the English quarters ... beer and wine, green geese, rabbits, storks, quails and cheese, enough fuel for the kitchens – '[1]

As so often with 'summits', we ask ourselves what negotiating pinnacle there was to all this vast gastronomic, sartorial and athletic infrastructure. I should be happier, and my curiosity more satisfied, if I could match it with a corresponding tally of clerks, scriveners and courtiers, and of indents for quills, ink and parchment. I can only vouch for those of my own day. But whether it be under the Plantaganets milling around northern France, or Wolsey to-ing and fro-ing over much the same ground a couple of centuries later, their legates and their small mobile embassies seem then always to have comprised much the same assemblage of 'commissioners' and 'councillors'. As for the 'Counsellors of Embassy', not to mention the First Secretaries, attachés, cypher-clerks and admin-officers, these all lay far in the future. The Field of the Cloth of Gold, like its less spectacular predecessors, seems to have entailed a minimum of paper-work. It is the fanfare and the fun of the setting that have survived.

It did not, of course, work. So the Field of the Cloth of Gold remains a legend pathetic or tawdry as you see it, for the most part passed over by historians, a lath-and-plaster memorial to a splendid young man whose grandiose potential as a king went awry. It is also an early demonstration of the application to diplomacy of what now are called public-relations techniques. Diplomacy by jamboree, by durbar, which is not quite the same – by in effect a form of 'royal progress', has not been unknown since. At Guines the 'great horses' of war – the Shires and Percherons of today – were caparisoned into incongruous elegance much as, on analogous occasions now, their modern equivalents, the great armoured tanks and giant missiles, are paraded garlanded, with

[1] *Henry VIII* by J. J. Scarisbrick (pps. 110–11), Methuen 1976

blossoms wreathing their terrible guns and war-heads. Nothing is ever quite new, under the sun or the satellite. The Field of the Cloth of Gold culminated in the ritual embrace of the two rulers, as on today's television screens a whole world has witnessed the embraces of Messrs Sadat, Begin and a President called Jimmy. Instead history recalls for us a brace of monarchs called Henry and Francis, with an Emperor called Charles looking on dubiously from the wings. And taking notes a lawyer, Master More, Sir Thomas of that name, diplomat and, some would say, saint.

Meanwhile, back home in Whitehall, a more pragmatic Wolsey was laying the foundations of his balance-of-power, and by no means with his master's youthful affability. Wolsey's diplomacy, like his destiny, was flawed by arrogance and bad temper. Even as his master jousted behind Calais, Wolsey was laying hands on the Papal Nuncio and threatening him with the Tower rack. Yet ultimately the pupil was to see better than the teacher that the balance-of-power must rest on the possession and application of power. The same royal master who turned brutally on the overweening servant also had the realism to bolster his foreign policy with sea-power, and the new balance-of-power with the new Royal Navy.

I have always seen the Field of the Cloth of Gold as a watershed of sorts in European diplomacy, and so, given its timing, in world diplomacy too. It represents not quite a 'last', nor yet quite a 'first'. Rather it is a perceptible stage in the progress of diplomacy, from the tribal, pipe-of-peace, post-battle, chieftain-centred dialogue of which it was the over-statement, to the trans-national summitries of today. True, the ensuing centuries were still, now and then, to resort to bilateral encounters of the traditional style. Yet even those are remembered now, as often as not, for their more spectacular incidentals. No one for example who has read *War and Peace* – or G. M. Trevelyan – will ever forget that when two Emperors met at Tilsit in 1807 it was aboard a raft on the Niemen.

Precisely this injection of public relations seems to me to derive from Henry VIII's contribution to diplomatic history. Its trace may still be visible, both in the great international congresses of later centuries and in the so-called 'razmatazz' of the Camp Davids and Guadaloupes headlined in recent years. More than an echo lingers too in the corridors of the United Nations. As with the

League of Nations before it, in my youth it was hoped that these standing international bodies would supersede our forbears' less idealistic approach to international co-existence. They have not, and the ambassadors still come and go around the world. So, increasingly, do their 'masters' too.

Chapter IX
Vienna, Paris, The 'Old Diplomacy'

Anything more comprehensive than this brief retrospect would soon find itself in competition with various excellent histories of diplomacy already available. Anything less so would conversely run up against that model of concision, the opening chapter of Satow's *Guide to Diplomatic Practice.* Either enterprise would be rash as well as repetitive. So this different and intermediate perspective on the newest variant of diplomacy will seek only the essential minimum of comparison between its past, its present and its probable future.

The points of reference I have chosen serve that purpose. The question they aim to answer is whether the latest version of conference diplomacy is a full mutation, or just an updating of the old. Has diplomacy, the implementation of foreign policy, become by now one more function, or even the victim, of high-speed air travel and the hot-line – perhaps for good, perhaps for evil, perhaps even for the entire superseding of traditional diplomacy? Or is it just the old formula, enlivened by a little technology?

As criteria go, my samplings are unrepentantly subjective. In the long procession from the primordial foot-slogging troglodyte-diplomat, via the ecclesiastic on his well-fed mule, to the earliest plumed and gold-braided 'Excellency' identifiable as such to us, it was at the Field of the Cloth of Gold that I found the first real relevance to latter-day summitry. So the emphasis on the previous chapter is arbitrary and wholly personal. Equally arbitrarily I am leap-frogging the whole seventeenth century, if perhaps with some sense of neglect towards the year 1648 and the three year Congress culminating in the Treaty of Westphalia. With a similar twinge of conscience, and the same short shrift, I am also bypassing the eighteenth century; at least I have already credited it with having finally institutionalized diplomacy as a profession. In Britain indeed it was Edmund Burke who in 1782 made it an official arm of government, when the Northern Department of His Majesty's Government was reconstituted as the Foreign Office, with its own Foreign Secretary – assisted incidentally by the playwright Sheridan.

To be sure, the first eighteenth-century 'unionizing' of the diplomatic craft seems in retrospect more of a gentrification; it took the nineteenth century to broaden the basis of recruitment and qualification. The twentieth century was to broaden the base still more – perhaps indeed to the distortion of the apex; there have lately been signs, on the whole I think regrettable, that at last, in Britain too, domestic political considerations are again beginning habitually to impinge on the highest diplomatic appointments. As already inferred from consideration of Dr Kissinger's summitry, it may well be a harsh reality of the modern state that the thicker the available democracy is spread lower down the pyramid, the less there will be left for the top, whatever our philosophy, ideology or effective system.

On reflection my neglect of the eighteenth century may anyhow be more apparent than real. I have singled out, as the next and most natural stepping-stones towards the present diplomacy of the Concorde and the jumbo-jet, the Congress of Vienna of 1814 to 1815, and then the Treaty of Versailles of 1919. And it is entirely arguable that the first was just as much an eighteenth-century phenomenon as was the second a time-lagged aftermath of the nineteenth. In diplomacy, as in furniture and fashion, the clock of the Victorian age seems twice to have struck late. Only with the accession of the 'Young Queen' in 1837 – some would even say with the death of the Iron Duke in 1852 – does the eighteenth century itself seem at last to have died. In 1901 the death of the 'Old Queen' may have synchronized nearly enough with a precise centennial of the Gregorian calendar. Yet her spirit pervaded our nation and its institutions, including its foreign policy and diplomacy, for a full generation longer. Victorian Britain lingered on, until the General Strike, the Hungry Thirties, the crescendoing mutter of an unbalanced German named Hitler, the Abdication and, finally, the sure premonition of a second Great War.

The great watersheds of history are often sited by material factors as much as by the thoughts, writing and aspirations of men. Inventions such as the stirrup and the steam-boiler have made empires out of nomadic tribes and Highland clansmen. Lord Gore-Booth[1] observes that Castlereagh took twenty-eight days to reach Vienna for the Congress of 1815; a generation later not even as many hours would have been needed by train. Similarly, another century later, transatlantic then world-wide air-travel were expediting still further the intervening contraction of the world by Victorian steam-power. Until the Imperial Airways flying-boats of the 'thirties even the most expert Phileas Fogg could only just reach Cairo from London via Brindisi inside a week. Today, though his mail may take longer to reach him, he can be there in person between two meals.

The Congress of Vienna, to which Castlereagh ambled by coach, has enough of the same consciously flamboyant quality and setting as the Field of the Cloth of Gold to justify its sharing also in the genealogy of twentieth-century summitry. That circus quality earned for it the imperishable accolade of the cynical old Prince de Ligne, that if it did not walk – or work – at least it danced – 'Le Congrès ne marche pas, mais il danse.' Indeed, much of the attendance seems to have been there just for the fun. Starting at the top, Duff Cooper[2] lists two emperors, plus their two empresses, four kings, one queen, two heirs to the throne, two grand-duchesses, three princes, minor royalties galore, and all their innumerable attendant courtiers. It had been much the same at the Field of the Cloth of Gold; virtually the whole of England's aristocracy, male and female, had gone along for the party.

But at Vienna, behind the socializing, an impressive achievement in organization and output took place in six months flat. Napoleon's 'Hundred Days' interregnum between Elba and St Helena barely ruffled it. Castlereagh's fellow-negotiator, Wellington, confronted the interruption with an effortless and notoriously successful quick-change back into his more usual military role. At the core of the proceedings was a surprisingly small and compact team of negotiators. Talleyrand himself, though inflating his status as Foreign Minister by a retinue of no less than three fellow-plenipotentiaries, evidently used them for domestic-political and decorative purposes only. He prepared his own instructions, in a mastery brief-cum-background-paper which has become famous. At the actual negotiating table he was accompanied only by one

[1] *Satow, op. cit.* (p. 519), Note 1
[2] *Talleyrand* (p. 245), Jonathan Cape 1932

top Foreign Ministry official, a professional of his own choosing.

Two-by-two seems to have been the rule for this select conclave of 'The Big Five', who briskly, competently, and with much attention to procedure, agreed between themselves what then went to the Congress as a whole to become, by June 1815, the Final Act of the Congress. Out of this informal standing committee of Foreign Ministers grew the Concert of Europe, which for the most part functioned surprisingly well till the First World War. It can be argued that out of it grew also what was to be the Security Council of the United Nations.

Though by the end of the eighteenth century there was no further doubt about what a diplomat did, it was a sub-committee of the Congress of Vienna that finally codified what he was. Its definitive 'Règlement sur le rang entre les agents diplomatiques' was a surprisingly democratic product for a body often criticized by historians for its excessive deference to the principle of 'legitimacy', as sanctified by the existing order. The 'Règlement' instead simply established the seniority of Heads of Mission on a basis of tenure. Life becomes much easier when prestige in the shape of population statistics, Gross National Product, or the military power of the sending country, can be discounted for all formal purposes by the receiving government; priority goes automatically to the oldest inhabitant, by accreditation, of the local Corps Diplomatique. Something of the same criterion applied even to placing at table can be very practical; I have seen fancied offence deflected by the poker-faced suggestion of alternative placing, higher or lower, on the basis of a wife's age or the husband's income.

The nineteenth century was the golden age of all these ceremonial niceties, enshrined under the heading of 'protocol', and stereotyped sartorially in the diplomat's alleged alternative uniforms of ostrich-plumes and 'striped pants'. In practice this was the age in which the serious organization of diplomacy was proceeding apace, and the conventions of the eighteenth century were harnessed to the aims and apparatus of the nineteenth. In Britain the 'Clerks of the Foreign Office' – which with their quill pens, letter-presses and jellygraph duplicators they literally were – found themselves, along with the young men of the still separate Diplomatic Service, recruited under the aegis of the Civil Service Commission. True, there remained more than a whiff of privilege in the still strict pre-examination screening, including the requirement of a personal recommendation to the Secretary of State.

Similarly hand-picked were the young men who went to the embassies overseas, in the Diplomatic Service that only absorbed the Foreign Office men in 1920. That amalgamation did away with the earlier requirement of a minimum private income of £400 a year. By that restriction Lord Hardinge of Penshurst, in the fulness of time Ambassador at St Petersburg and Paris, Permanent Under-Secretary at the Foreign Office, and Viceroy of India, had a narrow escape from exclusion. His father gave eight children a traditional country-house upbringing, the five sons 'all sent to the very best school, no expense being spared.'[1] Yet Hardinge refers to him as a poor man, and was perceptibly aggrieved that when he joined the Foreign Office in 1880 his allowance was only two or three hundred pounds, happily eked out by a small but timely legacy. The 'FO' had evidently joined the Armed Forces and the Church as a career for impecunious younger sons. That they brought with them genetic privilege as well as the other sort emerges from their achievement, as well as being a tribute to those early, slanted but rigorous selection procedures.

There are of course exceptions not just to rules but also to personal predilections, such as my own contention that Victorian England survived till my between-wars boyhood. Behind the silent films, and the far from silent early motor-cars and saxophones, the tempo of life went on for a while much as before in the countryside and provinces. So it did too, I dare say, in the corridors and cubby-holes of the Italianate 'FO'. That we can still admire – at any rate from without – across St James's Park.

Yet behind its mansards and cornices changes had begun to stir within a few years of the death of Queen Victoria and of her son Edward VII. The deeper sociological and political impact of the First World War and the trenches may have reacted with a delayed shock, fully penetrating British society only after the Armistice. On its war-time re-organization, however, the catastrophe had allowed of no time-lag. Not even the old Foreign Office was spared upheaval with, initially, its couple of hundred staff at home and little more than twice that number overseas.

[1] *Old Diplomacy* (p. 3), John Murray 1947

So it was to their great credit that by 1917, via the unlikely person of Mr Alwyn Parker, the Librarian, the Foreign Office were already preparing, indeed drilling, an entire peace-making staff in readiness for the end of hostilities. In other ways too Mr Parker seems to have been ahead of the game – and his time – devising what would now be termed a managerial visual-aid, akin evidently to the 'Swingometer' of election-night in our present colour-television era. Harold Nicolson has his own techniques for conveying irreverence without unkindness.[1] He deploys them impartially in his descriptions first of Mr Parker's device as a planisphere or 'reeling orrery', and then of Lord Hardinge of Penshurst – attended by its inventor like Jupiter with one of its moons – as the 'Organizing Ambassador'; Nicolson's utilization of inverted commas is none the less eloquent for being something of an addiction, which I too confess to sharing.

It is significant, but not surprising, that at this point the trails should cross of my three favourite precursors of diplomacy-by-conference. Hardinge, Hankey and Nicolson – these truly were pioneers, harbingers, fore-runners. It is no coincidence that this was the original meaning of the ancient Greek 'Prodrome', the telegraphic address so cryptically used by the FO and by all embassies overseas. It has mystified generations of telegraphists; yet take it simply as meaning 'ahead of the pack' or 'anticipating events', and it makes clear professional sense. If Lord Hardinge of Penshurst, the very apogee of the Old Diplomacy à l'anglaise, finally dipped a toe-tip into the new diplomacy-by-conference, the first Lord Hankey was probably its inventor, at any rate as an administrative concept. Harold Nicolson, in Paris at the 'sharp end' of the treaty-making, as we so trenchantly say today, was both an early practitioner, and the chronicler, of the new fashion.

All three see, and present, the Paris treaty-making in their own quite different way. Hardinge's approach is utterly ambassadorial, as a member of the Conference of Ambassadors, which was the connective tissue between the intermittent muscle-flexing of the constantly irrupting Lloyd Georges and Clemenceaus. It is after all no bad aspiration for a diplomat to see his profession as the continuing lubricant in the machine of international relationships; Hardinge's preoccupation with, and recurrent false modesty

---

[1] *Diplomacy*, Constable 1939

about, his various dinner-party manoeuvres and conversational triumphs are even today not to be derided. If at times he seems to convey that his part was the whole of the treaty-making, it was in reality a by no means insignificant role. The conciliation of personalities, and the fine adjustment of their frictions and temperatures by a skilled and dedicated practitioner, are none the less important under today's only superficially changed social criteria.

Lord Hankey, to the contrary, saw the peace-making episode as an extension of his other and probably greatest administrative achievement – his contribution to Britain's political evolution by the virtual invention of the Cabinet Office. What insistently concerned him was the need to make sense and order out of war-time to-ings and fro-ings which had had no parallel in pre-railroad diplomatic history; he reckoned on writing his memoirs that since 1914 he himself had attended nearly five hundred international meetings. Even before 1914 such conferences were beginning to figure as a useful innovation, on technical subjects such as the Red Cross, nascent civil aviation, quarantine and so on. Out of them had grown bodies that we now take for granted, like the Berne Bureau for Posts and Telegraphs and the Hague Tribunal. Hankey attributes to Sir Edward Grey the device of the conference of ambassadors which now, in a regional form, is used to bring together all of Britain's ambassadors in a given area of the world – a highly useful technique now adopted by most other foreign ministries.

Those were still of course the days of trans-European monarchy, in which Head-of-State visits had a family flavour, while the Foreign Minister went along too for the opportunity of useful diplomatic conversations. Only occasionally were there 'lone' overseas trips by British ministers. They would not even make headlines today; yet Hankey finds that of Lord Haldane, Secretary of State for War, to pre-war Berlin, rare enough to merit special mention. Save for the great 'Congresses' of the day, international conferences were not usually attended by statesmen of the first rank; the Algeciras Conference of 1906 for example, on German interest in Morocco, was a mere 'conference of ambassadors', though at the international level.

It was World War I, and the need for constant logistical and industrial liaison, that led to the need for continuing contact – to begin with Anglo-French alone – outside the apparatus of conventional diplomacy. There is a rueful echo with our own times when Hankey says, of these 1915 Head-of-Government contacts, that 'in a single day's conference more was accomplished to bring about unity of policy than would have been effected in weeks of intercommunication by ordinary diplomatic methods.'[1] Similarly in early 1979 Britain's then Prime Minister, Mr Callaghan, maintained that the summit-meeting at Guadaloupe had done more in forty-eight hours than could have been done by forty-eight thousand Foreign Office telegrams. To be sure, bolder headlines were achieved by his asertion, on that same occasion, that he was unaware of any crisis in Britain during his absence. So politically costly an observation perhaps therefore also justifies some reserve towards his, and indeed Lord Hankey's, similar assessments of the uses of conventional diplomacy.

Where Lord Hankey and Harold Nicolson are in evident disagreement is when both come to the immediate post-war years and the actual negotiation of peace. Nicolson, despite his reminiscent teasing of the excellent Foreign Office Librarian, Mr Alwyn Parker, shows the greatest respect for the machine which he and other Foreign Office officials had prepared, and which competently housed a British delegation of two hundred and seven officials, plus as many ancillary staff, at the Hotel Majestic in the Avenue Kléber, with the Hotel Astoria for offices.

What the spectator sees usually depends on where he stands, and these devoted if swarming functionaries were presumably the same 'hordes of officials' whom Lord Hankey found so irksome; according incidentally to Lord Hardinge of Penshurst, only eighteen of them were Foreign Office men. Harold Nicolson agrees with Hankey to the extent of referring to them as a 'vast delegation', but disagrees in that he sees the British Delegation as on the whole magnificently prepared, its only weakness arising from bad liaison inherent in the conference's initial inter-delegation organization, or lack of it. Here again one man's meat is another man's poison; what Harold Nicolson saw and praised as good staffing, Lord Hankey's verdict deplores as the idle curiosity, and propensity to leakage, of innumerable and intrusive interlopers and hangers-on.

In fairness, Nicolson acknowledges that not all Paris delegations

[1] *Diplomacy by Conference* (p. 15), Benn 1946

were as active and conscientious as the British. Quite possibly the persistent North American cliché of the cookie-pushing diplomat goes back to the palm-courts of the Hotels Majestic and Astoria, and to those delegates who, unlike the British, really did have time to drink their tea there at 'le five-o'clock'. Yet is was Lord Hankey's impatience with all the time-wasting and rubber-necking that led him to yet another major administrative innovation, that of a Secretariat to canalize the immense volume of paperwork increasingly generated by those other delegations that really did function. The machinery of war-time liaison had prepared the way for the apparatus of diplomacy-by-conference. In 1919, at the Paris Conference, the 'Council of Ten' was just the old Supreme War Council under another name. The affluence to it of countless inquisitive or merely self-important 'experts' led to the 'Council of Four', and so to the 'small room' solution imposing privacy by physical exclusion.

Perhaps the Security Council of the United Nations has itself something of the 'small room', even though it is installed within a very big one, and is vulnerable to the intrusive eye of the television camera. Certainly it is of the essence of summit meetings that they should provide for the 'petit comité'. The whole privacy of a Camp David vis-à-vis the outside world is that it can comprise either a 'small room' in Hankey's literal sense, swept and garnished against all intrusion, or the corner of a woodland footpath where two strolling Heads of State can pause and chat, inaccessible to even the most carefully aimed directional microphone. President Wilson not withstanding, however open the eventual covenant may be, it is not necessarily best arrived at too openly.

Lord Hankey was clearly unlikely to see eye-to-eye with Harold Nicolson on the niceties of delegation organization. Yet his insistence that 'small is beautiful', at any rate round the negotiating table, has much in common with Nicolson's own wider view of the diplomat and his function. Hankey liked a small Secretariat because he believed that personal friendship influenced statesmen and enhanced statesmanship. Similarly Nicolson saw diplomats as a world-wide community whose personal friendships reduced professional abrasiveness without prejudice to national loyalties. 'The most important elements of success in diplomacy by conference,' says Hankey,[1] 'are elasticity of procedure, small numbers, informality, mutual acquaintance and if possible personal friendship among the principals, a proper perspective between secrecy in deliberation and publicity in results, reliable secretaries and interpreters.' For these same reasons the corridors of conference diplomacy have always proved as important as the council-chambers, as we shall particularly see when we consider the United Nations Organization.

It is perhaps surprising that at this more intuitive point of his analysis, and as long as a generation ago, Lord Hankey should have taken the plunge, and decided that the old diplomacy is superseded. No doubt the diplomats will continue to be needed for background information and other intermediate functions; but he sees the responsibility to parliament of our domestic form of government as requiring actual negotiation exclusively by Ministers; the intermediaries must be cut out.

Yet, in fairness, Lord Hankey is writing of a particular time, its climax a Treaty which all too soon demonstrated its deficiencies. Challenged in this way, my own mind goes back in sympathy to Harold Nicolson, writing – I cannot recall where – of himself, toiling away at a more workaday level of the same peace-making marathon. Arriving rather early one morning, at his office in a small room of some desolate requisitioned hotel – probably Mr Parker's self-same Astoria – he finds himself overlapping with the departing office-cleaners, as he sits at his desk in the middle of a bare wooden floor, with the flood-line of the charladies' dawn-time scrubbing receding around him, as it dries towards the skirting-board.

I too have had this identical experience, and more besides, in the Downing Street Palazzo – as Geoffrey Moorhouse calls it – that we owe to Lord Palmerston and Sir Gilbert Scott. In the early and austere post-war 'fifties I habitually found it more cost-effective of energy to prepare of an early morning for my own sessions of conference-diplomacy, rather than late at night. So when briefing myself for a United Nations General Assembly I always pursued the principle that the two hours between eight and ten a.m., before the telephone started ringing, were worth far more than three or more slowed-down hours in the office after

[1] *Ibid*, p. 37

seven the same evening. So each morning I walked my little son to school, took the District Line, and passed through the King Charles Street archway good and early. And when – in those impenitent days – I watched, and even helped, the old ladies humping in the buckets with our meagre day's ration of 'nutty slack', my thoughts would go back to Harold Nicolson, ensconced like a disconsolately triumphant King Canute in his receding tide-mark of wet floor-boards. And a sense of destiny behind the drabness would comfort me for myself, as it reassures me for the diplomat's future now.

Chapter X
The Old Diplomacy - The Substance

Lord Gore-Booth reminds us in his memoirs[1] that foreign policy is what you do, and diplomacy is how you do it. By the same token the 'old diplomacy' is 'how they did it then'; and from one such account this chapter-heading is taken. *Old Diplomacy* – the Reminiscences of Lord Hardinge of Penshurst, K.G., P.C., G.C.B., G.C.S.I., G.C.M.G., G.C.I.E., G.C.V.O., Ll.D.[2] covers the years 1880 to 1924 which the author spent in the Diplomatic Service. It was published rather more than thirty years ago, when my father-in-law sent it to me, both as a Christmas present and as a cryptically defined object-lesson in 'what to avoid in the "new" diplomacy'. It remains one of my chained and favourite books, even if its fascination is often incongruous, almost morbid, in the light of today's world. I cherish it as the ultimate statement of the old diplomacy, at its frequent best and usually unwitting worst.

There are of course innumerable other diplomatic memoirs which illuminate what many would consider the Victorian and Edwardian high-noon of, especially, British diplomacy. By my check-list another fifty-odd have appeared in the last twenty years alone. Diplomats, even more perhaps than most travellers, tend to be prone to write their memoirs; for theirs are not just travellers' tales, but the tales of professional, indeed paid travellers, subconsciously craving no doubt to make restitution to their life-long sponsor, the British tax-payer and public.

And quite rightly too. Most diplomatic memoirs make good reading, and will also provide invaluable cross-bearings for future students of world affairs. I myself have a particular liking for the less portentous specimens of the genre. The late Sir Geoffrey

[1] Op. cit., p. 15
[2] John Murray 1947

Thompson's *Front Line Diplomat*,[1] already singled out, grows out of the self-same world described by Hardinge; Thompson joined the Service from World War I, the outcome of which Hardinge was helping to negotiate. Yet its version of diplomacy is at a much more down-to-earth level, with an underlying sadness and misgiving found neither in Hardinge, whose earlier world had not altogether vanished around him as he worked, nor later in our own contemporaries who, the vanishing of their former world being well behind them, can afford, or contrive, to be imperturbable, and look forward again.

Most interesting of all are those memoirs that straddle both the old and the new diplomacies. Sir Laurence Grafftey-Smith's *Bright Levant*[2] and *Hands to Play*[3] do just this. He overlaps both chronologically and geographically with Hardinge's narrative, though his overflows with a vision of the human comedy of which Hardinge was quite incapable. For Hardinge, who must have missed a lot of fun, has little in common with the Psalmist who reflects

> Lord, my heart is not haughty, nor mine eyes lofty;
> Neither do I exercise myself in great matters,
> Or in things too wonderful for me.

To the contrary, Hardinge's memoirs bring out his obsession not just with the study of power, and the analysis of it for his government, but with the possession of it for himself. He admits so spontaneously, frequently and explicitly – by today's less extrovert lights almost naively, though the power imperative is not less potent in the new diplomacy, as later instances will show. He began his diplomatic career as a first-class reporter of foreign affairs, soon evolved into a negotiator, and finished up a Viceroy. To all intents therefore the one-time 'plenipotentiary' became an actual ruler.

In the process Hardinge carried one stage further the axiom demonstrated by the Sir David Kelly in his book *The Ruling Few*[4] – that the successful diplomat is the one who makes a bee-line for the sources of power in whatever country to which he is accredited. Hardinge did just that – and just as implacably at home too,

[1] Hutchinson 1959
[2] John Murray 1970
[3] Routledge & Kegan Paul 1975
[4] Op. cit.

back at base. In fairness much of his vast professional success was demonstrably due to his energy, ability and the gift of communication which his own writings exemplify. It was also due to the fact that he was evidently a consummate lobbyist for himself, a ruthless careerist and, literally, a courtier when the ultimate seal of power, if no longer its seat, was still the throne, most of all in the foreign relations of a still largely monarchical Europe.

Hardinge's was an utterly different life from that of his equivalent today. His happiness and enjoyment in it are transparent. His only real anxieties seem to have been when his ambition was threatened – interludes usually of short duration. Twice he recounts how he out-manoeuvred contemporaries one place below him in the pecking-order, when they looked like huffing him on the promotion list. The moral outrage he deploys in frustrating them is however strangely absent when later, and repeatedly, he outflanks in his turn whole phalanxes of his FO seniors.

It was a life of caviar and champagne that Hardinge recalls, though with typhoid and intermittent hardship as a concomitant. Admittedly these ingredients are still available to the present-day diplomat – I have enjoyed all four myself. But today the average ambassador will have to eat out for his caviar with the occasional business super-star, or at the local embassy of some piscatorially over-privileged nation. In Hardinge's time this archetypal luxury was not too prohibitive for even the youngest and most penurious Third Secretary. From my own early days, having once briefly bought the best caviar for a pound a pound, I cannot begrudge it to today's big-spending gourmets, even if I never taste it again. As for Hardinge's typhoid, today we have our 'shots' and – if they let us down, as did mine – antibiotics to come to the rescue. So if the new diplomat's life is to lack the expansiveness and optimism of the old, it should be spared some of its precariousness also – though it is a thought worth considering whether the old diplomacy's typhoid or the new diplomacy's terrorism is the greater risk. That other unrelenting occupational hazard summarized under the representational heading of 'protocol and piles' will presumably prove as intractable to the new diplomacy as to the old.

A certain fatalistic hypochondria has always been characteristic of the profession, and Nicolson's fictional, or semi-fictional, renderings of diplomatic life are redolent of it. His Titty of

Chapter I – Nevile Titmarsh MacSomething-or-Other; the surname is never made clear – was inevitably a chronic malingerer. And not without reason; he escaped cholera in Istanbul only to die of the Spanish influenza in Buenos Aires. The valetudinary tradition may even survive till today, by a kind of professional atavism. I was not so long ago assured by a distinguished ex-Chief Clerk of the Foreign and Commonwealth Office that mass radiography had substantiated that the Diplomatic Service were much healthier than the Home Civil Service; though he could not swear whether the discrepancy was an index of the diplomats' clean living or of their hypochondria.

Even today the diplomat faces real and special health hazards. One young British 'high-flyer' posted to Bagdad took sick and died there, between breakfast and lunch, of an instant polio. An older ex-'flyer' today confronts his later years without a urinary sphincter, thanks to the bilharzia parasite and some unlucky tropical surgery.

Above all however, Nicolson already conveys the impression of a penumbra between the old and the new diplomacy, which is common to all the more eminent diplomatic memoirs of recent years, though in his case perhaps more poignantly than in others. Nicolson's initial picture, whether of his ambassadorial father's life or his own, depicts the bright afternoon of the old diplomacy. A generation of colleagues only slightly later – William Strang, Gladwyn Jebb, Paul Gore-Booth, in due course peers of the realm all – recapitulate eventful careers that begin already in the twilight of the old diplomacy, and lead on to an elegant adjustment to the new, even to a significant part in its formulation.

The fact of such an evolution does not mean that the whole of the old was jettisoned and left behind. A vast area of routine activity and function is common to the old and the new. And though history is alleged never to repeat itself, situations and predicaments constantly do. The merit of diplomatic memoirs, especially to the aspirant not yet of a seniority to write his own, is the illumination they cast on his own past experience, and the yardstick they offer for what is to come. As the rawest of raw recruits myself I soon concluded that in any emergency I would far sooner have as my chief a wise old man rather than a brilliant young one. Usually the sagacious and elderly ambassador has himself once been a brilliant and promising young secretary, a 'flyer' of his day. So too in the fulness of time his own juniors will absorb from him the best of both his worlds. He has seen and lived it all before; nothing comes as a surprise to him, and he is never taken aback – or at least seems not to be.

He will also have a tendency, however steel-cored, to be kinder and more understanding than he lets on or looks. Some of the soundest advice of a lifetime came to me from just such an ambassador of the old school – not one of our own, and well beyond the conventional British retirement age. He began by pulling me up for failing to conceal a particular disconcertment – 'You have to make a good face!' Later, when I knew him well enough to express appreciation of his guidance, he cheerfully denied all altruism. When in my turn I was an ambassador, he assured me, I too would always devote much attention to the young; it was a torch to be passed on. First of all, secretaries have a way of growing up into ambassadors, and of remembering kindness shown in their youth. Second, the young secretaries do most of the work, the 'travail brutal', and so know what is really happening; often also they can open up access to a normally intractable ambassador. And anyhow they and their wives are usually refreshing company for ageing ambassadorial couples.

Talleyrand and Metternich would have agreed with him, I daresay. So by action and reputation have also those more recent others whom I have cited above. Their wisdom has been learnt – as no doubt will be that of their successors in the new diplomacy – from the daily round of diplomacy, seldom trivial, usually enjoyable, always arduous. The double helix at its core is a day-in, day-out intertwining of 'making representations', and 'reporting', the last often involving counselling the home government; negotiation is simply a refinement of both, and conference diplomacy their three-dimensional-chess equivalent. Conferences, treaties and agreements are the main identifiable product of diplomacy. So is its tip that of the iceberg.

Not all conferences, however, presuppose a treaty, nor does every treaty presume a conference. Contrary to current popular dogma, conferences, even summit meetings, are by no means the whole be-all-and-end-all of diplomacy. Treaties can manage very nicely without conferences.

Here some arithmetic must break in; after all, as recently as Machiavelli mathematics figured along with Latin and Turkish as indispensable for the diplomat. That there is a high ratio of treaties to conferences stands out in, for example, the vast number of treaties, as against the relatively short list of conferences, that British governments negotiated in the last fifty years of comparative diplomatic normality, before the onslaught of the great post-war treaties of the mid-forties accentuated the trend yet further. Over the entire century from the Congress of Vienna the official Foreign Office score-book[1] lists only fourteen major international congresses and conferences, plus four meetings of the sovereigns or plenipotentiaries of the five Great Powers and seventeen specialized conferences. From Westphalia to Vienna – 1648 to 1814 – the total score had been only nineteen. Satow's list is slightly but not substantially longer. Yet between 1892 and 1942 Britain negotiated and signed one thousand two hundred and forty-three treaties.

Such at any rate is my calculation, relying largely on a pocket-sized assemblage of micro-chips which, on reflection, may itself be the small harbinger of a computer-revolution for diplomacy too; it would certainly have been a godsend to an aspiring ambassador in the darker days of the old diplomacy, when the office accounts were the new recruit's traditional and most dreaded chore. Now the disproportion between treaties and conferences is even higher. Since World War II the annual crop of treaties seems to have grown exponentially, from our erstwhile twenty-odd a year to three figures, plus or minus. Why this should be is another matter; perhaps simply the lives not just of individuals but of nations too are becoming more regulated which, in a disorderly world, might even be a blessing in disguise.

Most of these items were 'ambassadorial' treaties, bilateral and of a largely routine, 'do-it-yourself' and on-the-spot category. They were not as a rule the outcome of great conferences and encounters of Heads of State. They dealt with fishing rights, extradition, patents, epidemics, the mutual treatment of criminals and lunatics – the bread-and-butter of bilateral relations. Usually there was no hurry about them; problems arising from their protracted negotiation could generally be handled by diplomatic bag, by sending for an expert at the right moment or, given real urgency, even by a thriftily concocted cypher telegram.

[1] *See* FO Peace Handbooks Vol. XXIII, 1918/19 and Satow, Edition II.

My first-hand experience of the process includes negotiating one such treaty for and at the request of a fellow-Commonwealth government; this friendly mutual facility is less common now – a pity, for it can save time and money all round, and betokens a real good will and an authentic 'special relationship', in effect a family relationship. A purist might quibble that my little *modus vivendi* was not a treaty at all. But a *modus vivendi* is indeed a treaty, and on the best authority. So my small staff and I set to with a will, and patiently hewed out the rough outline of the desired text from the sometimes obdurate local granite. Whenever it showed signs of flawing or splitting, or if a refinement or technicality beyond our purely British competence cropped up, we consulted or even called to the rescue an expert from our Commonwealth cousins' nearest embassy. To unveil the finished article a top official from that country was given 'full powers' by his home government, and flown in as 'Special Ambassador'. At this point we edged unobtrusively from the limelight, and he signed the agreement, acknowledging us however with an honoured place at the concluding celebrations. In due course also, and 'through channels' a cordial expression of official appreciation was expressed by his Secretary of State.

Just occasionally the same informal, almost casual technique has been used with major international instruments. It is pleasantly remarkable that the same process of advance correspondence and informal contact should have been found suitable with both my own little *modus vivendi* and the Japanese Peace Treaty signed at San Francisco in 1951. It too had been negotiated previously, to the last comma, vicariously, and not by the eventual plenipoteniaries themselves.

There must have been scores of such workaday but essential little treaties as mine, as against each one of the great evocative place-names that resound down the long highway of diplomacy, via Kutchuk-Kainarji and Vienna, onwards to Versailles and Yalta, from a starting-point without doubt more remote than the recondite ceremonials recorded in the caves of Altamira and the Dordogne. Such recurrent and unspectacular proceedings represent a living continuity between the peaks of international encounter which may not be underrated. For each one a team versed in negotiation has been needed, with technical experts at call, and with a plenipotentiary there on the spot to sign, whether the commentators of today choose to call them diplomats – or himself 'Your Excellency' – or not. Successful negotiation is best assured by the experienced diplomat's easy-seeming but hard-earned familiarity with a country, its people and their ways. It springs from the same talent and training that provide the home government with honest and reliable information about that country. For this reason negotiation, and intelligence in its authentic and unambiguous sense are, precisely, the diplomat's natural business, and the two inseparable sides of his coinage.

My references to the 'plenipotentiary' function of the diplomat on the occasion of signing agreements, major or minor, may seem self-contradictory without a little elaboration. For such technical occasions the standing designation of 'Ambassador Extraordinary and Plenipotentiary' does not necessarily mean that a diplomat has, equally technically, 'full powers' to sign virtual blank cheques in his government's name.

At first sight therefore it would seem that the word 'plenipotentiary' is a contradiction in terms, and does not mean what it says. I myself can recall an occasion of extreme personal vulnerability when, having been kidnapped for my country, I had to concede that my ambassadorial position was 'more extraordinary than plenipotentiary'. The reason for the apparent paradox is that some full powers are fuller than others. An ambassador is 'plenipotentiary' enough to negotiate for, and make representations on behalf of, his government at any time. He does not need to brandish a blanket-style full power, much less a special one for the occasion, every time he sets his foot inside the local Foreign Ministry, or even initiates a specific process of negotiation. For this his credentials suffice; his Letter of Credence gives credit to all he says on behalf of his government. But before he finally signs an agreement in his government's name he certainly must have a specific 'full power', and most formally drawn up; a 'scrap of paper' will not do, though I have known a flimsy copy of a telegram, assuring that the formal document is on its way, to break just such a ceremonial log-jam.

Governments are – and presumably will remain, even for the new diplomacy – remarkably cautious and legalistic at moments of signature. And even the full powers to sign may not not necessarily confer final validity on the signature. An ambassador torn between urgency and, say, personal misgiving over a particular clause, can always sign *ad referendum*. If his government accept the point he has queried, then his signature to the whole instrument is valid. But even then this authentication does not necessarily make it law. Ratification by both governments, usually involving parliamentary and Head of State approval, is still the rule. Much of the agonizing about the SALT II agreement of June 1979 in Vienna was due to the immediate availability of the US executive, in the person of President Carter, there on the spot, yet with continuing uncertainty as to its congressional endorsement, personified by Senator Henry Jackson back in Washington.

So the plenipotentiary's traditional full powers seem increasingly to be notional – 'a certain fiction', as Grotius, referring to ambassadorial claims to incarnate the monarch's person, unkindly and rather prematurely termed that doctrine. Such indeed are these reservations that international law has a specific word for the exceeding of full powers. 'Sponsion' is defined by the Oxford English Dictionary as 'an engagement made on behalf of a State by an agent not specially authorized.' Such a commitment can be disowned by his government. It is a professional predicament unthinkable to the British diplomat; the word itself is almost a stranger, being largely a United States usage and concept and, I strongly suspect, as academic a proposition there as here too.

With all due respect to Grotius there are also certain special circumstances which, for the monarchically inclined British, may make their diplomats feel more full-time in their inherent plenipotentiary status than do others, even though the British must produce *ad hoc* full powers for special occasions just like ordinary republican mortals. One vestigial symbolism of the old diplomacy is perpetuated by the British diplomat's possession of the Queen's Commission, and by the ceremony of 'kissing hands' on appointment and departure as a Head of Mission overseas. The formality is a figurative one so far as concerns its pictorial accuracy; nobody's hand is kissed any more. Yet the terminology is probably responsible more than any other single factor for the inner confidence of every departing British envoy that wherever accredited, he stands for the Monarch's person and integrity abroad. He thus personifies his country in rather more than the conventional and ceremonial sense.

With all this, a good British ambassador is never on his high horse. He does not use his immunities, prerogatives and plenipotentiary status for trivial and personal purposes. Especially, being British, he will have absorbed from the very Crown he represents the lesson that the potency of legal and constitutional prerogatives lies generally in the refusal to exercise them. So his file of parking-ticket and other abuses in the local Foreign Ministry will be slimmer than most or, more likely, entirely empty. His local personal repute will be all the higher, and his professional credibility correspondingly more so.

This inward and built-in certitude is a discipline and also a reassurance. Both count increasingly in the area where the new diplomacy is at its most typical – in its growing involvement with the information media. And nowhere is the fundamental and continuing plenipotentiary status of the ambassador more manifest than in his never being 'off duty' or 'speaking entirely personally'. The blurring of reality and entertainment, especially by television, is now a commonplace. A reporter may genuinely think that he means it when he asks for 'Just a personal view, Ambassador?' In practice there is no such diplomatic phenomenon. Once the impromptu verbal arrow has imprudently been shot in reply into the electro-magnetic air, no rebuttal will call it back. It is 'on the record'; his government will find it hard to disown. Mr Andrew Young, for example, United States Ambassador at the United Nations, castigated British colonial history many times. He has done so in terms which his State Department must surely have considered, if perhaps not have disciplined, as *ultra vires*, as in fact a 'sponsion' of sorts. Yet a diplomat, as long as he is 'en fonction', is always primarily an institution rather than a person. So it is virtually inconceivable for him to be spontaneous. At least to seem spontaneous is perhaps his noblest public achievement, certainly his most arduous, when he knows that publicly he is in fact never more than a projection, the holograph, of his government and people. In the wider sense of the word he is always and unremittingly the plenipotentiary.

In another and more functional sense, that of sudden blanket authority or of full discretion, the role of plenipotentiary can always be delegated, and not just by the young diplomat's first intoxicating taste of the Chargé d'Affaires' new wine; to the allure of that particular heady brew all memoirs of the old diplomacy pay unfailing tribute. The educational technique of the deep-end launch into the swimming-pool has been a familiar process since human time began; so at least it has been to those whose concept of leadership does not stop at seeking and monopolizing it for themselves, but who go on to teach it to posterity for the greater good of the community. In diplomacy as in all activity the 'good chief' conducts his experiments in leadership-potential by constantly delegating responsibility; and it is often only in retrospect that the guinea-pig recognizes the fact, as have I on more than one occasion.

The first and most typical of my dry-runs was the handiwork of an ambassador whose name figures in what Geoffrey Moorhouse[1] evocatively calls 'the hyphenated litany of bygone ambassadorial names.' My own name happens to be a simple and straightforward bi-syllable. True, an elderly and deaf French lady steadily called me Monsieur Klaxon for several years; but at least mine is a name devoid of impropriety on translation into any known language. Here I am more fortunate than two war-time itinerants, Messrs Tyzack and Cusack whose names, brayed pointedly at the head of every receiving-line in the Middle East, galvanized countless official receptions by their profound anatomical scurrility in Arabic. So innocuous is my own surname that I even like to think that the 'KCMG' now by extraneous circumstances attached to it, must surely mean 'Kindly Call Me Geoffrey', unlike the more supernal derivation perpetuated in Mr Moorhouse's book.

Certainly in the case of my former and late ambassador his particularly double-barrelled name, like the eminence of his rank, was for me but the guinea-stamp. And for a' that I thought him even more of a man when, owing to a two-way split of official commitment, he delegated to me the entire responsibility to summon, at my discretion, a cruiser from the adjacent ocean. This twilight involvement in such an epitome of the old diplomacy was, I suppose, technically even a size larger than gun-boat diplomacy. Yet it has always left me unrepentant, and with an honest taste in my mouth. Its prime purpose was not at all to impose Britain's imperial will – there was already enough of the new diplomacy about to deal with that, one way or another – but to save lives; and not only British lives at that.

My ambassador did not elaborate on such nuances. He informed

[1] *The Diplomats* (p. 47), Jonathan Cape 1977

me succinctly that he handed over the eventual decision entirely to me. If it proved a wrong or foolish one he would, even so, back me to the hilt officially and publicly, but he would 'give me hell' in private. In the event I sent the necessary signal and called up the cruiser. The remote-control effect was so instantaneous and calmative that before she could even arrive I had sent a chaser ordering her back again. The ship's company, it duly emerged, were as disappointed as my ambassador was gratified. He bothered to tell me so; and his thanks remain a treasured memory, along with a comparable expression of appreciation from the late Ernest Bevin, on a quite different occasion a year or two later – both cases being nicely outside the official statute of limitations on their respective documentation. In another instance, involving neither discretion nor self-congratulation, I am always on re-reading touched to see even the single-minded and sinewy-hearted Hardinge of Penshurst capable of recalling in old age, and with emotion, occasional kind words spared him by the potentates of his youth.

Another relatively major delegation of authority occurred when, by a quirk of succession, my ambassador at the time – equally affectionately remembered – proved never to have had authority over an enormous war-time bank-balance, the disposal of which was approaching final negotiation with our host-goverment at the time. The sole signature had been transmitted down the years from one second-in command to the next; so the British Government's 'plenipotentiary' for the final cashing-in was, willy-nilly, myself. The negotiation ended suddenly and successfully, with myself at the Foreign Ministry wearing a pin-stripe suit and ski-boots as a last-minute part of an amiable but unrelenting mutual bluff. The Secretary-General of the Ministry had released me from our sparring to go off for some Christmas ski-ing, only to summon me back promptly from the mountains that same night. It had meant ski-ing down to the railway-station in a 5 a.m. blizzard; and it struck me on arrival in the capital that there was a certain eloquence of its own in my travelling combination of charcoal-grey formality as per protocol, and barely melted snow on my ski-boots. Sitting in the Minister's antechamber, it occurred to me that there was no reason why one-upmanship need remain a one-way transaction. I decided therefore not to change into the conventional black Oxfords which I had available in my brief-case.

The strategy certainly broke the ice of several gruelling months of Indian-wrestling.

Friends have often attributed to me a professional series of what they call my off-beat records; my precocious but diminutive first embassy was one of them, and yet another my being reputedly the last British diplomat to summon anything so awesome as the cruiser just mentioned. But to date my largest financial record had been a cheque for a mere million and a half pounds, which I had endorsed to my government as a very juvenile official of the then Consular Court in Cairo.

This time however the transaction was for thirteen million dollars. I signed it with a suitably nonchalant air, and passed it to my ambassador. He was twinkling at me, I noticed. 'Well,' he commented, 'At last I can stop worrying about those confounded Venezuelan air schedules.' I was surprised – 'Oh, you didn't tell me you were planning a leave trip.' 'Not me – you! All these months you've been sitting on the sole signature to a fortune; and we have no extradition treaty with Venezuela!' I reassured him. He need not have worried. My exclusive full-powers, or at any rate the sole signature giving access to this astronomical sum, had at no moment prompted me to think dark thoughts of embezzlement and French leave. Who would want to live the rest of their life at La Guaira airport? Or – on reflection – might they not just, in certain circumstances perhaps?

In practice and in retrospect therefore, the definition of 'plenipotentiary' can be almost infinitely broad, extending from the precise implementation of his specific full powers, via a general sense of responsibility towards the accreditation conferred by his government, to a habitual reflex of common-sense and realism in the performance of routine duties. Nowhere are such reflexes more consistently required than in another principal area of the old diplomacy due soon, it is often contended, to be superseded by events. I am referring to the area of 'reporting', of keeping one's government informed, of intelligence in its 'respectable' sense, despite a widening tendency of late for authoritarian governments to class as espionage the compilation of even the most basic economic data. Driving through Montana in the USA I remember marvelling at the huge road-signs exhorting the tourist to view the generating-plant in the foundations of the great Coulee Dam, and proclaiming 'This Way To The Missile-Sites!' I reflected a little wryly that, in certain less open societies, the very egg-production statistics were probably a state-secret, their investigation by the unauthorized subject to the direst penalties.

This unwelcome development, with its train of expelled attachés and imprisoned tourists and businessmen, is usually objected to as something abnormal, a throw-back to harsher times. Optimistically we assume that man's progress must be continuous and automatic. On that understanding the current debasement of personal and international standards of behaviour, the hand-to-mouth pragmatism of our epoch, are just a temporary hiccup in the smooth running of human affairs, including diplomacy. Yet it can seriously be contended that what seems to us a novelty and a freak is really only a reversion to type. Personal and physical violence, precariousness and brutality, may well be in reality the normal human lot. Our recent and comparatively brief enjoyment of domestic law-and-order, and our present fumbling for its international equivalent, may equally have been a short interlude of rationality, an aberration that we have naively taken for a norm.

The very existence of the old diplomacy lends substance to this contention. Its immunities were a safeguard, created in part to cater for the tendency of the then majority of authoritarian regimes to treat the ordinary seeker of information about their country and people as a common spy, and to mete out rough justice to him accordingly. Diplomats were therefore immunized as licensed spies – 'honest spies', as Ayrault said in 1588. Frederick the Great of Prussia, who had much going on to hide, did not care for diplomats. They nosed about; while as for their ostensible function of inter-state communication, was not one monarch quite capable of writing to another? Yet he had to accept the diplomats even so. In the same way the harshest regimes come to terms with, and adjust to, international coexistence by relaxing their grosser restrictions on the size and freedom of movement of diplomatic representation. It happened in the Soviet Union, in China, in Egypt after Nasser, and it will happen in Albania, Vietnam and Cambodia in the fulness of time.

In June 1979 the British Library mounted in the British Museum a novel, neat and quite beautifully selected exhibition on 'Diplomacy'. In it the first Queen Elizabeth's Secretary of State, Sir Francis Walsingham, figures rather in another capacity, that of 'spy-master'. Yet making allowances for a more ruthless age than ours, Walsingham seemed to me, as I contemplated the exhibit, far less the manipulator of a Tudor-style 'dirty-tricks department' than a competent bureaucrat, securing necessary intelligence from autocratic and suspicious neighbours for a ruler unlikely to suffer incompetents gladly. Today, though oppression still views the diplomat with misgiving, he remains a single mutually convenient principle of order, in a world increasingly disorderly for the layman. The western businessman, journalist and now broadcaster has, over late decades, on the whole grown used to going where he wished. Recent tendencies have put such travellers at risk; the USSR and Iraq are cases in point where, for the exchange of overt espionage agents, *bona fide* tourists and businessmen could well become a negotiable currency, there for the taking. The essence of the diplomat is that he is not negotiable in normal circumstances, and indeed should not be so in any circumstances.

In such increasingly closed societies the diplomat too will more and more have to depend for his facts on the information put at his disposal by the receiving government. The skill of the old diplomat was always to add flesh to these dry bones, to supplement by observation and interpretation the meagre or misleading statistics of productivity, defence capacity, population trends, education and the like. A natural corollary of this information function is that of interpretation, from which it is only one step to recommendation – to advice in fact. The common assertion – that by the end of the old diplomacy an ambassador was just a taker and relayer of instructions, a postman – never took into account the extent to which it is the ambassador himself who, by advice and feed-back, forms and modifies those instructions. Inevitably they are primarily the expression of the will of the government of the day; but in the formulating of it the counsel of the local diplomat, of the legendary man-on-the-spot, will be ignored or bypassed by them at their peril. Such was the case with the rise of Nazi Germany; and so seems to be the as yet incomplete verdict of history over the Suez tragedy.

The now celebrated valedictory despatch of 31 March 1979 from Sir Nicholas Henderson in Paris goes only one single, though crucial, stage further than any normal despatch of substance to the FCO. It does so by virtue of its internal domestic gloss on the inward-bound advice it proffers, and by its almost uncanny timing, given an internal political transformation, in the form of a General Election, which as yet lay in the lap of the gods. Nor as a rule were the despatches of the old diplomacy 'leaked'.

Chapter XI
The Old Diplomacy - The Style

What is now known as packaging is neither a modern nor a purely mercantile invention. When Sir Nicholas Henderson writes a historic valedictory he is – in furtherance of its more serious purposes – in effect competing for attention to its substance. Even from so major a post as Paris he must engage the scrutiny and influence the thinking of men – and, by the turn of the 1979 electoral coin, eminent women too – who are daily swamped with advice. To survive they must refuse to drown in the tidal wave of paper conveying it to London. Selectivity is crucial. So the presentation, the wrapping, can still influence the reception of the material, however important the theme and the source.

The Foreign and Commonwealth Office uses the excellent and democratic system of starting incoming paper on its progress from the bottom upwards. It is a method which has the additional merit of accustoming the novice to responsibility from the start. He soon learns to intercept whatever will only waste his masters' time. Equally at his peril he is allowed only one bite at initialling-off into heedless oblivion the kind of incoming report which, the higher it climbs up the scaffolding of power, will bring each successive reader that much nearer the edge of his revolving chair.

With incoming telegrams it is of course different. There is a built-in procedural safeguard which ensures that authentic pyrotechnics simply cannot fizzle out in the obscurity of some departmental Third Room, as the starting-point of the FCO conveyor-belt is still called. Nor is it wholly unknown for ambassadors to have their own private systems for ensuring that a particularly heartfelt communication is fielded promptly on arrival, and hurled straight at the wicket.

That wicket is in the last resort the Prime Minister. It should normally be the Foreign Secretary, and usually is so, save for the eventuality of a very dominant Prime Minister or a Foreign Secretary weaker in action than in principle. In the older diplomacy the ambassador's prime imperative may well have been to please, say, the Empress Catharine of All The Russias by his youth, good breath and clear complexion. There was always however his Secretary of State at home, whom today he must also please by more practical and intellectual attainments. Between him and that Secretary of State stretches in addition a minefield of officials, low, high and very high. His reporting must negotiate this obstacle first. The troops, every bit as much as their general, must cope daily with floods of important but exhausting and often boring paper. So if Our Man in Erehwonia can make his despatches and semi-official letters, and despite blesséd abbreviation his telegrams too, interesting and enjoyable to read, their reception benefits; however eminent their source and weighty their content, their vital progress upward will be expedited.

If in this way he acquires a legend, so that his reports are even awaited eagerly, then most of his battle is won. When the Foreign Secretary himself begins to wonder out loud how long it is since he saw one of those splendid despatches from So-and-So, the word spreads fast. When hard-pressed juniors at the starting end unconsciously expedite through the machine the contributions of a So-and-So who regularly brings interest, even amusement, into their work – then that So-and-So becomes known as one of the better ambassadors at both ends of his line of communication.

Another decade or so, and the output of one or two outstanding recent practitioners should emerge from under the thirty-year barrier. Diplomacy has always been able to prove that wit and humour need not conflict with accuracy, insight and wisdom. And a modern ambassador who can bracket 'Opus Dei' with 'vox populi' may be sure, with Belloc, that however scarlet his procedural sins, at least his words were – and will be – read.

Apart from its style of reporting, the old diplomacy was conducted 'with style' *per se*. It had a style of its own, which incorporates, but is more than, both literary style and life-style. A good diplomat's person and work are infused with his own quality of what in Spanish is called 'categoría'; I know of no exact English equivalent for the word, save perhaps in the strictly American slang idiom that someone or something 'got class'.

Two examples of such personal 'style' come to mind. The more recent nevertheless reaches back into, and is a link with, the old diplomacy, largely through the happy prolongation of the late Sir George Rendel's life till the age of ninety. His book *The Sword and the Olive*[1] provides a window-seat view of the Hitlerite encroachment across the pre-war Balkan landscape, though its title, rather movingly, has something of the ancient flavour of a much earlier and wholly Christian vision of diplomacy; its business, said Bernard du Rosier in his *Short Treatise on Ambassadors* of 1436, was peace. So it was with George Rendel's retirement years too. From the Singapore constitution to post-Suez finances they were charged with one unspectacular but complex assignment after another.

George Rendel's story has all the Edwardian vitality of that of a Hardinge of Penshurst, but without its consciously monumental and so faintly vulgar quality. This quality of 'style', emanating principally from elegance, simplicity, intelligence and, above all, intellectual integrity, could well be that one essence of the old diplomacy most indispensable for, and communicable to, the new.

The same qualities are visible, in a form perhaps more emphatic because so stamped with the ethos of the time, in an earlier manifestation of the old diplomacy. I came across it in a way thoroughly consistent with its own 'style' – as a reading-aloud accompanying a friendly dinner with a religious order. They followed the civilized practice of eating in total mutual silence. Instead of chit-chat, readings are chosen, of a kind to encourage contemplation without discouraging digestion. After a couple of very brief theological exordiums, the main book-at-bedtime is normally of a wholly secular content. In my case it did have a certain clerical connotation. The choice was fortuitous, but for my present purposes fortunate. The reader for the evening had selected an excerpt from Noel Blakiston's *The Roman Question*,[2] a compilation of the despatches and letter of Odo Russell – later Lord Ampthill – from Rome between 1858 and 1870.

Russell's status as an envoy in Rome was for much of his mission indeterminate, given the uncertainties at the time of the Italian body-politic and the Holy See, and of their political relationship. In effect he seems to have enjoyed a lengthy secondment from the Piedmontese court to Rome. So protracted, and

[1] John Murray 1957
[2] Chapman and Hall 1962

pleasant, was it that there is a rather touching letter of 1863 in which he pleads most earnestly, in the full knowledge that it will cost him both money and rank, against a promotion which would take him away from 'a mission full of historical interest and useful labour.'

I read this letter with particular sympathy, since yet another of my own 'off-beat records' is that I was apparently the first FO man to ask for a second tour at a certain Latin American post hitherto regarded traditionally as an exile. Personally I had found it of immense political and economic interest, of great beauty, culture and charm, and quite adequately accessible. That the aeroplane had meanwhile replaced the river-steamer and the narrow-gauge railway was a development that evidently had not yet penetrated the corridors of the Downing Street Palazzo.

One difference between our respective petitions was that Odo Russell's ends 'So pray, my dear uncle, leave me here as long as you possibly can!' Mine did not. The uncle in question, Lord John Russell, was for most of his tenure his Foreign Secretary too. In my case this was not so, however aptly the word 'avuncular' applies to the affectionately held memory of the late Mr Ernest Bevin, my own Secretary of State at the time. When I used to interpret for him he was certainly aways avuncular with me, indeed equally so, as often as not, with whichever ambassador to Britain it was who completed our bilingual triad. But no nephew of Ernest Bevin was – and I suspect never would have been – one of his ambassadors. In the British Diplomatic Service of today such advantageous kinships are still exceptional, even if an approximation to them is not entirely unprecedented.

Yet the Russells' version seems to have been a very qualified nepotism. It in no way guaranteed Odo's future. His eventual father-in-law – yet another peer – seems to have accepted him with amiable fatalism as 'as likely as anyone else in his stagnant profession to advance – ', a comment which, especially being addressed to the Permanent Under-Secretary at the Foreign Office, creates no particular presumption of avuncular 'pistonnage', past or prospective.

The overriding impression created by this assembled correspondence is of the sheer professional efficiency of the parties to it; its elegance, good humour and readability come as a bonus. Thus Russell not only obtained sight of a secret cypher message from

Napoleon III to the French ambassador. He memorized it ver-
batim, but took the precaution of cross-checking his recollection
of it with his informant before reporting it by secret despatch to
his uncle, the Secretary of State. Such technical competence is all
the more impressive to a generation as increasingly reliant as ours
on electronic aids to the recording and retaining of our facts.

Despite the tumultuous situation pertaining between France
and the Papacy Russell preserved excellent relations with all the
participants, including his unwitting informant, the French Ambassador de Gramont – who doubtless read his secret communications too. It may have helped that Russell spoke French, and other
languages, not merely well but superbly. With the French only
the best is good enough for their language from a foreigner; a
mediocre command of it vexes rather than flatters them – today's
generation of Frenchmen would probably riposte sharply in good
English – whereas an unexpected elegance and precision will
always dissolve and totally disarm any good Frenchman. Not so
evidently with their ladies; as a young man in Beirut I was assured
that the French High Commission mothers always warned their
daughters against young Englishmen who spoke French too well.
Odo Russell may have had a hand in the parentage of this discouraging legend; it seems to be the descendant, or possibly a
variant, of a similar but pleasantly qualified throw-away line by the
formidable Prince Bismarck – 'Never trust an Englishman who
speaks perfect French – except Odo Russell.'

The tribute endorses equally Russell's integrity and his linguistic prowess. Both were part of the old diplomacy, as were the style
and pace of Russell's life. Both also emerge delightfully from two
final quotations, each of which goes on in its context to exemplify
the business-like reality which underlay the literary elegance and
the at times almost Watteau-esque *mise-en-scène* of their presentation.

The first is a private letter of 1 May 1860 to Russell's uncle and
'master':

'I have literally nothing wherewith to trouble you today. I have
called on my diplomatic friends and found them idle and their
Chancelleries deserted ... The Duc de Gramont was planning a
day at the quails and Cardinal Antonelli, ever cheerful and pleasant, finding I had no news to give him talked for an hour about
his flower garden and the fish of the lake of Albanao ...'

The second is a secret despatch to the by this time Earl Russell some four years later. Though its main body comprises some tough and down-to-earth talking, it opens with the courtliest of verbal minuets:

'Despatch No. 8 Secret of 15 January 1864.

I had the honour to be received this morning by the Pope at a private audience. His Holiness welcomed me with even more than his usual benevolent kindness. I told the Sovereign Pontiff that I had the honour of being admitted to the presence of Her Majesty the Queen before leaving England and that Her Majesty had been pleased to enquire after His Holiness's health with interest. I also added that Their Royal Highnesses the Prince of Wales and the Princess Royal . . .

The Pope seemed much gratified and said that he deeply venerated the high public and private virtues of Her Majesty the Queen, and that no Sovereign in the world inspired him with more admiration, sympathy and respect, and that he felt sure Her Majesty understood his position and pitied his misfortunes more, he added with a smile . . .'

The author of this despatch is the same man who, only a little earlier, had been reporting to the same Secretary of State, and uncle, in the most graphic and military detail, the atrocities committed by the papal soldiery, under a Colonel Schmidt whom His Holiness promptly promoted to Brigadier-General. His economic reporting is equally competent and professional, descriptive yet unemotive in the best tradition of the old diplomacy.

Tradition is the supporting fibre of continuity; and continuity is the essence of diplomacy. Even diplomatic immunity – an institution much abused, regrettably in more senses than one – has continuity as its true purpose. In popular mythology diplomatic immunity is exclusively identified with duty-free cigars and champagne, and arrogantly unpaid parking-tickets; it is the occasional airy over-indulgence in these privileges which most provokes the resentment, possibly envy, of the bystander. In reality immunity exists ultimately to safeguard the person of the envoy, thus ensuring that, whatever tensions may arise between nations, there is always a functioning mechanism available to maintain an indispensable minimum of contact – once again that quasi-scientific but useful neologism, an 'interface'.

It is perhaps this inherent and inward traditionalism that

exposes the diplomatic profession to the charge of anachronism, even archaism, of an ostentatious and backward-looking élitism supposedly obnoxious to a supposedly egalitarian society. Yet if truth is the daughter of time, so diplomacy is pre-eminently the child of history. A profession which builds on precedent may not fail to think of the past while living in the present and looking to the future – an intellectual contortionism which surpasses as an achievement even that of the English common law. The external symbols of historical involvement, and so of tradition, and by extension of representation, are a particular bone in the throat of those who cannot accept that the envoy is not a protégé of privilege but only an abstraction, an institution on two legs. The old diplomacy had learned the hard way, and long ago, that the trappings had always applied to the nation, not the man. The tradition surrounding him did not exalt him, but rather honoured his country. Very few diplomats forget it; but of these awful tales are told. Woe betide His Excellency the day he thinks he actually is excellent.

Among the more vulnerable sanctuaries of tradition are the embassies, the residences, those overseas versions of the stately homes of England that are an affront to so many visiting legislators, a delight as a rule to the natives, and as much a national heritage as their equivalents back home, surviving by dint of day-trippers and the National Trust. Tradition is something involved in, but distinct from, representation, an activity perhaps better considered under the separate heading of prestige. Now and then prestige architecture has reacted on recent British governments with all the potency of a hallucinatory drug, the search for immediate tangible prestige encouraging the illusion of an instant new tradition, which is a contradiction in terms. Thus the regrettable new British Embassy in Rome is a justification of those who, in the brutalist 'Sixties, fought to preserve the skyline of St James's Park, and can now imagine what neo-traditional barbarity might have been rearing its silhouette there in place of the elderly Palazzo, for the prestige of a fad which has not even lasted to be a fashion. Even the much maligned gnomes of Switzerland, while ruthlessly gutting and re-installing their traditional buildings, leave the façade and outline intact.

The nuances between prestige, representation and tradition are exemplified in the quite different philosophies of Her Majesty's

Government towards Embassy property abroad that they rent, as against that which they own outright. The Supplies Division of the bygone Office of Works has long since been absorbed into the vastnesses of the Department of the Environment and the Property Services Agency. Yet I have no reason to believe that their pattern of thought has changed. To rented property their attitude was always correct but unenthusiastic; so were the furniture and fittings they made available to the official occupying it. But the decision to buy – with overseas property usually a sound one, in terms both of current expenditure and long-term investment – always worked an instant transformation in their approach. For government-owned property only the best is good enough, and thereafter only the most meticulous stewardship. For it the Aladdin's cave opens not just its doors but its floodgates. Supplies and maintenance are lavished with a dedication which amounts to affection – enhanced, I have gratefully experienced, if such efforts, and especially the department's visiting representatives, receive the warm welcome that enthusiasts and authentic connoisseurs deserve.

One or two ambassadors have apparently received them with Victorian aloofness, as if engaged in trade; as a result any such throw-backs were rumoured to be in the bad books of the men from the Ministry, whose miracles accordingly took longer. Usually however their punctiliousness and *pietas* is shared by the diplomatic trustees of these national heirlooms abroad. The ambassador and his lady have to live with the official Sheraton and the Lawrences all the time, to justify and cherish them when their hair is down too, and not just when the receiving-line is forming and the Scotch whisky and the champagne beginning to circulate. The difference of degree between the concept of tradition and that of mere representation and prestige was charmingly and unwittingly demonstrated when my wife and I once visited privately the rightly celebrated British Embassy in Paris. The ambassadress, a lady not only beautiful and intelligent but also kind, and now a distinguished author, noticed even before we did that her jean-clad daughter was about to plump herself astraddle an exquisitely frail window-stool. She arrested her daughter's descent in mid-flight with a word, explaining 'It's survived since Napoleon's sister, and I'd hate to see it shattered now!'

I understand that at home in Russia the Soviet government

show much the same *pietas* once they set about restoring and maintaining the survivals of their own artistic and architectural heritage. Overseas too something of the same nostalgia often showed, in ways in which the elements of tradition and prestige were at times uncertainly proportioned. Very soon after the war I noticed for example that the wives of my Soviet colleague had particularly beautiful furs for formal occasions. On one such anniversary at the Soviet Embassy the whole décor was stunningly Tolstoyan. Even the cold buffet incorporated as a centre-piece a refinement most of our generation will only know from old copies of Mrs Beeton – a convoy of cold roast pheasants, re-upholstered in all the splendour of their original plumage. The whole gourmet vista especially appealed to the lady ambassador of the United States who, with total spontaneity and sincerity, burst out to our hostess, the Soviet ambassadress, that this was perhaps the most beautiful table she remembered in a life-time. 'So it must be,' came the answer. 'Only the finest is worthy of a great nation.' Mr Gromyko would have approved. So too, I am sure would the Empress Catharine of All The Russias.

At one of our Latin-American embassies – a particularly elegant and well-designed specimen of a smallish diplomatic residence – the focal point of the drawing-room was an excellent copy of the Lawrence full-length portrait of Castlereagh. Though his name figures honourably in at any rate the pre-Castro history-books of Latin America, his successor Canning's is the name that counts there. So Castlereagh's magnificent likeness emphasized Britain's artistic tradition rather, at the expense of the diplomatic; he had the reputation of being both the handsomest man in Europe and – pathetically for his times and his tragic end – uniquely faithful to an extremely feather-brained wife. However evocative the picture though, obviously something was lacking. The infallible Supplies Division had the answer. With their help we were able to call in a new Canning to redress the balance of the old drawing-room. So Canning now looks across at Castlereagh above the fireplace, to the correction of historical imbalance and the vast satisfaction of the local anglophiles.

I understand that the venue itself of these two portraits is currently endangered, thanks probably to the controversial 'Think-Tank' of 1977. Inevitably there has been some echo outside its ranks to its thesis that many of our diplomatic premises overseas are by now far too pretentious for Britain's reduced circumstances. So the suggestion is to sell up, buy cheaper, and move out. Experience teaches however that such economies tend not to be cost-effective, and to prove costly too in less quantifiable ways. Rationalizing prejudice and perhaps ideology as thrift, they make an exception to one tradition, or at any rate one old saw, by demonstrating that occasionally it is wise men who build houses for the foolish to sell, and thereafter for even wiser men to buy and live in. Spacious premises in spacious gardens from spacious times can easily be adapted to modern exigencies, sparing the need to trade-in prime real-estate for an inferior substitute. When a misguided nation emerges from its crisis of biliousness and induced panic-action, it will find itself weakened by the surrender of irreplaceable assets and, by break with tradition, of important overseas symbols of stability and continuity.

The modern British diplomat, inside whom Sir Henry Wotton's honest man still wrestles tirelessly with Machiavelli, likes of course to see himself as fusing traditionalism with infinite adaptability. Such ambivalence is not the norm of home-based officialdom. Your Whitehall man proper is not as a rule so complicated; his instinctive reflex favours the latest conformity, especially when his native caution is untroubled by extraneous irritants such as Think-Tanks. I remember one happy day when I was able to report to my ambassador that I had found him the ideal embassy residence, in time furthermore to have it finished it to our government's specifications. Exasperatingly our country was just then enduring one of its recurrent bouts of financial stringency and cutbacks in capital expenditure; so Treasury policy was that though leasing was possible, purchase was unthinkable. As a result it seemed a major coup, a break-through, when a most reputable local and indeed international bank volunteered the option of a loan for the purchase-price, and at a derisory three percent. The repayments would in fact have amounted to less than the rent we would be paying, with the British taxpayer owning the freehold within a generation.

All in vain. I have often thought since, and with rueful amusement, of the thunderbolt that struck back from Olympus – 'Her Majesty's Treasury does not borrow from foreign banks!' So on the strength of this famous-last-word we leased, instead of buying a bargain, but prudently contrived a succession of option-to-purchase clauses in the lease, giving the Treasury the chance to change their mind, should they meanwhile have recovered their senses, or the British economy its historic robust health.

This detour into the property-market may well have blurred rather than clarified the distinction I have sought to make between tradition and prestige; perhaps the whole squabble about the diplomat's representational capacity is precisely that representation falls into the grey area between the two. The old diplomacy seems to me to have cared more for tradition than for prestige, the difference between them being one of dimension and even ethic. Prestige is for impressing others. Tradition is for impressing – or at any rate fortifying – yourself. Thus Britain's Motor Show is for prestige – or should be if it works – whereas the State Opening of Parliament is for tradition. The two can of course overlap – hence Trooping the Colour or, overseas, that most beleaguered of all diplomatic functions, the Queen's Birthday Party.

The danger with prestige is that, being less soundly based than tradition, its pursuit slides easily into a sterile and egocentric nostalgia. Too much is made of the present because too much uncertainty envelopes the past. Hitler, with his monster rallies, his Wagnerian mythology and his neo-pagan assault on traditional Christian values, demonstrates horrendously how the pursuit of prestige can spring from an acute sense of inferiority about the recent past. A concern for tradition demonstrates instead a healthy equilibrium between past, present and future. While on tour a predecessor of mine at the same post received the naval salute due to an ambassador from a rusty revolver instead of a cannon. He was delighted by the improvised traditionalism as he was unabashed by the unprestigious setting, turn-out and weaponry; his reception-comittee were giving him of their very best – all indeed that they had. A naval friend of mine had an analogous if slightly more ambiguous experience on a naval visit to one of the lesser-known ports of a Central American republic, itself alternatingly lesser known or over-publicized, depending on the fluctuations of its non-stop leadership struggle. In his case the number of guns prescribed took the form of successive volleys of rifle-fire. For the safety of those on board these were aimed into the nearby man-grove-swamp. Out of it instantly poured a stream of villagers, immersing themselves into the comparative safety of the shark-infested shallows. The shelter of the jungle, to which they habitually withdrew whenever their national defence forces made an appearance, had this time proved illusory, thanks to this antiquated ceremonial honouring a passing maritime 'gringo'.

Not far away, in a not dissimilar jungle in an adjacent republic, a friend of mine was required to present his credentials to a president who for reasons of his own liked to keep on the move. In the tropical heat, in full broadcloth and gold braid, in cocked hat with ostrich-plumes, he drove in his Land-Rover down the forest trails to the presidential whistle-stop in its village clearing. He did not so much mind, he explained to me, the small boys running ahead of his convoy, proclaiming in vociferous sincerity 'Here comes the circus!' It only visited their jungle villages once every two years, and they were entitled to enjoy it when they thought it was coming. The real injustice was that His Excellency the President, who had insisted on both the pilgrimage and the pantomime, finally received my colleague's credentials in shirt-sleeves, under peeling adobe and a leaky palm-thatch in a tropical downpour. My friend's tradition had been sacrificed to the President's prestige.

Evidently there is a relativity, a reverse progression, to which the diplomat's sense of values is subjected. Its downward gradations might be expressed in some such way as: 'I am concerned with tradition; you are concerned with prestige; he is concerned with precedence.' Like protocol, of which it is the dubious offspring, precedence – 'I come first' – is a useful servant and a deplorable master. It can lead to self-importance and an obsession with the shadow of one's nation's interests rather than its substance. Prestige too tends to be the terrain of the touchy and nostalgic – a symptom of having seen better days and resenting it. Of tradition to the contrary the worst that can be said is that it is the creed of the romantic. Yet of him in turn it may be said that the romantic, in diplomacy at least, tends to think like an idealist while acting like a pragmatist. The product should logically be a patriot who yet remains a member of mankind.

In this synoptic sense tradition has the further merit of giving the old renewed validity. Some years ago in one of the old Empire's trouble-spots a British diplomat achieved a small immortality by what might well be termed a verbal 'sponsion' (see Chapter X). He proclaimed that the British Government would 'never' take a particular course of action. They promptly did so, but not before a shudder had run round the diplomatic world. 'Il ne faut jamais dire jamais' – 'Never say never!' – is more than a diplomatic rule in any language. It is a tradition; the reminder was salutary among the nations.

Another tradition was recently substantiated, and indeed encapsulated memorably, in the British Library exhibition of 1979 in the British Museum, recapitulated and generously illustrated in Mr Peter Barber's companion book *Diplomacy*. He shows how, from the beginning, the diplomat has suffered from an overdose of enforced mobility. Having myself once painfully been known in the Bagdad chancery as 'Waiting-to-Proceed Jackson', that particular tradition came as no surprise to me; it still stands, though its companion, that of chronic diplomatic penury, fortunately does not at present.

For all too often the investigations and wayfarings of those early ambassadors are best recorded in their plaintive appeals for the reimbursement of their expenses. Much of Britain's finest family plate was in fact royal plate, not returned to the Crown as supposed at the end of a ruinous mission, but retained by some ambassadorial nobleman of the time in lieu of an expense account ignored. Such extremes are not inflicted on his latter-day equivalent; but the peripatetic tradition still survives. At the height of the first European parliamentary election campaign the BBC asked the British ambassador in Bonn what understanding the German public were showing towards British aspirations. His answer was detailed and knowledgeable, so much so that his interrogator, obviously not counting on so much expertise, asked him how he knew all this. Because, the ambassador explained, by the time he had gone around making speeches, up to Hamburg, down to Munich, and back again, he had a fairly clear idea what the German people were thinking. Even Cardinal Wolsey's proto-ambassador, the Florentine Thomas Spinelly, would have approved, though from the forlorn tone of his correspondence in Mr Barber's exhibition I doubt if he ever had a refund of his travelling expenses in those same parts from his all too meteoric English employer.

Today's diplomats receive subsistence allowances, known by some as 'per diems'. They can even draw advances on account of their travelling expenses, and in hard cash. My earliest advances even of salary were for some years effected by 'drawing a bill'. I never quite grasped what this roundabout transaction was meant to achieve, even when bills-of-exchange in the commercial world had become part of my stock-in-trade as a suitably aggressive, down-to-earth, export-driving and trade-promoting diplomat. With each bill I drew in those earlier days I simply had a primitive suspicion that, like Spinelly, I was being done down by the system, and blessed the day when an unequivocal cheque on a local bank took its place.

To me the mercantile facet of diplomacy was always an honourable tradition of its own, on its own historical merits. It was not one of these periodic novelties, somebody's gimmick about which we were supposed to enthuse briefly, probably at the expense of other functions, such as our regular and more generalized reporting. Whatever may have loomed large in the foreground, as trade always did, the background too had to be painted in, faithfully and in its entirety. In countries where the waters were endemically troubled – and my wife and I have lived through some nine major coups, revolutions or upheavals – it was always my prime intention that these episodes should never come as a surprise to my government.

Geoffrey Moorhouse anticipates one such of history's vacillations, and a mighty one indeed – the zenith of the Iranian 'bonanza', when Tehran was a boom-town for the free-spending of the world's oil-money. At the moment the British Embassy allegedly decided that they 'didn't want a lot of elegant reports . . . about social conditions in Iranian villages.'[1] If so, it was a pity. Admittedly pressures from home have made it desirable, even fashionable, for the diplomat to espouse trade work with something of a flurry. But there is nothing trendy about trade, and its social-economic setting has always been a barometer to its future. Even the lordly Hardinge of Penshurst knew all about this. The between-wars diplomat too was taught from the beginning to keep his eyes prudently and legitimately open. The state of the roads, or of people's shoes, a switch from tram-cars to trolley-buses or, alternatively, to donkeys – all these can be early-warning signals of impending economic and political change.

I remember two diplomats who as young men used to tour those self-same mountain villages on horse-back; one even had

[1] Op. cit., p. 296

173

the humour to team up, for mutual efficiency, with the Muscovite observer lurking uncomfortably at his heels. This journalistic, resident-correspondent tradition of the old diplomacy might well have diagnosed, from those same neglected Iranian villages, the faint preliminary tremors which were to grow into shock-waves that have sped around the world. Perhaps, by the more sophisticated sampling techniques of today, they were indeed so sensed, but greeted with incredulity. It would not be the first time that vast financial commitment at the home-base has proved unreceptive to the first intimations of bad news from the field; in its time the automobile industry has been a case in point.

But the old diplomacy always had a man, or regularly sent one, wherever the strata were unstable and the tremors most eloquent. This philosophical, often humorous acceptance of the delicate role of mobile sensor, or thermo-couple, is a diplomatic tradition of its own, as testified by my equestrian predecessor who made a virtue of his own invigilation. A reassuring instance of its continuing existence was repeated by a recent weekend paper quoting a British diplomat home from those parts. What a relief, he concluded, to be back home where there can be eight people in a room without thirty-two plots in progress. And what an insight also into his own balance and versatility.

So tradition, not so much in method as in ethic and underlying philosophy, was a principle arm and an invisible strength of the old diplomacy. Its role and potency are reminiscent of those nonexistent Papal divisions which so provoked Stalin's derision, yet within a quarter-century of his death materialized as though by magic, in Poland, behind a Polish Pope.

Chapter XII
The United Nations

My late colleague Sir George Peregrine Young, Bart., was a British diplomat classic to the extent that, with the looks and the style of a Regency 'blade', he was really a very modern man. As circumstances required he could function as efficiently under a Labour Foreign Secretary as he might have in later years, flying supersonic with a Conservative successor to some distant summit conference. Like his wife, he died young, not long after World War II. But he was outstanding among his kind, and has left various remembrances, not least a son who, in his own way as idiosyncratic and colourful as his father, has literally bicycled his way into public recognition and parliament.

His father's finest hour dates back to one of those intermittent Fashodas which come as occasional but necessary blood-transfusions to the French stereotype of Britain and, more especially, to the frustrations of France's presidents.

The scene was wartime Beirut. The occasion was a set-to between Generals Spears and Catroux, on what today would have been denounced at the United Nations as French neo-imperialism in the Levant. Free France evidently viewed the occasion to the contrary as a legitimate reassertion of Gaullist irridentism, in anticipation of impending peace. So behind closed doors the fur was flying. They opened briefly for 'Sir Young' to step outside, where an anxious group of officials and military at once bombarded him with demands for a progress-report. 'So far so good,' came the answer, with an archaic smile worthy of those early envoys of Thucydides – 'Open countenances, openly arrived at!'

President Woodrow Wilson's 'open covenants of peace, openly arrived at' were among the major naiveties of the inter-war period. Yet their costly artlessness had then a certain innocence that differentiates them from today's often suspect clamour for 'open government'. Such onsets strike against that decent secrecy which even the most enlightened government must maintain over critical areas of its activity. Qualitatively then, and still more quantitatively there is a difference of dimension between the old League of Nations of Geneva and the United Nations of New York. The regular meetings of the League of Nations Council were only 'summits' to the extent that they were normally attended by at any rate the Foreign Ministers of the member-powers. In size too the League was not comparable with the rising one-hundred-and-fifty-strong body which has grown out of the original fifty signatories to the Charter of the United Nations, on the 26th of June 1945 at San Francisco.

Though Heads of State were not there to sign, there was already a whiff of 'summitry' at San Francisco, as there had been at its preliminaries. A much lamented American author of those days built some of his best underworld stories around what his villains called 'the greatest non-stop rotating crap-game in New York.' Until recently some of his epithets might well have applied to the nascent United Nations too; its magnetism for the leadership of the world's powers, small, great and super, made of it a permanently available standby summit. The annual General Assemblies of the United Nations and, particularly, the crisis meetings of the Security Council, have therefore served as staging-posts on the way to the new summitry to which they have by now habituated the world.

If the League of Nations grew out of a peace-treaty that failed through the League's subsequent incompletion of membership, the United Nations grew from a peace-settlement that is still uncompleted, despite a membership-turnout so complete as to seem at times a positive plethora. Some of the smallest and newest nations sensibly economize on the number of embassies they establish around the world. Not one of their Presidents would however deny himself the access to the summit afforded by representation at UN Headquarters, New York. As a result the General Assembly Hall at what was Turtle Bay on the East River now tends each autumn to be a summit for the small. The summits of the great seem to gravitate more and more to their own capitals, or to carefully chosen neutral ground.

Today's summit diplomacy then can be said to be the product of the partial failure of the United Nations; the more it has grown the more it has in effect turned the great powers back to the private forum that it was meant to supersede. Both processes – the centripetal, westwards and inwards to New York, and the centrifugal, eastwards and outward, back again across the Atlantic – are logistically the offspring of the long-range bomber of World War II. In the 'thirties neither the Imperial Airways flying-boats nor the Yankee Clippers had materially influenced transatlantic mobility, while the sea-route would have been too slow for recurrent summitry. Lease-lend, coming after cash-and-carry, changed all that. The Atlantic Charter of August 1941 had been a largely maritime affair. On New Year's Day 1942 the Declaration of the United Nations shifted the centre of international gravity firmly to the United States mainland. From then onwards more and more gentlemen of England and elsewhere were to shuttle across the Atlantic, for a while wrapped in blankets in the bowels of scarcely converted bucket-seated bombers. The Hot Springs Conference on Food and Agriculture of May 1943 was succeeded by another in Atlantic City on refugee issues. By 1944 the Bretton Woods Financial Conference, and in October the Chicago Conference on Civil Aviation, had in their separate technical ways shaped portentous patterns for the post-war years. In August 1944 at Dumbarton Oaks the first outlines of a United Nations Organization took shape.

Dumbarton Oaks was a true summit-meeting – a summit of officials however, though very high ones indeed. For whenever two or three Permanent Under-Secretaries and Directors-General of their Foreign Ministries are gathered together, it is still a summit of sorts. I remember one such eminence suggesting to me that when the permanent head of a Foreign Ministry decides that good might come of a long chat, a real *tour d'horizon*, with the ambassador of a major power, then this too is a summit, or at any rate a mini-summit; and more of them are convened than one might think.

Interleaved between these diplomatic conferences, as World War II drew to its end, were the great, authentic, historic summits – Tehran, Yalta, Potsdam. Winston Churchill, being a mere Head of Government, had regularly yielded precedence to those leaders also Heads of State. At Potsdam even that traditional wartime seat among the mighty was abruptly wrenched from him by the electoral reversal of 1945. Politically it was among the more brutal displays of instant elimination; but a still crueller human mortality had more than once intervened in this new airborne diplomacy. On the way to Yalta in January a converted bomber, out of fuel and seeking to ditch in the Mediterranean, cart-wheeled to its end over a submerged reef. It took with it half of the British delegation, including a good friend who had been our house-guest in the Lebanon only shortly before. Half a year later another such 'plane vanished without trace, flying eastward across the Atlantic with several of the British delegation from the San Francisco Conference.

Today we take entirely for granted the routine safety of the great jumbo-jets and the elegant Concorde. We push to the back of our minds, and memories, the sombre toll which the early summit diplomacy exacted from its first practitioners. Today's battle is no longer with the elements and embryonic science. Instead every summit-bound aircraft travels in silent and so far successful combat with the competing weaponry, technology and ruthless ideology of transnational terrorism.

At least however by San Francisco the Charter of the United Nations was signed. All that remained was to institutionalize it, implement it, and set it to work. Like all infants the new apparatus must also first have a name. The origin of this one enjoys various attributions, and in fact probably 'just growed'. Already on New Year's Day 1942 there had been a 'Declaration of the United Nations' to sign. Lord Gladwyn tells how even by 1943 it had become a habit to refer to an eventual post-war authority as 'The United Nations', President Roosevelt having previously used the term as a rallying-cry for the allied powers. Lord Gore-Booth, who was also in at the birth, pin-points the formal baptism as May 1945, in Commission I of the San Francisco Conference. There Mrs Eleanor Roosevelt proposed, and he formalized in a motion, that the title 'United Nations' be adopted for the new body. I myself recall that some nations and commentators boggled at the collective plural, and insisted on an orthodox abstract noun, in the singular and for use with a singular verb. So for many years 'The United Nations Organization' still now and then reared its head, more often as 'UNO' or, in the Latin languages, 'ONU'. In the end brevity has prevailed; we are back where President Roosevelt started, and more so, with 'The UN' as a title used quite unselfconsciously even in the spoken form.

Before however 'The UN' set up shop in its final American

home, post-war London was very properly granted the preview of this new world body. In August 1945 the Preparatory Commission of the First General Assembly of the United Nations began to function. Seconded to it as Executive Secretary was the British diplomat Gladwyn Jebb, later Lord Gladwyn, to such effect that he had what he evidently considers a narrow escape from becoming the first Secretary-General of the United Nations – or perhaps from a prototype Soviet veto – by ceding his candidature to the Norwegian Trygve Lie.

Organizationally and administratively the Preparatory Comission did its work well. The General Assembly, which opened – on time – in Central Hall, Westminster, on 10 January 1946, was by any such standards a British triumph. In broader human terms its triumph was hollow. Shortly after, while temporarily in Iraq, I received from the Lebanon a pulse-racing special item from a local paper which intimated that suddenly, thanks to the London meeting, lions were lying down with lambs and bears, prisoners were being set free, Soviet troops were withdrawing from Central Europe, with free elections to follow everywhere – a whole millenium had exploded. Shortly before that however I had celebrated my thirty-first birthday to a more sombre message, Winston Churchill's 'iron curtain' premonition at Fulton, Missouri. So my Lebanese prophet's overnight cornucopia of glad tidings explained itself when I noticed his date-line – April 1st! As 'poissons d'Avril' go it was too skilful by half, a poignant evocation of the might-have-been for a desolate and divided world, like the United Nations itself in a Middle East so soon condemned to false hopes. But for one delirious split-second I too had been taken in, and delighted in it.

From that first General Assembly a more durably enjoyable legend had already filtered through to balance these melancholy reflections. At all good conferences a major banquet is included in the ticket; and His Majesty's Government had apparently decided to do the visiting statesmen proud as a change from prevailing austerity. The banquet was convened in St James's Palace where, I was assured, the royal gold plate was brought out from its wartime safe-keeping in some remote grotto, to dot the 'i' – or gild the lily – of renascent hospitality. As the proceedings closed, and the illustrious guests trooped out into the night, one of them was neatly detoured into a side-chamber where, without fuss, an equally elegantly white-tied gentleman deftly abstracted from the envoy's tail-pocket a small side-plate or coaster, as massively and royally armigerous as its sheen was eighteen-carat. The culprit represented a people not a thousand miles removed from the site of my April Fool's Day spoof, and which like him has survived down the ages by its unfailing and unashamed eye for the main chance. His surprised explanation was accepted; he had quite naturally assumed that a souvenir gilt ash-tray went along with the ambassadorial menu on so historic an evening.

Or so it is told. But by the time I heard of it Mr Lie and all his new Secretariat were winging their way across the Atlantic to what was to become the UN's home-town, though at first in very improvised accommodation. I only made its acquaintance some three years later, and it never seemed to me that Flushing Meadows on Long Island was New York, certainly not when battling to and fro between our Empire State Building offices and the UN's half of the converted bombsight factory which was its temporary home. Even the name 'Lake Success' seemed to me contrived, the work of some ad-man, or a devotee of the Coué system of self-indoctrination.

Yet behind the façade of breeze-block and chip-board, with occasional indiscreet vistas of machine-tools glimpsed through gaps in the conference back-drop, patterns of the new diplomacy were taking form. Procedures dating back to Church House and Central Hall in London, and to Harold Nicolson's Paris before them, were becoming established. So when finally the Secretariat settled down – or rather up – in its new skyscraper that so often mirrors the passing clouds against a blue sky, Assembly life went on much the same. To the Secretariat officials, and to those diplomatic magnates who hobnobbed with the Secretary-General up on his thirty-eighth floor, it had become more vertical. To the ordinary delegate, scurrying between perhaps as many as six committees, the General Assembly Hall and the Security Council Chamber – not to mention the cafeteria if he had a moment for eating – life was as horizontal and extended as at Lake Success. Only the corridors were longer, especially one endless promenade-deck linking the main council-chambers. Its nylon carpeting stretched into infinity; and no one had foreseen that its mileage would generate in the wayfarer a charge of static electricity that shocked innumerable delegates almost into insensibility when finally earthed. The spark was frequently discharged via the metal door-knob of a particular men's lavatory, strategically placed at the corridor's farthest end. After a while however some technological wizard covered it with a rubber insulant, and this favourite spectator-sport ceased.

Domination of the physical environment is a part of survival, whether the setting is a water-drop microcosm swarming with ferocious pond-life, or the slightly larger goldfish-bowl of the United Nations by New York's East River. It is not therefore immaterial to the progress of diplomacy that the nearest washroom to the main Delegate's Lounge – i.e. the bar – should initially have been bedevilled with a high-voltage door-knob. For the diplomacy of the United Nations is essentially, strikingly, literally, one of lobbies and corridors of power, or at any rate of influence. For this reason it is not quite the same as the earlier conference diplomacy of a Hankey and a Nicolson. It has more of a parliamentary flavour, with less of the British quality perhaps than of the American congressional, and now probably, and increasingly, of the European. It is a diplomacy of blocs and caucuses, mastery of which is a special skill, an essential expertise.

For it is also a system open to manipulation; and when different blocs join in voting in the same sense for entirely different reasons, it makes for ominous and strange bed-fellowships. Several assorted and quite differently motivated anti-colonialisms – indigenous, Latin American, Soviet, North American – concerted to precipitate by a fateful decade or so Britain's progressively phased time-table for her decolonization programme; Africa's stability may well be paying one price now, with others to come elsewhere. It could also well be that, by those same artificial and often premature 'target-dates', such ephemeral bloc alliances falsified the whole life-purpose, and expedited the death, of Britain's Sir Andrew Cohen, perhaps the truest friend of the emerging nations, and one of the United Nations' founding giants.

Equally the physical apparatus of the United Nations has become the archetype of the modern conference machine and its committee organization. Though the United Nations is anything but a government – its Secretariat is jealously invigilated against any such 'empire-building' pretensions – yet in many ways the Secretariat does play the consistent material role which a host-government assumes at any major international conference or congress. It provides the setting, the premises, the rooms, the furniture, the endless paraphenalia of communication, now that the media and their electronics are a part of conference diplomacy. Delegates must also eat, drink and relax, publicly or privately as they choose. They must snooze, wash, and indeed – as already hinted – occasionally even relieve their bladders, this too with selective degrees of privacy; that nearest door stencilled with a masculine silhouette – or no doubt feminine too as time goes by – has more than once served as a useful political extension of the adjacent committee-room. Electric typewriters, translation and simultaneous interpretation, radio and television facilities, documentation – all these Martha-functions of the great occasions in modern conference diplomacy are increasingly the province of the United Nations and its subsidiary bodies.

Its lay-out and structures of activity are now virtually standard when governments host their own conferences – regional, Specialized Agency, Andean Pact, at Monrovia or Punta del Este. The committee organization, with its Plenaries, Committees of the Whole, Ad Hoc and Special Committees, Working Parties, Drafting Groups – all will be much the same, and such that all or several of them can be functioning simultaneously. So the diplomat has had to learn new administrative skills. Dexterity in handling, using and serving this new machine must be part of his repertory.

The United Nations offers a post-graduate course in these latest crafts. Of the newer supplementary diplomatic skills chairmanship is probably the most important. Ambitious young diplomats achieve it by climbing a long and painstaking road, as Rapporteurs and Vice-Chairmen of progressively more important committees. With such training a good chairman can cope with any committee, outclassing the sea-lawyers whom their debates always breed by his sheer superiority in procedural techniques. Nothing will come as a surprise to him. He will know which of the recognized methods of adjournment or putting to the vote he may encourage, use or evade, thereby protracting, postponing or terminating discussion of an awkward item. He will deflect, or crush, 'points-of-order' launched by artists in this device; for he understands it even better than they. He will know when a so-called 'procedural motion', with its different majority requirement, is in fact just a stalking-horse for a quite different substantive purpose; the achievement of substance by procedure is a United Nations technique as old as the organization itself. By it I have watched a celebrated Indian practitioner pursue and realize his purpose behind the subtlest of diversionary smoke-screens. His speech notes, scattered like winnowed corn, were retrieved for him in the nick of time by distraught acolytes, crouched at the foot of the Assembly's automatic podium, of which meanwhile he was juggling the controls, so that it rose and fell like an early Wurlitzer cinema-organ. Yet another, in the Suez debate of 1956, moved that the condemnation of Britain should be voted first and debated after – and got away with it procedurally; I was reminded that, when Alice was in Wonderland, it had been the sentence first, and the verdict after, there also.

These occasions are the great moments of the General Assembly. Its routine annual Plenary Sessions can however point to one major weakness of public summitry, when involving the presence of Heads of State. The set speeches in Plenary of visiting Heads of State are not really composed to be listened to. They are addressed primarily to their home press, and not to the attendant delegations; in practice these Plenary audiences, after a few weeks of it, are usually few, all but a handful of reluctant volunteers being already busy elsewhere in committee. Such set speeches, in the actual negotiation of a specific summit conference, can slow the course of events still more than in a United Nations Plenary. For even Heads of State – as at Vienna in 1979 – can lack full powers; and long speeches requiring constant reference back to parliaments – or grey eminences – at home, can lead to very slow decisions. Conversely, of course, a Head of State who is an authentic tyrant can expedite matters remarkably by exercising his absolute full powers, even by remote control from far away. Stalin did so at San Francisco in 1945, over-riding from Moscow a rigidly briefed Gromyko by a flat reversal of fundamental policy on the attributes of the Security Council.

As well as his tenacity to his brief, the same indestructible Mr Gromyko has frequently also demonstrated the basic diplomatic skill of keeping several oranges spinning in the air simultaneously. Its prime components are a card-index memory, decisiveness, and a gift of communication; the conference diplomat must know his brief and its precedents, and be able to expound them. Other attributes – charm, linguistic ability, drafting skill, good connections, eloquence, and the like – though helpful are secondary. In a separate and exclusive class of its own comes identifiable moral integrity, which elevates mere competence into something greater; Dag Hammarskjöld was always redolent of it, though arguably in the wrong place, time and office. In short, diplomacy is a management skill like others. Only its dimension and imperatives are different, since its executives act for peoples and not for shareholders; and nations still represent a higher authority than corporations.

The organization of modern conference diplomacy being therefore a management task, the acquisition, retention, transmission and utilization of information lie, as in all management, at the very heart of a good delegation. The speed and volume of information-processing – the telex, mechanical cyphering, the overnight air-bag, the press-conference and television interview – have radically affected the conference diplomat, and have much to do with his prospects and likely future. In addition a United Nations General Assembly, like any large conference, is protean by nature. It will be dealing with any number of themes; the very names of the standing committee and councils of the United Nations emphasize their diversity. These themes require many specialized skills, and correspondingly expert individuals to apply them. So the tendency of a delegation in action is for its components to scatter in their various directions and, all too easily, to lose touch in the horizontal and vertical labyrinths of the United Nations Headquarters. Talleyrand, and Hankey with his 'small room', had no such problem. Unlike them the Head of the Permanent British Mission to the United Nations, and at the General Assembly his visiting political master too, must positively exploit this quality of dispersal. Each morning the delegation spreads out through the committee-rooms, council chambers, delegates' lounges and corridors; within the United Nations Headquarters only the Secretariat have offices to which they can withdraw and sit, the Delegation never. So at some time, and point, it must be made to coalesce once more; otherwise much of its intervening expenditure of energy, and acquisition of data, will have been dissipated and wasted.

The delegation has in any case another built-in tendency to fragmentation and entropy. Nearly half of it comprises 'the Permanent Mission'. They live there all the time; they have homes and families awaiting them at the end of the day, however long; they know each other, and also the corridors and escape-hatches of the Secretariat, and its personnel too. The balance, 'the Visiting Delegation', are strangers, transients living from a suitcase, with a life-style different and – unless some sort of a 'mandarin' – perhaps solitary, even lonely. Though experts at home, they are novices on the spot. Any mutual exclusivity or élitism, however unconscious, can virtually split a delegation. All these disparate elements must be made to work together functionally and economically, and at the best happily and synergically.

I can only recall one occasion when the morning diaspora of the delegation regularly failed to recapture its overnight unity, and also when 'permanents' and 'temporaries' tended to go their separate ways. It was the one time, of many Assemblies and conferences, when an elementary but indispensable ritual, the 'Delegation Meeting', was neglected. The rubbing of minds comes naturally in the Foreign Office, where departments tend to drop everything at four-thirty for a communal cup of tea, the tea being the least important part of the few minutes' proceedings. Similarly if the outside world telephones an Under-Secretary at the wrong hour of day he will be inaccessible, being locked in conclave with the Permanent Under-Secretary, and all the other Under-Secretaries, at 'morning-prayers'. The British notoriously speak most frivolously of that which they take most seriously, and this ceremony is duplicated overseas at British Embassies the world over.

To say that the delegation meeting has become an integral part of conference diplomacy is neither a statement of the obvious nor an over-simplification. It is the basic invention which reconciles the temporary devolution of authority over a broad area with the retention of a consistent policy line. It ensures that no one, from the humblest lobbyist to the Head of Delegation, needs to be out of step. An informal system of 'runners' can suffice to keep the various components of a delegation in contact during the day's conference proceedings; hence the small *billets-doux* that are constantly slipped to 'the Chair' while committees are in session. But at 'morning prayers' the delegation memory-banks are cleared and up-dated for the new day. And when the leader of the delegation has listened for half an hour to all his staff and their mutual interpellations – and vice versa – he runs slight risk of being summoned out of the First (or Political) Committee by one of those nightmare 'phone-calls from London, demanding what the devil his delegate in the Sixth (or Legal) Commitee has just been telling a startled world.

Earlier mention of lobbies and caucuses points to the fact that these innovations of conference diplomacy are themselves also derivatives of the evolution in communications. I am told that what are called the synapses of the human brain cross-link and inter-communicate with a complexity which makes even the most advanced micro-circuitry seem crude and primitive. There have been times when I could have been persuaded that the caucus system of the United Nations is more sophisticated than either. Individual nations can have interests which overlap – and possibly conflict – to the extent of qualifying them for membership for several pressure-groups simultaneously. Not all of these are power-blocs, or official United Nations caucuses. Nigeria for example can find itself pulled in many different directions as a member of the African caucus and the Commonwealth Group, and also be influenced at the United Nations as both an oil-exporting country and a 'needy' member of the 'developing nations' group. It is however very exceptional for a delegation formally to disassociate itself from the agreed position of its geographical caucus once a matter has reached the stage of a public vote in committee or in Plenary. As a result the aim of the United Nations diplomat is to influence decisions while still in a formative condition in caucus. Since caucus meetings are on principle closed to outsiders, to do so is difficult without incurring the charge of interference, with all the odium intrusiveness, or entryism exposed, entails.

The problem is dealt with, and if done properly the odium averted, by what to everyone but the actual lobbyists is regrettably known as lobbying. They themselves prefer to be known by their official designation of 'special advisers', a term which to them is no mere euphemism of the 'rodent operative' category. I could rightfully say 'to us', since at several General Asssemblies I was special adviser on Latin America, and at one, for an uncomfortable space, simultaneously on the Arab countries too. After grappling with both these fistfuls of quicksilver for some weeks I reverted to my normal quota of Latin American delegations, a mere score or so, with not even a couple of hundred names and faces to photograph mentally. A very large number of them became good friends, as we met again year after year.

The Latin American caucus, as the oldest, is perhaps the most typical of the United Nations blocs. Its palmy days are long gone though; for a while it was the belle of the United Nations ball, when twenty votes out of fifty-odd could make or break a two-thirds majority. For a long time thereafter its weight could by sheer gravitational pull still swing the voting of newer voting-blocs, and till today it produces statesmen whose quality and influence rise above the tragic ideological differences of that marvellous sub-continent. Even on colonial, economic and humanitarian themes the bloc's constant reconciliation of total regional solidarity with compromise and decent common-sense could augur well for its peoples, once their rulers' ideological polarization settles down into something like a normal, restless, uncomfortable but working set of democracies.

Observing the lobbying process applied to the various caucuses with as much detachment and humour as is possible to a participant, I used to comfort my occasional sense of moral outrage by trying to rationalize it to myself, as just one more manifestation of traditional diplomatic technique updated to new criteria. There were visibly, for example, quite different national schools of lobbying methodology. Some were primitive but effective; wining and dining, and even darker appeals to the senses, and to plain greed, have always had their successes. So too does subsequent moral pressure – as it were – when these appeals have been accepted too heedlessly. Such occult techniques are not however for the corridors and lounges of the United Nations, where most of the contact takes place.

A main purpose of lobbying is, perfectly properly, to form some sort of advance picture of how the voting cards are likely to fall, and if necessary to influence their falling. As a result much lobbying is a matter of urgency, and wholly public. It is also usually sedate, even discreet, but was not always so. In those early days, when the Latin American vote was crucial, I had occasion to extend my advisorship quite informally to my United States equivalent, who had been wondering aloud why his flock had lately become so recalcitrant. I reminded him of a certain cartoon scene popular at the time in the cinema, and still a television favourite with new generations. In the foreground some standard anti-hero of the Mickey Mouse school is being remorselessly over-hauled by the forward-line of an American football-game. Catching up on this tiny fleeing figure is always the same phalanx of gigantic robot-like figures, granite-jawed, helmeted and shoulder-padded, looming larger and larger till, like charging buffalo, they overwhelm him and, bursting by illusion out of the screen, steam-roller the viewer too. This, I contended, was his team when the alarm-bell for a lobbying exercise was sounded. Its targets, I warned him, detested being manipulated, even man-handled, and still more forming part of a public spectacle which the rest of the Assembly found highly diverting. In terms of the then current nuclear debate, his version of lobbying was achieving over-kill.

Though not offended – we were good friends – he was certainly incredulous. So I promised him that I would alert him the next time that, from the onlooker's view, the action stations klaxon sounded. I did so. He watched with me, and the forward-line never charged again. It had been a classic demonstration of counter-productivity. The arm-twister – another unheedingly used synonym for lobbyist that we authentic special advisers axiomatically reject – measurably produced a lesser return than the operative who used classic diplomatic method for this new situation. Negotiation, persuasion, reinforced if needs be via the 'usual diplomatic channels', a transaction between equal parties, a deal if you wish, the promise of support given for support received and, if impossible, the abandonment of any *quid pro quo* till another time, without resentment or recrimination – if these methods fail, success by the others will be illusory. Perhaps the highest refinement of the art is to lobby, gratuitously, for the thesis of a friend-in-need – with of course prior authority, if you are wise. Such bread upon the waters can return in minutes rather than in days.

A small but characteristic instance of this process caused to overlap for an instant two lives whose names figured on quite different pages of my little General Assembly memo-pad. One, the late Cyro Freitas Valle, was a Brazilian ambassador – and statesman – whom I liked and respected. Behind the florid complexion and rather hyper-thyroid blue eyes of a theatre-version English country squire he had a fine and patriotic mind, with a considerable regard for our own country. The other protagonist was the New York correspondent of a great British daily of simplistic editorial policies, and whose formidable proprietor was the only being or phenomenon this otherwise intrepid pressman held in unholy dread. I had been able to help him out professionally once, when I found him pale and unusually silent at the delegates' lounge bar, having just received a telegram announcing the despot's imminent descent upon him for an instant survey of the United Nations scene. 'The Beaver's coming through!' he went on repeating hollowly, gazing blankly into the distance behind the barman.

It was to him I in my turn could have recourse, after I had been summoned – to the same bar – by Ambassador Cyro, to be told of a 'phone call he had received from London. My journalist friend's paper had that morning included Brazil in a list of Latin American countries pillorying Britain's colonial position at the United Nations when, to the contrary, their delegation had at my urging been at vast pains to give Britain credit, time and room to manoeuvre. My whole small edifice of mutual confidence had come tumbling down. My pressman friend listened compassionately but pronounced, memorably, that 'a recantation wouldn't get past the youngest sub-editor.' Instead however he guaranteed that within the next twenty-four hours there would be an article on some totally different front, but singling out Brazil for lavish and well documented praise. All parties were satisfied, and remained in a relationship of pleasant mutual obligation.

It was very kind of Ambassador Freitas to be so forthcoming when, even so comparatively recently, times were much more overtly hierarchical and I was small United Nations fry compared with him. Very obligingly however the Latin Americans operate on the old Gallic basis of 'Once an ambassador, always an ambassador.' So thanks to my mini-embassy in Central America I too was 'Embajador Jackson', and an 'Excellency', which helped. For emergencies I had an even stauncher ally, a friend over many years, in whom from the first I had identified an exponent of a new diplomacy, excellently camouflaged in the most formal trappings of the old. Victor Andres Belaunde himself had seemed very old to me when I, at thirty-five, first knew him on the Peruvian Delegation to the Fifth Session of the United Nations General Assembly.

Ten sessions later, as Head of the Delegation, he seemed hardly to have changed at all. With the benevolently saturnine looks of a somehow saintly Mephistopheles, his Assembly technique too conveyed a built-in contradiction. His façade was that of a professional orator, his substance that of an expert and indefatigable conciliator. He and I had become friends over a pun – mine, in Spanish; an unfortunate African lady delegate had been struggling vainly to extricate herself from a misleading sentence in a committee debate on the Introduction of New Members. Yet he combined his elegantly Rabelaisian humour with the strictest moral principles and propriety, which permeated all his professional activity. He never allowed an Assembly to separate him from his wife, and together the old couple attended the six-thirty Mass every morning at Saint Patrick's Cathedral on Fifth Avenue.

It was perhaps because I knew and enjoyed Spanish that I appreciated his art where those who listened to him via the simultaneous interpretation could not. Spanish is very much an orator's language, and the older Latin American delegates tended to perpetuate the orotund *bel canto* school of nineteenth-century speechifying. Two or three of them were rightly dreaded as bores and windbags, their booming tones guaranteed to empty a committee-room or council-chamber in seconds. Ambassador Belaunde however was different in quality and kind. Listened to at first hand, his play on the endless resources of the Spanish language and literature could be spell-binding; simultaneous interpretation sterilized and desiccated it, much as updated renderings of the Gospel do with the King James and Authorized versions. Behind the façade of eloquence, the substance too was impeccable and the brief thoroughly mastered, whether a disarmament, colonial or membership issue.

But at a still deeper third level sat the real Belaunde, cool, sophisticated, cynical often, detached always, studying the course of the debate and the impact of his speech from behind a deliberate screen of his own masterly oratory. I can recall no one else who could constructively meditate while making an excellent speech. He would use such a speech as a bull-fighter uses a cape, then go off to a caucus-meeting to turn the results into a mediation, or an amended resolution for the next committee meeting.

Thanks to him I was shown a mark of confidence which in my then capacity acted on my morale like a private accolade. He invited me into the holy-of-holies, a Latin American caucus-meeting, firmly over-riding a number of vocal protests that the presence of an outsider was improper and unheard of. From these voices my real friends were more clearly identifiable; it was a feature of the Cold War days that individual delegates of certain friendly nations could nurture ideological sympathies discreetly contrary to the practice of their government. It was only the once; and my stay was short, and quite sufficient to convey a not really very important message. But it ratified an authentic 'special relationship' with the Group; and to set his seal on it Senor Belaunde sent for a photographer to take a formal picture of the occasion, and signed it. I prize it all the more because, before he died, his qualities had become acknowledged sufficiently universally for him to have become President of the United Nations, at the Fourteenth Session of its General Assembly.

The ultimate extreme, *ad absurdum* possibly, of this new diplomàcy of coulisses and corridors was, as I have indicated, its polite extension even to the washroom facilities; of these many a multi-lingual anecdote is told at the expense of the elderly ambassadors who of necessity frequent them most assiduously. Many a procedural reconciliation has been effected, in the interval of an acrimonious debate, when in the white-tiled annexe one party has courteously stood back to cede to the other the first haul at the roller-towel dispenser. It was, I think, in 1958 that a ferocious First Committee debate on Cyprus was briefly suspended, but long enough for the word to go around, and a significant hush to fall on the busy subterranean corridor. With the synchronized precision of manoeuvring starlings, if less obtrusively, delegates edged towards the fateful door with its 'Men/Hommes/Hombres' stencil. When through it stepped together, arm in arm, the Greek and Turkish Foreign Ministers, chatting and smiling urbanely, the enthusiasm was evocative of the effusive crowd emerging from nowhere, to the help of victory, after the shoot-out scene in the late Gary Cooper's famous film, *High Noon*. This reconciliation too, alas, proved fragile, and temporary – the only moment of light relief in a long, harsh and tragic saga. Within minutes the peevish tit-for-tat of alternate quotations from Durrell's *Bitter Lemons* was resumed, with tragedy growing steadily out of farce.

The diplomat's recent and novel adaptation to public polemic is something sudden, in which the United Nations has played a formative part. World War II had already transformed the whole concept of public-relations. Before the war I certainly had been drilled to an instant evasive reflex if the press even hove into sight. And only the mighty ever confronted those coffin-like microphones of the early radio; television did not even exist to panic us. The Ambassador alone ever made a speech – or perhaps the Consul-General – and that usually on Prize Day at the local British school. A decade later the diplomat, as so often in his history, was instructed to change his spots overnight, and dutifully adjusted himself to an instant new tradition. We were to run with outstretched hand to meet the press. On tour from overseas head-quarters we were not to shrink from the intrusive hand-mike, or to wince at the inevitable question 'What does it feel like . . .'. Most of us learned the hard way to face the worst ordeal of all – the television studio, even the TV panel. Now, I understand, the young diplomat may take TV classes, just like the business executive learning to prop his chin, while composing his thoughts, between thumb and index-finger in the prescribed TV way.

The pioneers had no such advantages, least of all in the aboriginal territory of these new and terrifying techniques, the United States of America. The trail-breaker, and by scale of achievement not merely for Britain alone, was Lord Gladwyn, in the early Cold War days at the United Nations. It was he who showed how it could be done. His duels with the late and odious Andrei Vyshynski, notorious from his prosecution of Stalin's show-trials, became a feature of early American television viewing. Vyshynski's murderous past made him a natural 'baddie' for the viewer, perhaps even more than did the ordinary man's bitter realization that World War II had left his planet more divided and precarious than before.

The regular reader of histories and biographies may find it difficult to credit the frequent assurance that Britain's star UN performer disliked his role, and the particular TV celebrity it brought him. It was, I believe, in 1953 that I was sitting right there behind him, on the back row of the British Delegation stalls. I was able to observe him in the process – to his credit impressively rapid – of making up his mind that a more than usually scurrilous Vyshynski onslaught on Britain's attitude to 'Measures to Avert War' must be challenged. I watched the faint and momentary flicker of distaste, the stoical straightening of the shoulders, and the steady walk down the gangway and up to the new podium. Gladwyn Jebb was certainly taking no personal pleasure from what he had to do. But as so frequently, he then gave a badly needed demonstration that double-think and double-talk could not thrive in the free air of open discussion.

The extreme adaptability of British diplomacy to these new criteria was, I believe, timely and influential. Whatever the diplomat's future is to be, the United Nations experience will have affected its course as indelibly as has any other factor in his past. In whatever future drama or comedy the diplomat is to be cast, the healthy response of the new United Nations body to Cold War experimentation will most surely leave its mark on the role attributable to him. Conversely, such partial success as it has had, against impossible odds, it owes to the diplomat and his reflex, stronger and more ancient than all the dynamic of new ideologies and the inertia of new bureaucracies.

Chapter XIII
Conference Diplomacy

The previous chapter contends, then, that the United Nations has made its own contribution to the evolution of diplomacy. The signs are, even so, that the novelty of that contribution is wearing thin. The United Nations, for a couple of decades after its inception a prima donna among the world's voices, no longer holds the spotlight. She lives on, not so much prematurely retired as withdrawn from the footlights, coaching aspiring young nations and also running, as a sideline, an unobtrusive but quite successful catering and security-guard business.

Any more than a free lunch, there is no such thing, they say, as a youthful *femme fatale*; but it does seem that, in only early middle age, the United Nations has already instead become unnecessarily dull. Certainly most of its drama is now restricted to the Security Council. As for the General Assembly, it has largely become an international sounding-box. Instead of its earlier crisscross of variegated political interests its division is now preponderantly North/South, of developed as against developing nations. Its weighting is increasingly economic and humanitarian; in political terms it has – for example in the Middle East – lost all credibility. Nothing politically urgent is allowed to reach the General Assembly forum; such matters as peace and disarmament are steered towards the Security Council, with its built-in veto.

During the decolonization period the Fourth Committee (Trusteeship and Dependent Territories) could always be relied upon for a lively performance, in committee and right through to the Plenary debating of its resolutions. Lately the territories, and issues, falling under that heading have so dwindled that soon little but Southwest Africa/Namibia and Zimbabwe/Rhodesia were left for Committee IV. Its earlier protest function seems if anything to have been taken over by the Conference of the Non-Aligned Nations.

Owing to an intellectual thimble-trick eventually exposed as 'The Salt-Water Fallacy', surface-to-surface or overland colonizing did not count. Such cases were never, in the crusading heyday of the United Nations, allowed to fall within the terms of reference of the Fourth Committee. Some colonies were always more colonial than others; no intervening ocean, no colony. So its anti-imperialism was always selective, and its proceedings unlikely ever to be enlivened by the admission, and oratory, of petitioners from such colonial outposts as, say, Vladivostok or Port Arthur, let alone Santa Fé or Los Angeles. The USSR and the USA were somehow deemed incapable of colonialism. In the idiom of Real-politik – or sophistry – it is even more doubtful that the Fourth Committee's dwindling anti-colonial agenda will ever be replenished by pleas for the independence of, say, the Kuriles or Hawaii. Yet their off-shore status ought logically to leave them wholly vulnerable to the Fourth Committee's zealotry, in the absence of the usual overland exemption. Perhaps the difference was always one of will. Nations weary, or ashamed, let go. Those which are not do not.

It seems in any event inevitable that the glory and the glamour should have departed from the United Nations. So far as the political summits are concerned, the organization is an archaeopteryx surviving in the diplomatic aviary, a coelocanth in the bath-tub – a recognizable ancestor, but outstripped on the evolutionary ladder. Certainly the FCO's annual Assembly routine leads to this conclusion. From memory I could myself easily reconstitute a composite of those earlier preliminaries to the autumn General Assembly – the crescendoing departmental meetings leading to the formation and briefing of the British Delegation – all the logistical challenges of placing assorted political spokesmen and departmental experts in their right places at their right times – and then bringing safely home again all these important statesmen, and women too; for the British Delegation, over a decade or so, by some happy coincidence always ran a fine and famous line in handsome ministerial red-heads. The return trip usually in fact exposed them to no more serious hazards than those of one or the other of 'The Queens', a civilized recuperation, after the rigours of up to three months of air-conditioned wheeling, dealing, and speechifying far into the night.

Not any more. The annual trek to New York of the General

Assembly Delegation is no longer an administrative event, let alone a tour de force. Habit and expertise build up after many years; and I have the impression now that the annual inflation of the comparatively small Permanent Delegation in Now York, by a General Assembly temporary influx from London, has no longer the exhilaration of a salmon-run, but rather the sedateness and predictability of the autumn migration of the caribou. At the New York end the visiting delegation is fielded unerringly by capable and capacious hands – captained by another of those red-heads the dear colleagues accused us of breeding. A well-versed team provides everything from a bedroom to a desk, and a brief to read at it, compiled by the appropriate geographical department back in the FCO. During the Assembly it will be that same geographical or specialized department with which the particular expert will dialogue on his particular theme. Normally he will do so by overnight diplomatic bag, telex or routine telegram. Thanks however to the time-zone differential he will sometimes use a late evening 'phone-call or priority telegram, to rouse the Head of Department or the Resident Clerk from his bed, in the small hours of a British morning hard on the Greenwich meridian. In compensation however the London end will have all the next morning to compose their thoughts, while the New York Delegation sleep in their beds, to receive the FCO's lunchtime reply in nice time for 'morning prayers' at the Delegation office, and with an hour in hand before the General Assembly and its Committees start to function for the day.

By this stage of the Assembly the United Nations Department of the FCO, back home in the Palazzo, should be able to relax. The Department has done its job, and can leave particular cases to the FCO specialists, till the Assembly is over and their task of collation begins once again. So too can Protocol and Conference Department relax. Their General Assembly contribution has been a familiar choreography of simple and by now routine logistics, its only hazard being the occupational unpredictability of all ministerial and parliamentary programming. Increasingly now it is instead in the one-off, *ad hoc* realm of international summitry that the adrenalin will stir in Protocol and Conference Department, and its departmental blood flow fast again.

Of the 1979 Zimbabwe/Rhodesia conference at Lancaster House it can safely be said that there can never be one quite like it again, and not merely as the final bow of the old actor-manager from the colonial stage. Not the least of its achievements was its demonstration that Commonwealth Conferences, against all the odds, remain very much of our time. They are no longer a mere intermittent improvisation, but a recurrent feature of the international political scene, a new diplomatic tool of unexpected efficiency and temper.

Most nations have already accepted, or grasped, diplomacy by conference as a fact of life, and taken the necessary material measures to participate in it. So much so that many of the newly emergent nations – according to one disillusioned and globe-trotting conference expert of my acquaintance – lend to the construction of a spanking new Conference Centre a top priority, away above new roads, harbours, hospitals, or excursions into the intermediate technology.

The Cuban government did just this for the 1979 Havana Conference of the Non-Aligned Nations. Perhaps after all they are more subtle than we. Though many such an international conference may seem to us a mere cartoon version of bureaucracy out on a picnic, such a Centre may well recoup its outlay in far more than empty prestige. For the human inter-reaction of national leaders, meeting on such occasions in person, seems more and more to effect a negotiating catalysis beyond all purely managerial prediction. Britain has arguably lagged behind in and neglected the necessary material provision for this necessary human chemistry.

Summit conferences involve by technical definition the presence of Heads of State, Heads of Government, Foreign Ministers and, increasingly, Finance Ministers. Britain, with recurrent conferences arising from her Commonwealth and now her European Community involvements, has over recent years developed both a considerable expertise in their handling and an international reputation for it. Much of her expertise is in fact only expediency, a regrettable necessity in response to the all too familiar challenge of budgetary stringency – the making of a better brick with ever less straw. For a generation she has been struggling and hoping to catch up, by building eventually her own International Conference Centre with countries in what has been called the 'wretched of the earth' category who have already built theirs. Successive plans have been rejected, and budgetary appropriations missed – though as a providential byproduct of chronic procrastination successive waves of architectural brutalism have also passed harmlessly over our heads; otherwise who knows what monstrous incongruity might by now have confronted Westminster Abbey across the way at Broad Sanctuary.

It is largely indeed by luck and tenacity that enforced improvisation has seen Britain through the birth-pangs of this newest diplomatic method. 1977 was the *annus mirabilis* mentioned earlier, in which the FCO was confronted with hosting four major summits within two months. These were the NATO ministerial conference, the annual Economic Summit of the Seven major industrial powers, the Commonwealth Conference, and the Council of the European Community, not to mention six minor summits preparatory to or arising from them. To have a permanent International Conference Centre in London, complete with standing material facilities and staff, would merely have involved activating an existing facility, and thereafter successively re-activating it, admittedly perhaps with the risk of overloading, given the spate of arrivals. In the total absence of such a permanent facility inventiveness took over – the legendary British genius for improvisation.

The FCO have refined their cumulative conference expertise to the extent of maintaining both 'inward' and 'outward' specialists in their Protocol and Conference Department. In preparing any summit anywhere there must be those who push and those who pull, those who expedite the great, and those who receive them, and their retinue, and nurse them from the first crucial moment when the first institutional toe touches the asphalted apron of the receiving airport. In 1977 the department in question, confronted with a concatenation of conferences, and with no International Conference Centre yet to receive, accommodate and shepherd them, took thought of the amoeba, and budded itself into a Conference Unit and a Presidency Unit. The Conferences Unit looked after 'nuts-and-bolts', the 'nitty-gritty' – mid-Atlantic technical argot for the wondrous logistics of transforming, say, the neo-classical splendours of Lancaster House into a passably functional Conference Centre, its new installations and electronics inexorably – and thriftlessly – dismantled once their purpose was served.

Behind the logistics the professional diplomats were, as ever, producing the paper-work – the briefs, the submissions which would be implemented, or not, according to the political will of their Ministers. The documentation of the Conference itself – the agenda, its circulation, the press material, and so on – all this would be handled, in the case of a Commonwealth Conference, by the Commonwealth Secretariat. This permanent and amply staffed body has headquarters worthily and not too nostalgically located at Marlborough House on Pall Mall, under a Guyanese Secretary-General of Indian origin, holding two excellent British decorations, his predecessor having been a Canadian.

But the European Community, also in the queue of that congested year, is not a Commonwealth body, and so needs its own conference secretariat. Britain responded to the freak pressures of 1977 by another *ad hoc* invention, a 'Presidency Unit' which can be reactivated every time Britain's turn for the six-month presidency of the Council comes round. Such a Presidency Unit will probably always be necessary, even when life is simplified for the host-country to a conference by its possession of a modern and permanent Conference Centre which, on the accordeon principle, can always be expanded temporarily, to cope with a summit conference imposed by its occupancy of the Presidency. Such a standing cadre will serve the purpose executed at a Commonwealth Conference by the Commonwealth Secretariat, similarly managing the agenda and its documentation, press material, and – when for example the host-country is Britain or one not too dissimilar – the important function of conference relations with a national parliament vigilantly addicted to its parliamentary Question-Time.

Not all countries yet have the resources and facilities to cope with so sudden and intense a call on them. In such cases a pleasant innovation swings nowadays into action. A fellow-participant in the summit conference comes to the rescue, for example lending experienced personnel to stiffen up, or even create, an indigenous Presidency Unit. In practice therefore we now see national secretariats functioning internationally. So once again summit diplomacy has not only caused diplomatic method to evolve. At the policy-forming stage, and at the administrative stage indispensable to it, the function of the diplomat himself, and his operational chain-of-command, have in this way been significantly modified, if not yet his accreditation and his loyalty.

For an all-English version of inward conference diplomacy I shall again have to call on memory, and seek to assemble a fairly representative composite.

On such occasions great activity, and anxiety, has prevailed on the administrative and logistical front. A Conference Unit is activated and, on what always seems to be a hot summer afternoon, the final office-meeting is convened, under the eaves of the old India Office corner of the FCO in King Charles Street. In this surprisingly large and once elegant room, with its quaint but attractive bull's-eye windows, a dozen senior officials come and go during the afternoon. Their summons had in theory emanated from the Chairman. In practice they have been convened by one of that breed of handsome and imperturbable middle-aged ladies of which the FCO – and the British film industry at its best – seem to have a world monopoly. One knows without being told that the planning of a summit conference is child's play to a lady who in her time probably ran a communication network behind enemy lines, in between repeated parachute descents. But very correctly she leaves the Chairman to it once the meeting convenes, and indeed he handles like a maestro the agenda on which she has so carefully briefed him; he is not perhaps quite so youthful as he looks, and very affably emanates considerable authority. But he also respects it in the committee membership, each one of which is an expert in his field. So the agenda flows briskly and amiably.

Security problems take no time; the large, slightly episcopal gentleman expounding on this theme finds that he needs simply to press the button on the excellent machine he installed last time, which was not so long ago. One of the three Conference Officers explains the arrangements made for supplying permanent passes to delegates. The criteria are severe, since hardly an international conference anywhere passes, he claims, without one or more delegates infiltrating into the closed sessions a 'secretary' who is actually – or so he thinks – his lady-friend, but is also in reality a press-woman in disguise, 'if not something worse!'

There is a decorous argument about the numerical distribution of these permanent passes to the respective delegations. The FCO man bear-leading the overseas visitors shows a fierce dedication to their rights at the expense of his own FCO colleagues; he even volunteers to lend his own Polaroid camera, to be available on the spot for late-comers accredited but passless. An Under-Secretary, who has self-evidently in his time been a rugby player, and even today would walk unmugged through any city in the world, gives warning of a risk of industrial action. There can be no certainty till after the weekend; but if the impending national strike of the Plumbers' and Joint-Wipers' Union is balloted, the delegates will have no toilet facilities at all, unless the new loos ordered after last time's debacle can be installed within the next forty-eight hours. The matter is left in the hands of a young man from Information Department, who turns out to be a labour specialist, and has the right connections.

A very silent and cherubic post-adolescent suddenly gives tongue, in an immense basso-profundo even more reverberant than that of the rugby player. He requires to be sure that all delegations receive parity of treatment in the distribution of conference documentation; we must not be seen to be doing ourselves more proud than our visitors. Not for the first time, what initially seemed a certain cussedness, though underlying considerable charm and fluency, turns out to be a simple but stubborn determination to see fair play for the visitors.

As the afternoon proceeds, smatterings of a new language are picked up by the newcomer. He learns that 'doorstepping' has to do with impromptu interviewing, and that its practitioners include both 'mutes' and 'vocals'. He is dissuaded from allocating to one sensitive group of delegates two convenient small rooms rather than one inconvenient large room, lest the press interpret the separation as signifying that its members have fallen out.

By the time the meeting disperses – on the dot – he has decided that these are a most impressive and reassuring cross-section of British officialdom, management, and manpower. In their different ways each one is strong-minded, intelligent, aggressive, civil and articulate. Any business company would be glad, and lucky, to have them at their board-room table – and all probability will, he suspects, in several cases soon. He accordingly concludes that at least the organization of the Constitutional Conference is going to be a success, whatever else may come of it. He has enjoyed his afternoon, and the company it has provided. Their government and his have decided what they must do. He and they are the ones now deciding for them how best to do it.

In this little flash-back I have referred to the remarkable diplomatic Norns who supervise the destinies of those leaving Britain's shores for summits and other conferences overseas. Their very real breed is one of the wonders of Whitehall, and infinitely more impressive than their fictional counterpart. Another of their number is the 'outward lady' who, it might be thought, would have an easy time of it compared with her mirror-image, the 'inward lady'. Far from it, to judge only from the ten-page questionnaire I recall from such occasions, covering everything from meals in the aircraft to the voltage of razors and typewriters, if electric.

In practice, an outward summit always requires an outrider, if not a whole advance-party. Much as with a royal visit, they go out ahead and walk the course meticulously, even callipering out the distances with an invisible drill-sergeant's pace-stick, and a very real stop-watch. Ideally of course it should not be necessary; the 'outward lady' should be spared this and similar remote-control responsibilities. Theoretically the FCO's worries over an outward visit should cease the moment the aircraft is airborne. But advance checking and liaison is always advisable, though the FCO experts can pride themselves that in the case of the reverse traffic, foreign governments sending delegations to Britain can do their liaisoning in a relaxed and confident spirit, and with minimal cross-checking.

Conference diplomacy, as now modified by recent technology and public-relations pressures, is here to stay, for a while at least. Today's diplomat has had to learn to dance to its tune, as the periwigged diplomat of my opening chapter had learned to excel in the minuet and other less courtly dances. What is not yet clear is whether governments, the political arm, see the conference diplomat as a participant, a partner, or as just a Thomas Cook, a valet-de-chambre, or a stud-groom. Yet on the apparently humdrum logistics hinted at in the last few pages hinge the relationships of nations, and the lives of their children.

This is why conference organization is so much a part of foreign policy, and so meticulously under the direction of the Foreign and Commonwealth Office. The men and women of the Diplomatic

Service who implement policy are also the ones who carry the responsibility for the smallest detail of that implementation. The two cannot be disassociated, which is why I believe that conference diplomacy signifies an intensification rather than a dilution or diminishment of the diplomat's function. It certainly seems to be keeping him busier than ever.

Chapter XIV
Grafting, Cross-Fertilization . . . .

For the apparatus and practitioners of British diplomacy the decades since World War II have represented one of their profession's more restless interludes. So much so that, as an alternative chapter-heading for it, the equally horticultural 'bonsai' of the Japanese, which applies to the still subtler art of miniaturizing trees, seemed instead briefly tempting.

There are those who would simply say that since the war the British diplomatic plant has been pulled up far too often, its roots scrutinized, and then dubiously replanted. Others, more sombre, would go so far as to endorse the 'bonsai' root-pruning analogy without qualification. If a perfect dwarf oak, or a lilliputian pine-tree, is a joy to the eye but of no earthly use to man or beast, so too, they would contend, are Britain's continuing diplomatic impedimenta. Though not wholly excluding some such risk of stunting, I would not yet concur. So on reflection I relinquished the 'bonsai' label.

In any case, the British diplomat of the post-war generation has proved himself an exceptional survivor. He has had to be, having been required to endure, *in vitro* and under local anaesthetic only, one major operation plus three public autopsies. Reassuringly they have all confirmed that he is not dead yet. They have also helped to inure him to a public scrutiny of his insides which, by 1977 and the 'Think-Tank', was to call on all his stoicism. Simultaneously he – and increasingly she – has lived through several *de facto* mergers with other departments. So he now knows, and has shared, all the managerial insecurity of the potentially redundant business executive, subduing his ulcers in the allegedly more exposed setting of the market-place.

Disconcertingly too his Service was meanwhile expanding – and occasionally sharply contracting – like an accordeon played a little uncertainly. Recruitment policies have been acutely sensitive to the fluctuating fortunes of the times and the nation, and to the changing call for particular age-groups within the Service. So another analogy for the perennial FCO phenomenon of 'bottle-necks' and 'log-jams' might well be that of a boa-constrictor, with the bulge of its latest dinner moving progressively along the slender elegance of its usual silhouette.

Today in fact, long after the first time that it was pulled up by the roots, the Diplomatic Service is far larger than it then was. I had believed that this trend to growth had been reversed of late. For at least a decade the administration has always been able to rebut any suggestion of expansion with all the outraged statistical virtue of a lady on a strict slimming diet; thus between 1968 and 1978 manpower was reduced by nine percent, and some fifty posts closed. Yet it seems that precisely the new incidence of summit diplomacy may well be quietly sabotaging this austerity. According to one hardened summiteer the very device of sum-mitry, which claims by the personal contact of leaders to outflank the armies of bureaucracy, is fast creating its own. Each summit is apparently proving to require an 'infrastructure', a massive supporting staff purloined from their more permanent occupations. All of which goes to demonstrate that pyramids have existed even longer than Parkinson's Law.

In 1914 it was a very small pyramid indeed, at both base and apex. The Foreign Office employed some six hundred London-based staff, a quarter or so of that number, including the porters and char-ladies, functioning back home in Downing Street. The equivalent number in 1969 was six thousand, with about half serving in London. By 1975 it had gone up to eight thousand, even though in between, after the Duncan Report of 1969, the closing of posts and premature retirements had gone on apace. This ambivalence of expansion and contraction had existed since the first of the uprootings – though it is perhaps misleading to classify the Eden/Bevin reconstruction of the immediate post-war under that heading. The 1943 'Proposals for the Reform of the Foreign Service' (Cmd 6420) were initiated by Anthony Eden, but implemented mainly during the tenure of Ernest Bevin at the Foreign Office. The document's succinctness and enthusiasm contrast favourably with later official reports on the same theme. Their philosophy too is different, being unreservedly expansionist.

There was already a long-term danger to the Service in this 'expansionism'. It was to mean that, in the first post-war years, some of the right things were to be done for the wrong reasons. The Eden proposals aimed ostensibly at dealing with a temporary situation:

'On the cessation of hostilities, however, the new Service will be faced with a problem which will demand an immediate solution. For a number of years there will have been no new entry. At the top of the Service there will be men who have stayed at their posts during the war against their inclination and who will wish to retire to make room for younger men. The Foreign Service will be understaffed while the tasks which face it will have multiplied.' (Cmd 6420, para. 7).

The error was to have taken the multiplication of tasks as more significant than the immediate understaffing.

The war was almost won. Eastward as well as westward the land was now bright, and its horizons vast and promising. The executants of the Eden proposals saw themselves in an expanding universe; the transfer of their euphoria to their own role in the post-war world, to Britain's diplomacy and to the diplomatic career itself, was understandable. At a moment of history when one Iron Curtain was being rent into tatters, and the imminence of the next unimagined, it was easy to overlook, or forget, certain transformations, relative and absolute, which had discreetly foretold the end of Victoria's England since long before the Old Queen had died. On top of such changes in the world-order must now be added the new bill yet to be paid. That wars have to be paid for was momentarily forgotten, though the cost to Britain's accumulated patrimony had already been hinted by the Cash-and-Carry of early wartime.

This imperception lay at the root of the unrealistic approach to the immediate future of Britain's diplomacy and the career serving it. It seemed to many as if the wartime crescendo of function and personnel would go on for ever. I was travelling around the Near and Middle East when first I heard of the Eden proposals. They came as no surprise – the pre-war Appointments Board at my university had forecast the Diplomatic/Consular/Commercial amalgamation when I had consulted them as to which FO examination would best suit my purse and extreme youth. But the first chance that I had had to discuss the new prospect had sent me to bed that night preoccupied, having listened to the version, if not the messianic vision, of a rather senior and otherwise apparently sane colleague. He pictured to himself a Near and Middle East dotted with a chain of small but diligent British Vice-Consulates – 'District Offices under another name' – reporting and responding to himself of course, or someone like him, at the embassy in their respective capitals.

The term 'neo-colonialism' had not yet been invented, and if it had would not have appealed to the post-war British mood, whether of electorate, parliament or Foreign Service. But if I had needed a corrective to a view so impervious to the self-evident reality all around us, I would have received it on my return to Beirut. In Tripoli our country was privileged to be represented by that admirable institution, an excellent Honorary Vice-Consul. A successful Lebanese industrialist, I respected him for his astute mind, and liked him even more for his amiable and imperturbable disposition. Speaking of the steady lifting of the wartime clouds, he commented to me, tongue noticeably in cheek, that it should not be long before the rich milords and ladies would be flooding back, to resume the traditional British love-affair with the Near and Middle East. I replied, rather ruefully, that to me it looked more like being the rich Near and Middle Easterners who would be flooding to England on their post-war Grand Tours. The corners of George's sensitive mouth twitched; but he did not contradict me. That was the last time I was to see him, though I have thought of him often enough since, and of our prophetic little exchange.

So I had always seen the 1943 reform not as an endlessly steeper curve, but as no more than a one-off expansion, catching up with the attrition of some six years of negative recruitment and 'natural wastage', as the various administrative implications of human mortality are now rather inconsiderately termed. Like all the subsequent reviews of Britain's overseas representation, it did in fact contain its own inherent quota of retrenchment; a component of thrift can always be relied upon wherever the Treasury godmother has been in attendance at the birth. I understand indeed that for a few short weeks the new Service had its own block-vote, but that the Treasury paw swiftly reached out and recaptured the escapee. The built-in element of economy was quite simply that of recruitment from within.

By it the former Diplomatic Service was initially enlarged by amalgamation, by the incorporation into it of the Commercial

Diplomatic and Consular Services. Recruited by effectively the same methods of selection, and of identical hierarchical grading, a high proportion of their members had also by now had much the same career training as the old Diplomatic Service. They were much the same sort of person too, even though the 1943 Command Paper makes much of 'democratization':

'Among the criticisms which have been brought against the Diplomatic Service the view has been expressed that it has been recruited from too small a circle, that it tends to represent the interests of certain sections of the nation rather than those of the country as a whole, that they have insufficient understanding of economic and social questions, that the extent of their experience is too small to enable them properly to understand many of the problems with which they ought to deal, and that the range of their contact is too limited to allow them to acquire more than a relatively narrow acquaintance with the foreign peoples among whom they live.' (Cmd 6420, para. 2).

It is true that till comparatively recently a private income of £400 a year had been a prerequisite of acceptance into the old Diplomatic Service; and even in 1943 life in the career would be none the worse for some such supplementary benefit. The Eden proposals accepted that by now the time for self-sufficiency had come:

'This knowledge (of foreign countries and foreign languages, of modern history and economics) can with difficulty be acquired without special study such as today requires the assistance of private means. This requirement places a limitation on the field of selection of candidates which cannot be accepted.' (Cmd 6420, para. 14).

Certain proposals followed which would have provided special advance training at the public expense for likely candidates. This particular reform never materialized; but the 'recruitment from within', plus the more open atmosphere of post-war Britain and its higher education, meant that the post-Eden/Bevin Diplomatic Service was certainly no longer that of Odo Russell, Hardinge of Penshurst, or even Harold Nicolson. If not yet a meritocracy, it was no longer an aristocracy, not a club, nor even an oligarchy. A vestigial self-consciousness of these 'exclusive' origins has left the present reformed Diplomatic Service unnecessarily hyper-sensitive to the updated reproach of what today is correspondingly termed 'élitism'. Even in 1943 however there were those of its members who combined experience of the state school system with some awareness of the purpose and surviving utility of finger-bowls, and other such accessories to the stereotype of diplomatic activity.

The process was to accelerate. Less than ten years after the war's end I heard one of Britain's first, and in a while highly distinguished, woman diplomats, over a Third Room family tea in the FO, confront a new recruit on this same theme. He had been vaunting rather aggressively his achievement as 'the only one here from an unpriviliged background.' The no-nonsense young lady challenged him to poll those present. Not one, even among those from leading independent schools, had not received some sort of state help at some stage in his education, some to the tune of one hundred percent.

So the Eden reforms were timely, generous and imaginative. In their way, and for their time in so swiftly evolving an epoch, they were also more fundamentally radical than other subsequent scrutinies of British diplomacy. They were the last to take wholly for granted the career of diplomacy as something akin to a vocation, and not implicitly to question it, by formalistic if not double-edged tributes to the diplomat's professionalism. The Command Paper is categorical:

'The diplomat must be able to keep His Majesty's Government informed of developments which may affect their foreign policy, submitting his observations and advice, which may or may not be accepted. While a diplomat may therefore be able to influence foreign policy by his reports, he does not finally determine it. This is the task of the Cabinet. The art of diplomacy consists in making the policy of His Majesty's Government, whatever it may be, understood and, if possible, accepted by other countries.' (Cmd 6420, para. 3).

The 'virtuous circle' of the professional diplomat has never been presented more clearly nor acknowledged more officially. The diplomat advises; his government decides; the diplomat executes and expounds. With any break in the circle – a main danger incidentally of political appointments – the process is no longer diplomacy, and its practitioner no longer a diplomat. That the Eden proposals also envisaged closed future relations between the FO and the then Colonial Service and the Imperial Defence

College – now the Royal College of Defence Studies – should not be mistaken for archaism or atavism. More likely, given their general philosophy and freedom from nostalgia, the suggestion, far from being retrograde, was a cautious response to, and recognition of, the growing 'foreignness' of what had been Empire.

There is no grafting without preliminary cutting; and these first hints of a grafting – though as yet without a whisper among them of the Dominions Office – were very relevant to that Department's earlier separation from the Colonial Office, and to its future integration with the Foreign Office. The history of the Dominions Office has its own text-book, from its inception in 1925, via its absorbtion in the India Office, to its transformation in 1947 into the Commonwealth Relations Office and, finally, after a renewed merger with the old Colonial Office in 1966, to its fusion into the new Foreign and Commonwealth Office, the FCO of 1968. I find that account, in Lord Garner's immensely informative presentation[1], particularly sensitive in its relevance to my present theme.

By the 'vesting date' of the 1st of January 1965, three years before its final culmination in the 'merger' of the two Offices and Departments of State, the officials of the CRO had already become members of a combined Diplomatic Service, a first step to the new integrated Department of 1968. This new Diplomatic Service, like the earlier amalgamated Foreign Service of 1943, was also a form of recruitment from within, in broader Whitehall terms. The CRO itself simply could not muster the personnel needed to set its sails to that 'wind of change' famous from Harold Macmillan's memorable speech of January 1960; it is incidentally curious that probably the most authentic of the claimants to have coined this phrase for him, Sir David Hunt (*On the Spot*, chap. 6 – Peter Davies 1969), eventually became a British ambassador himself by integration into the new combined Service. The Commonwealth Service just did not have the numbers – and so the cumulative resources in skills and experience – to man the many new missions needed, in capitals whose governments had in the past been content to leave foreign relations to the British Government in London. It could only draw upon its neighbour, the Foreign Service.

So it might have been an ordeal far more profoundly traumatic

[1] Joe Garner *The Commonwealth Office, 1925–1968*, Heinemann 1978

than in the event it evidently was, to lower the flag on a Service with the almost regimental *esprit de corps* and intimacy that Lord Garner describes, and to exchange these for the much larger anonymity of a new joint Diplomatic Service. Each Service had much to learn from the other. Perhaps in truth the British diplomat is today less 'pompous' and 'magisterial' – recurrent CRO epithets! – thanks to the Commonwealth Service cross-fertilization. Conversely the diplomats may have taught the CRO man something about the susceptibilities of independent sovereign governments, to which Harold Macmillan himself had shown particular sensitivity (Garner, p. 374). What Lord Garner himself describes as a 'range of activities more reminiscent of minor royalty than diplomacy' was liable to protract a vestigial 'maternalism' which has been known to set teeth on edge in 'Old Commonwealth' chancelleries, as indeed also in post-amalgamation British High Commissions; thus more than one High Commission lady needed to learn not to refer to the wives of her husband's Diplomatic Service juniors as 'my staff'.

Most good marriages rest upon a comfortable shedding of shared illusion, and so did the union of these two great departments of state. The Foreign Office – by now the FCO – had to adjust itself to the qualified perpetuation of what Geoffrey Moorhouse perhaps prematurely calls 'the illusory moment of Commonwealth'. (op. cit. p. 388). Conversely, as Lord Garner acknowledges, 'the staff in the two departments had grown much more alike – the FO, after the Eden reforms, had lost the image of being "stripe-panted diplomats" and the CRO, having cut the tie with the CO, was establishing its own tradition; the younger generation in each department were indistinguishable from their colleagues next door in a way that had not been true before.' (Garner, p. 413).

On the whole the CRO, by average grade of entry into the new combined Service, had done well out of the merger. Malcolm MacDonald recognizes in his Foreword that in Lord Garner 'they were led by a man whom they could trust to do his best for them, and to minimize the effects on their careers of being absorbed into a much larger organization.' (Garner, p. xiiii). By its accentuation of existing bottle-necks however, the old FO had done less well – or so it was believed – and was to pay a price in deferred promotion, middle-echelon insecurity and, conceivably, premature retirement.

Despite surgical shock and growing-pains however, this process of evolving a new type of specialist to confront new exigencies in his profession, is of the essence and history of diplomacy – which is perhaps why I have repeatedly insisted on dwelling on its past, as a component of its present and its future. The next landmark was to be the Plowden Report of 1964, which marked a major evolution in the process started by the Eden/Bevin reforms of twenty years earlier. It now admitted that the world had changed around Britain, and not to her advantage:

'The world in which the overseas services now have to operate is no longer the world of 1943 or even a world which could be foreseen in 1943. The international scene has greatly changed, and Britain's position in the world has altered. ... The United States and the Soviet Union have grown more powerful, both in absolute terms and in relation to other powers. In relative terms, the military strength of Britain, as well as that of other European countries, has declined ... while accepting the strength of our own nuclear potential, we must recognize the effect on Britain's power of her relinquishment of control in many strategic parts of the world since 1945. ... we have accepted that we no longer have within our control the economic resources of a world-wide empire.' (Cmd 2276, paras. 6-8).

This diminishment, Plowden affirms, has brought with it new responsibilities. Britain may not, in Churchill's words, be relegated to a tame and minor role in the world. 'What we cannot secure by power alone we must secure by other means' – i.e. by 'diplomacy' and 'persuasion'. 'In this our "diplomatic" services have an indispensable part to play:' (Plowden, para. 9). Economic and commercial factors will be crucial, 'and a first charge on the resources of the overseas services.' (Plowden, para. 10). These resources are over-stretched, not least with the new calls imposed on them by the emergence of new independent states, and by the new relationship of Britain with a transformed Commonwealth. 'There have not been enough people to go around' – thanks also to the extension of multilateral diplomacy and the proliferation of international agencies (Plowden 12-16).

It was all this new realization that had encouraged the firm suggestion of the 'vesting-date' of New Year's Day 1965 for the new combined Diplomatic Service. Its fresh dose of realism, though an improvement, was still far from complete. 'The continued Commonwealth link remains a bridge between the continents of the world. Nothing should be done to weaken it.' (Plowden, para. 14). True, as indeed was to show at Lusaka in the summer of 1979; though the precariousness and vulnerability of that bridge had been far less apparent in 1964. In its new recognition of multilateralism, hindsight shows that the Plowden generation greatly over-rated the United Nations, while ignoring – seven years after the Treaty of Rome – the nascent integration of Europe. Violence too as a factor in international diplomacy was foreseen, but attributed largely to extreme nationalism, to liberation rather than revolution, and not at all to ideology.

Plowden, as good a voice of Britain as any other, appropriately enough shows also some of her uncertainty. Thus 'our need for efficient overseas representational services is likely to increase rather than decrease.' (Plowden, para. 24). Yet 'some limit must be set. The existing scale of activity ought not, in aggregate, to be greatly exceeded.' (Plowden, para. 30). Eden's affirmative view of Britain's future diplomacy has thus already become ambivalent, an incipient contradiction in terms, though not yet the fundamental questioning of national assumptions which was to follow.

I have heard it said that the man who foretells the future tells a lie even though he speaks the truth. By this fatalistic standard the Plowden Report did less harm than its more dogmatic successors and, particularly by its firm and promptly implemented stand on the integration of existing structures, probably did far more good.

For the next uprooting very nearly became a root-splitting. The Duncan Report of 1968/9 is hard to justify, so soon after so weighty a predecessor, except on the understanding that in so short a time the basic values of British foreign policy, and not just of her diplomacy, had come to be radically questioned. Plowden was concerned with structure, Duncan however with total cost-effectiveness. Retrenchment, not merely of finance and personnel but of scope, was now therefore taken for granted:

'. . . the general trend is clear enough. Britain has hitherto needed, for a variety of reasons, something comparable to (though smaller than), the American scale of representation. In future she is likely to need something not differing significantly in size from

French or German representation overseas. ... The evidence available to us, however, suggests that the size and coverage of the British Diplomatic Service could be significantly reduced over a period without danger of Britain's effort being overshadowed by that of any other *major power of the second order*.' (Duncan, II 6-7. – my italics). Also:

'Quantitatively the Service faces a period of contraction, due primarily to changing national requirements flowing from Britain's altered role in the world.' (Duncan, II 34(c)).

The commissioning of the Duncan Report rested therefore on revolutionary assumptions as compared with its predecessors. One major change was Britain's withdrawal from East of Suez, twelve years after the Suez fiasco. Equally time-lagged was the belated recognition of membership of the European Common Market as a real possibility, and as a factor in Britain's equation, whatever the final outcome. For the first time swingeing foreign exchange economies were a prime objective, rather than an incidental bonus of reshuffling routine budgetary headings. Already Personnel Department officers were lamenting that they 'could not hear themselves think for the whistling of the axe and the screams of the victims'; for by 1969 the Diplomatic Service had its own Tolpuddle Martyrs, in the persons of 'The Thirty', expeditiously and prematurely retired that year – 'willing victims' in the fashionable euphemism.

The weakness of the Duncan Report lay in its very inventiveness. Its fertility in ideas engendered a whole new scheme for British diplomacy, which could be termed a magic formula, a gimmick, an 'Open Sesame', a revelation – or indeed a statement of the obvious – as the reader was inclined. As Churchill is alleged to have claimed for his past, in his own graphically idiosyncratic French, Duncan sweepingly divided Britain's world, for diplomatic purposes, into two rotund halves. More asymmetrically, these were to be the Area of Concentration and the Outer Area. Whatever the intention, this distinction was taken, inside and outside the Service, both in Britain and abroad, to divide the world into first and second-class countries. Devotees and denizens of what had already come to be called the Third World were outraged. They foresaw an apparent relegation of overseas aid to the outer darkness which would be the precise opposite of, in their view, the 'First' World's prime post-imperial obligation. Members of the British Diplomatic Service were equally dismayed by the corresponding designation proposed for their posts in these differing areas, as 'Comprehensive' and 'Selective' respectively. In view of subsequent hard feeling about domestic educational reform, it is ironic that, by a total semantic inversion, in diplomacy 'comprehensive' was to apply to the world's chosen élite, and 'selective' to the poor relations among the peoples, and to Britain's representation to them.

It was on this 'sheep and goats' rock that the Duncan Report foundered; it was in fact extremely 'undiplomatic'. What it said was in practice not unreasonable; but its pragmatism was insufficiently discreet and too dogmatic in its expression, and its proposed application over-regimented. Yet its actual analysis of Britain's problem was probably more acute and realistic than any of the other 'uprootings' before or since. Thus:

... the range of topics in the diplomacy of the future will be much wider with an emphasis on economic and social issues ... a new kind of diplomacy which is both more wide-ranging and more intensive ... a high probability that a considerably increased proportion of the world's trade will take place in the Area of Concentration and that an increasing number of policy decisions on commercial and broader economic issues will be taken in concert by these nations.' (Duncan I: 10).

Here the Duncan Report was foreshadowing among other unpredictables the Council of the European Community and the annual economic summit of the ten major industrial powers, which are now greeted quite nonchalantly, and with none of the chilling of the spine that welcomed the 'Area of Concentration' in 1969.

This ambivalence, both of philosophy and in its articulation, runs through the Duncan Report. The famous, or notorious, phrase already quoted – 'A major power of the second order' – could alternatively betoken either a healthy if tardy realism about Britain's world role and diplomacy, or conversely a surrender to short-term adversity and pessimism. I have often thought that its references to the upsurge around us of the two super-powers have some affinity with the status of Westminster Abbey, bracketed between those two high-rise newcomers, the Shell Centre to the south and the Park Hilton Hotel to the north. The diminishment of the Abbey is only relative, and its physical preservation, on the merits of its own absolute quality and category, all the more indispensable. Given such criteria it should survive its new neighbours. To think any less positively, of Westminster Abbey, of Britain, or even of her diplomacy, seems to me a capitulation to that pressure of a philosophical yet irrational nature which Arthur Koestler calls 'reductionism'.

Good sense, even if again vitiated by ambiguity, seems to me likewise to characterize the Duncan Report's definition of the 'New Diplomacy', one of the first, and still one of the best, that I recall seeing:

'... the increasingly regular contact at all levels between specialists from various countries in the complicated techniques of modern life and the switch to multilateral organizations of activities which would previously have been bilateral. The task of our overseas representatives is to adapt themselves to this process, to master a wide range of subjects, and to support experts from outside the Diplomatic Service. ...' (Duncan, V: 22).

Perhaps I have read a trace of reinsurance into this particular conclusion only because of its subsequent evolution into one of the more debatable recommendations of its descendant, the Central Policy Review Staff's 1977 'Think-Tank' Report. There we see an unequivocal dichotomy postulated between 'Foreign Policy Work' and 'Political Work' which, however intellectually attractive, has been rejected as no more feasible than the Duncan 'Area of Concentration' in terms of workaday diplomacy.

Equally perceptive, yet by extension just as ambivalent, is another prognosis, today already a reality within the enlarging European Community. It suggests that diplomatic staff need not increase because:

'It will be a growing feature of international relations within that area that members of Home Departments will deal regularly and directly with their opposite numbers on a visiting basis, rather than through diplomatic intermediaries. A good analogy available is the close contact which has developed between Central Bankers. ... More often, however, our posts on the ground are needed to prepare the way, to advise and help during the visit and to ensure proper follow-up action when it is all over. This role will remain essential.' (Duncan IV: 16).

The Duncan bet is therefore hedged, thus for the first time raising a make-or-break question. Will the first-class talent, on which all review bodies have agreed Britain's diplomacy has always drawn, be content to function as a stage-hand? Or conversely will a part-time stage-hand by trade be capable of assuming and fulfilling the diplomat's enduring function inbetween shows? In the event the Duncan Report posed more questions than it elicited answers, and the more radical innovations which it suggested were not implemented.

Chapter XV

. . . . and Root-Pruning by Think-Tank

Perhaps these pending questions had left outstanding at the political level the sense of a job left undone. So after Duncan there was inevitably more to come. And though no government, once in office, has a monopoly of selectivity in its assaults on public extravagance, Labour governments have perhaps been the swifter to seek out symbolic targets for their fiscal ardour. After the General Election of 1974 the economic climate was particularly conducive to retrenchment, above all in 'overseas interests and requirements'. (CPRS Report, p.v.).

Defence had already suffered, and in parliamentary considera-tion of foreign affairs Britain's diplomatic apparatus has tradi-tionally been a preferred and vulnerable target for attention, a lightning-conductor for bolts of token thrift. The British diplomat has lived philosophically with the knowledge that a healthy pro-portion of the Labour benches axiomatically consider him a luxury if not a parasite, and that the Conservative benches are not really that much better, serving both meanwhile with equal fidelity as custodians of the nation. He knows that this 'black legend' of extravagance and expendability cuts no ice with the Foreign Sec-retary, the Prime Minister, and those of the Government of the time confronting the harsh reality of the overseas world. But he also knows their more basic need to accommodate with the domestic political and electoral world. This equally harsh reality must inevitably leave him as the Oyster to the Walrus and the Carpenter when political expediency calls.

So when in January 1976 the then Foreign and Commonwealth Secretary asked the Central Policy Review Staff – the CPRS, better known as the Think-Tank – to review Britain's overseas representation, it was a safe assumption that they would not speak softly, and would carry a sharp knife, if not a big stick. Even so, its commissioning was generally welcomed, within as well as outside the Diplomatic Service, and in the press too. Though myself already retired, and 'otherwise engaged', I took a family interest in it. I had known at any rate one member of the Think-Tank in my time and, as a sample of what to expect, his energy and intellectual power had seemed a good augury. Set up under a Conservative government, the group was to report to its Labour successors. Its whole function, status and *raison d'être* were apolitical, reputedly applying Harvard-style selected case-study method to intensive factual analysis in an environment of complete intellectual objectivity.

Before such an approach the Diplomatic Service had no cause to quail. As times change the diplomat has always had to change with them, perhaps more than most; as I have tried to convey, he has been something of a reluctant but conscientious chameleon, even if, in Britain's post-war circumstances, multiple experimentation had momentarily left him rather in the legendary predicament of that unfortunate creature when deposited on a Highland tartan. And the diplomat himself was under no illusion how much the world had indeed changed around his diplomacy. Its resources, tools and techniques had changed, even if its enduring criteria had not; the most rigid sticklers for these tend anyhow to be the newly 'embourgeoisé' among the powers, as it happens. The British diplomat knew that, in all this changed world, he remained a meber of an honourable profession, and belonged to a good Service which rightly, though not always successfully, had for a generation been fumbling its way to a reappraisal of sorts. He also knew that much remained to be done.

He felt for example that his Service was over-administered and under-equipped. By the 'sixties voices were already heard urging the use of the computer for passports, visas, and even for filing and data-retrieval. The London end seemed to him far too vast, yet working from facilities drab, antiquated and cramped. Even so he did not necessarily want to see the old Palazzo bulldozed and replaced by some brutalist eye-sore during a passing 'wrecker' phase. Not only were far too many of his junior staff employed just administering themselves, but he himself had to spend increasingly more of his working day on his and their logistics, leave, career prospects and family welfare.

Despite all efforts there was a penumbra, if not a communication gap, between his Service and his outside world. At home business tours and leave courses were too perfunctory for a Service whose essential orientation had always been economic and commercial, while abroad British Weeks and Visiting Missions came and went, but seemed always a surrogate for real and persistent market penetration. He had a nagging suspicion that given a chance he could give better value for money. The top echelon of his Service felt insecure, the middle echelon felt even more so, while the junior echelon, if they let themselves think about it, contemplated a long and guilty vista of dead-men's shoes stretching before them. There was no clear career line ahead of them, even though 'career-planning' should have exorcised the 'rat-race' nightmare. Despite an excellent and energetic Diplomatic Service Association, a tradition of loyalty and reserve left the thinking of its collective members far ahead of its collective expression. Esprit de corps was on the defensive in a competitive and iconclastic age and milieu. The Service was becoming ever more impersonal; even the United States Foreign Service had its own residential club, with branches in Washington and San Francisco; whereas not all in the FCO felt up to the Travellers' Club.

The pollster's 'average man' has a tendency to embody a concentration of exceptions, even when he is also the average diplomat. The foregoing distillation of anxieties is possibly therefore rather over-proof. Yet it remains reasonable to say that, confronted by the Think-Tank, the FCO did not take it for granted that all was for the best in the best of all possible Services. The Duncan Report had been a disappointment, side-tracked by its own special vision, by a split image of two diplomatic worlds. So now was just the moment for a truly scientific scrutiny, uninvolved, apolitical, long-term. The CPRS investigation was therefore seen as a major opportunity, a potential climacteric in the history of Britain's diplomacy.

Its Report, issued the following year in 1977, after what must have been something of a domestic and world-wide crash-programme, went far beyond the stark iron-ration of material economies which might have been expected, or the twenty percent all-round cut which the Treasury supposedly awaited. Mr Callaghan's brief was bound to make it so. He had included in it every aspect of promoting and representing Britain's interests, both at home and overseas, in whatsoever capacity and whether executed by diplomats, the armed forces, home-based civil servants, or any other government agency. My present study, or speculation, and so its consideration of the CPRS Report's relevance to it, relate solely to the future of the professional diplomat. It is clearly therefore impossible to include in the few paragraphs here available all the wide-spread implications of a sturdy volume of some four hundred and forty 'A4' pages; even the laconicism of Command Paper 7308 adjudicating on it extends to seventy pages of either noticeably restrained commentary or, with commendably frequent impartiality, a terse 'Accepted'.

All too obviously also a similar restraint must apply to my own interpretation of, and indeed disappointment in, the 'Think-Tank's' contribution to the future orientation of diplomacy and to its British arm. On the credit side its net was flung wide, both administratively and geographically. Its mandate was briskly executed. As a mine of information its end-product is inexhaustible. Many of its findings will undoubtedly become standard practice, even if disassociated from its overall philosophy. As a source of data to future administrators, historians and students of our times it will be invaluable. As a testimony to its authors' diligence and ubiquity it speaks for itself.

Its intellectual objectivity, however, or at any rate its freedom from fundamental misconception, seems to come into question on the very first page of its opening summary. Rightly taking as an initial premise Britain's economic and therefore political decline, the Report goes on to infer as a logical sequence that 'there is very little that diplomatic activity and international public relations can do to disguise the fact.' (p. ix: 4). But that is not what diplomacy is there for; yet again the validity emerges of the Gore-Booth dictum[1] that 'foreign policy is what you do, diplomacy is how you do it', to which the Blue Book on the CPRS Report[2] has itself wisely reverted. To falsify an unfavourable image of one's country is a political decision, not a diplomatic activity or technique, and is in any event a short-term expedient of dubious efficacity. Any analysis of diplomacy since Machiavelli must be suspect if based on the presumption that the diplomat, like The Prince, exists to fudge, embellish or otherwise distort reality.

It is the first tenet of diplomacy that it must never be based

[1] Op. cit., p. 15
[2] Cmd 7308, para 8

on a lie. What is now a morality – so I choose to believe – doubt-less started out as an expediency. For liars are found out; and an ambassador who is mistrusted – 'without credibility' in today's jargon – can no longer speak for his country. One such, von Ribbentrop, rightly or wrongly ended on the scaffold. It was this fact of life too, rather than the agonizing merits of the Israeli-Palestinian conflict, that so spectacularly disqualified Mr Andrew Young as United States Ambassador at the United Nations in August 1979. He admitted that he had withheld the truth from his government, or told only a part.

The word 'disguise' is what has led me to question, on moral grounds, the negative opening premise of the CPRS Report as to the function of British diplomacy in the face of national decline. If instead it had denied to the diplomat the material capacity to 'rectify' or 'remedy' that decline I would still have disagreed, but on the practical ground of recent social and political circumstance rather than from professional ethic; i.e. he can be part of the cure, but only if so allowed. The difference is that diplomacy can do no more than what it is given to do, be it badly or well. As with the computer – 'garbage in, garbage out', and vice-versa. If diplo-macy may not falsify, indeed it can rectify. If the national will is there to halt and reverse decline, the diplomat can do much to implement the political decisions involved, all the way from servicing an export-drive to preparing the seed-bed for a currency support operation. What he may not do is edit the truth on which he is basing his mission. That is no longer diplomacy but 'dis-information'.

The Think-Tank Report was intended, indeed designated, not only to assemble facts but also to make recommendations on the strength of them. What is it then that differentiates between recommendation and interpretation, between the Think-Tank and, say, a chain-store efficiency expert seconded to Whitehall? Perhaps motivation. As an assemblage of data the Think-Tank Report is far more complete than its predecessors, whether dealing with defence sales statistics, overseas broadcasting, or FCO tele-grams traffic. When however it proceeds by induction from the multifarious particular to the dogmatic general, it is dealing in opinion, a highly subjective commodity on which to base a review of potential significance to the national future and survival. It is thus no more than opinion to state that 'dedicated and highly talented people are working with great efficiency on matters which are of limited importance to the national interest'. (CPRS, p. xvi). An equally valid opinion is that any competent Head of Chancery, or Head of Department at home, would promptly identify and eliminate any such professional dilettantism.

Many of the foregone conclusions which impair the work put into the Think Tank Report seem to be of an almost philosophical nature. Its underlying premise is revealed as an axiomatic pessimism. To accept – as most of us do – that by sheer magnitude the United States of America and the Soviet Union are now in a different category from the European powers, as will also be China, is not defeatism but adjustment to a fact of life. But as valid a fact – which the Report however ignores – is that Britain is still a significant community of some fifty-five million people, the same island as before, and in many ways more privileged than ever in its resources. Yet the Report assumes without explanation that she is somehow not in the same category as her neighbours, if not indeed in an irreversible decline. Even the temporary windfall of North Sea oil is minimized, as unlikely to expedite the recapture of lost ground or to produce a significant change within the time-scale of the Report[1]. It is thus taken for granted that Britain somehow cannot do what France and Germany have done already.

This assumption is only an opinion, and debatable, whereas the realities of Britain's present economic situation – both for better and for worse – are a measureable observation of fact. The two may not therefore be blurred, or equated as factors in the assessment of Britain's diplomacy and its future.

All too pointedly also the Report's assessments rest on an insistently egalitarian philosophy which, if not shared by the reader, renders many of them meaningless if not invalid. In complaining of the Diplomatic Service's tendency 'to err on the side of perfectionism', the specific charge is that 'the work is being done to an unjustifiably high standard.'[2] This evaluation has familiar socio-political overtones, akin to those which have frustrated the purpose of comprehensive education by the deliberate levelling of standards downwards rather than upwards. A similar class-consciousness is betrayed – or flaunted – in the attribution

[1] p.x., paras 5–6
[2] CPRS, xiii: 12/c

to the Diplomatic Service of 'conservatism', 'middle-classness', and 'élitism'.[1] It is paradoxically reassuring to an apolitical profession that at the same time other commentators have to the contrary found it a hot-bed of 'pinkoes'.

From damning the concept of *esprit de corps* with some very faint praise, the chapter in question proceeds to recognize that 'corporate attitudes can be changed without changing institutions' – which it concedes the Diplomatic Service has itself demonstrated in export promotion. An ominously Pavlovian hint of 'conditioning' follows however: 'But generally speaking changes in institutional structure will lead in the long run to changed attitudes.'[2] Just such a logical perception was what equally logically led to the forced collectivisation of Russian agriculture, to a transformation involving immense human misery, to the dependence of the Soviet people on North American harvests, and to the moulding of by now billions of minds as a byproduct.

Less tragically than this remarkable throw-away observation, the Report's assessment far too frequently precedes full examination of the subject. Here it is disarmingly reminiscent of that great wartime comedian Tommy Handley who, with unsolicited gifts constantly thrust upon him, invariably and charmingly exclaimed 'Isn't it lovely! What is it?' All these are symptoms of an essentially mechanistic approach which, for example, automatically equates *esprit de corps* with a closed mind, and the Eden/Bevin reforms with mere generalism, not recognizing the authentically 'revolutionary' quality behind their freedom from dogma and ideological implication.

This quality of 'tunnel-vision' emerges in the total failure of the Report to provide, or to seek, an image of what diplomacy and the diplomat actually are. There is no recognition that, for example, the 'generalist' in question as often as not is in fact a 'multiple specialist'. One Deputy Under-Secretary of my acquaintance is simultaneously a highly-qualified practical Arabist, a recognized expert with the news-media, and a principal authority on the European Community, as well as being a formidable administrator. Another, now a distinguished public figure, as a young man sat with me on the old Overseas Negotiating Committee. Eventually he became our petroleum specialist; and a future

[1] Chap. 21 : 22
[2] Chap. 22 : 24

Chairman of Shell told me privately that within a month he was a better oil-man on their sub-committee than the companies' spokesmen themselves.

In general the Report gives the impression of not realizing that there is an enduring function which, by any other name, is always 'diplomacy'. Thus its whole section 'Multilateral Economic Work'[1] is rightly, and politely, treated as a statement of the obvious in the Government's response.[2] For it is patently just our old friend 'conference diplomacy' under another heading. In stressing 'the disadvantages of a powerful institutional ethos[3] the Report in effect denies the reality of diplomacy as a function and a profession.

As mentioned under the consideration of diplomatic immunity, this analysis already enjoys the dubious endorsement of President Qaddafi, who has lately sought to replace his ambassadors with committees of Libyan students. The experiment is not original. The Soviet Union too did away with its diplomats for some years after the 1917 revolution, inflicting on its envoys the ungainly new title 'Polpred'. After some years of ambassadorial relegation to the bottom of the diplomatic totem-pole, away below even the Chargés d'Affaires, national and professional pride found it best to resume the traditional hierarchical classifications. All such occasional aberrations seek to deny the continuing function of the negotiator, but in the end it is always needed. Those regrettable neologisms 'ongoing' and 'interface' apply so exactly to the diplomat's *raison d'être* that, if the CPRS Report had indeed succeeded in abolishing him, it would soon have been necessary to re-invent him.

If I seem to have been selective, indeed heavy-handed, in my recollections of the Think-Tank's Report, it is because its positive achievements – which are many, and usually to do with procedures rather than principles – have been amply identified for me by the 'Accepted's' attached to their various paragraph references in the Blue Book presented to parliament as Cmd 7308. They are in any case immaterial for the most part to our present study, which specifically concerns the future of professional diplomacy. And along with such positive acknowledgements, the Government's commentary notes as many or more of the Report's

[1] Chap. 5:4
[2] Cmd 7308, p. 22:5:1
[3] Chap. 1:10

proposals as 'Current Practice'. This endorsement confirms that the Report has great merit, and use, but as a compilation and as a case-study – a check-list of sorts. Its content is important, even if its result was not. The Report as such mattered far more than the recommendations it made.

It is a pity therefore that this particular CPRS exercise was tendentious before it was born. Even during the compilation of the Report it was surrounded by controversy, indignation even, of a sort which makes it difficult to judge other than politically. Its text alone demonstrates that it was approached in a sociological if not ideological spirit, incomprehensible, obnoxious even, to a Service axiomatically non-partisan. There seems also to have been a certain unkindness in its procedures, an adversarial approach more appropriate to a certain type of television confrontation than to the eliciting of cooperation from loyal, serious and rather anxious officials. It is legend that, at one post overseas, the visiting inquisitor opened the office-meeting called for the occasion by the ambassador with the words 'You must view this whole enquiry as a facet of the class-struggle'. If true, such an opening gambit would invalidate the whole investigation, all the more so perhaps if not meant seriously. A joke in such dubious taste at the expense of a captive audience would amount to an elaborate discourtesy and a conscious unkindness quite incompatible with its author's serious function. Humour is all too infrequent in government enquiries. But they are no place for teasing, let alone baiting.

The Britain of the 'Sixties had been characterized by a satirical school in which a quality of jeering, of 'send-up', substituted for the authentic anger of true satire. Though its practitioners grow up like everyone, its echoes have persisted. Whether the Think-Tank Report will be filed by history under a 'satire' or 'diplomacy' reference rests to be seen. But historic it is in its way, and far more than a culmination to the process begun by Anthony Eden in 1943. All its predecessors had been products of a same process, though of different intensity. The Eden/Bevin reforms were an exercise in upward egalitarianism, any economy motive pursued by recruitment from within. The Plowden Report was essentially a managerial document, its economies geared to cost-efficiency. The Duncan Report was an undisguised retrenchment operation, its economies to be derived from the trimming of size and numbers. Unlike all these, the CPRS was a product of lateral thinking, its whole dimension different philosophically, possibly even ideologically. Certainly the element of economy was to be pursued quite differently, by a sweeping transformation and reduction of function. Its impact was meant to restrict the category of work attributable to the Diplomatic Service rather than, as hitherto, the man-power and the money made available for it.

With any living organism, or organization, to achieve stasis is a form of dying. I own a fossil sardine, from B'charré by the Cedars of Lebanon which, the palaeontologists tell me, made the mistake of achieving its fishy best some sixty million years ago; as a result its offspring have made no progress since. So it would be an ominous portent of mortality if a human institution like diplomacy were to be frozen in its techniques and range of action. Stress, reform and evolution, to the contrary, are symptoms of vigorous health and life. The wartime Eden/Bevin reforms were of this category.

It only became apparent after World War II that Britain was in more ways than one not just convalescent, but a very sick country. The common weakness of the Plowden, Duncan and CPRS reviews is that they all represented accentuating programmes of cosmetic surgery on one of the components of a larger body politic, whose profound total sickness was meanwhile being left largely untreated. In this sense their reports were irrelevant.

They also correspond to a time when, to the great prejudice of our country as a whole, the evolution of its ostensibly radical political wing had been virtually paralysed by a cult of 'irreversible change'. As the late Professor Bronowski has fortunately reminded us, the concept is scientific nonsense in relation to cultures and societies; the only irreversible change is that of biological mutation.[1] The engine stuck in a siding can and indeed must reverse.

But persistence in error is even more expensive than retreat from error. Already convalescent from her two world wars, Britain was by now undergoing an accentuating crisis of under-productivity, and so of over-spending. A hard-headed observer of the economic scene has summarized it crisply: 'Britain is now in-

[1] *Ascent of Man* (p. 48), BBC 1973

significant – a mere five percent of the economy of the free industrial world.'[1] This estimate continues the corresponding downward curve, for the Organization of Economic Cooperation and Development, instanced by the CPRS (p. 5, 2:2), from a share of 7.6 percent in 1955 to 5.7 percent in 1975. Without benefit of hindsight it is fair to say that successive British governments of both parties were happy to turn their eyes away from a macro-economic prospect horrifying to close study, in favour of token demonstrations of small-scale fiscal and administrative vigilance in between crises.

My own experience of surgery is that doctors prefer a patient to be clear of hepatitis or chronic bronchitis before removing his appendix or draining his sinuses. In the same way I cannot see how any of these three successive task-forces could ever have been expected to produce a valid long-term report based on the data of an interim situation, in one organ, of a body which was already in its entirety an undiagnosed patient. When a total view of the nation's state and prospects does not exist, it is too early for the piecemeal scrutiny and patching of its individual components in isolation from the whole.

For this reason I believe with regret that every review of the Diplomatic Service since the Eden/Bevin reforms has been untimely and unnecessary. Certainly wastage must be avoided, recruitment harnessed to function, the scale of overseas representation geared to international political change. All these are however administrative matters, perfectly capable of internal departmental control, subject to normal ministerial and parliamentary scrutiny; thus the practice of compulsory retirement at sixty has been tacitly modified in a number of recent ambassadorial appointments, without review, report or recommendation. It was I believe wrong to wield three times in fifteen years a public sledge-hammer in lieu of a perfectly adequate departmental nutcracker. It would be still more wrong to do it again.

These successive reviews have increasingly fallen between two stools, between the 'grandiose' approach of a public relations operation, mounted for effect or distraction, and the excessive preoccupation with detail of a conscientious office audit. As a result all three, having been commissioned to examine a Service,

[1] *Economist*, 18 August 1979, p. 13

have seemed to be making an example of it to the public. The common error was to have approached the 'Service' as an end in itself, and so a thing of itself. But it is not an isolated entity. It is a function, one of many means to a much larger national end of which it is only one part. The Duncan terms of reference for example reflect nothing of this larger vision, corresponding regrettably to that mood of our times which would probably sum up Shakespeare as so many grammes of carbon and hydrogen dioxide, with some tracer-elements.

The gradually narrowing oscillations of her political compass suggest that Britain needs, and is approaching, a national re-appraisal, a rethink rather than a Think-Tank. In advance of it, tinkering here and there with the fundamental structures of major departments of state has generally been an error. When as a nation we have finally seen clear and decided for ourselves what Britain's place and role in the world is to be, then will be the time to review and update our country's diplomatic machine. Till we have regained our sense of purpose and direction it should be left without further uprooting, applying its own care-and-maintenance to the task of servicing the nation's current business abroad.

Here it may well be said that I too am allowing myself the subjective luxury of opinion and recommendation. But then this is not a report. And one man does not make a Think-Tank!

Chapter XVI
Which Way Now?

I have tried, by a sort of sampling, to show something of the diplomat's history, out of which the 'Old Diplomacy' of our recent times grew and briefly flourished. If there is to be a 'New Diplomacy', I hope that I have identified and illustrated the main factors extant and influencing it. I have used mainly – but not wholly – the British Diplomatic Service as my model, believing that memory from within is as important a testimony as observation from without. In any case, I have little doubt that the human and administrative problems of other national diplomacies are much the same as our own – even those of, for example, the Soviet Union, despite radical differences of philosophy and material power. For this same reason I believe that various negative influences overshadowing Britain's diplomatic organization are largely those which are also tending to diminish and prejudice the world-wide institution of diplomacy as a whole.

For its immediate state is not encouraging, either as an instrument for mankind's welfare or even, at first sight, as a career for one's successors. So much so that behind this short-term disarray looms the ultimate pessimism of total 'redundancy' for the profession as such. There are indeed those who sincerely believe that the diplomat could and will be abolished, or at any rate allowed to become extinct. Such a proposition is, to an interested party, almost too bad to be true. Any member of the endangered species, past or present, will be at obvious pains to approach it with cautious detachment.

Nevertheless the straws in so chill a wind are undeniably both numerous and ubiquitous. One is summitry, another the growing equation of the traditional diplomat with conflict and uncertainty. Given détente, given even a reasonable balance of terror, the 'resident diplomat', as against the special envoy à la Kissinger for *ad hoc* crises, may well by this thinking be superfluous. Similarly the present cult of pragmatism, of living even internationally from day to day, could render obsolete the diplomat's historic skills of foresight and extrapolation. I remember wincing inwardly when a US colleague once cheerfully assured me that political and economic forecasting by his post for two years ahead would not make him popular in Washington, while for five years ahead it would get him fired. Events of state too are often trivialized, when the intention was to humanize, by the intervention of 'ambassadors' from the world of entertainment – names have figured ranging from the Beatles to Miss Elizabeth Taylor – as if history were a television programme requiring 'commercials' to sustain it. The technique of the Potemkin village has indeed reached its extremity when not only the buildings are façades, but their inhabitants too.

In a converse scrapping of protocol, a British Prime Minister can publicly congratulate himself that, in conference on an idyllic tropical island, he and his fellow-summiteers can 'sit down without a lot of observers and officials.' The implication is one of relaxation and informality, conducive to wisdom, harmony and the 'grande vision'. In reality the product of these jamboree techniques is as often as not an outbreak of what has been termed 'spasm diplomacy'.

One particular visual presentation has stayed in my mind as the true and dismal embodiment of this ultimate pessimism for career diplomacy. It was a photograph rounding off the publicity of a small summit held in Bonn. At a ravaged breakfast table in the British Embassy sat the German and British Heads of Government. In the foreground there were crumbs, and half-empty coffee-cups – all the detritus of that sad and singular anomaly, the working-breakfast. But of His Excellency himself, at his own post, in his own home, at his own table, there was not a sign. Only the two summiteers sat smiling.

Perhaps summitry and the cult of personality are inter-changeable components in the public relations approach to international negotiation. So if the 'star' principle is accepted for diplomacy, and by a logical extension the star of the performance is going to need a stunt-man for what is dangerous, difficult or tiresome, then equally logically he must be off-screen for the close-ups. So here is yet another assignment for the diplomat, shot at, kidnapped, held hostage, reconciled as he already is to being scene-shifter or research-assistant to the Kissingers of the day.

After this depressive glimpse of the diplomat's scene at its worst, some cheer is probably now justified. And indeed my thoughts go back happily to a remarkable anti-hero of his time, one Colonel Julian, otherwise the Black Eagle, a famous negro aviator and eccentric known even better for his picaresque adventures on the fringe of the international arms trade. For some improbable reason he contrived to call on my Under-Secretary at the Foreign Office, an austere and desiccated man who insisted on my chaperoning him with so exotic a visitor. The colonel and I took to each other, but not so the Under Secretary, who grew more and more aloof and uncommunicative with each passing moment and soliloquy. Finally, in full flight, the colonel paused and drew from his pocket a fistful of assorted pills and capsules, swallowed half, and thrust the remainder under my Under Secretary's nose, with the exhortation – 'Take some of these, sir; they will help restore your lost vi-rility!' For my part, all that I was offered was an almost imperceptible wink from – and to – an utterly expressionless face. 'Julian, thou shouldst be with us at this hour' is perhaps the sole moral of this digression.

To redress therefore the balance of optimism, I hasten to display the reverse of the professional medal. Is there really anything new in the diplomat's playing second fiddle? And does he object to it? At least he is not as a rule playing fiddler to fools, as was long ago his intermittent role when functioning as low-born backstop to high-born nincompoops. Accrediting one such, a Duke of Tuscany is reported to have commented that 'We have fools in Florence, but we do not export them.'[1] Updating him, Lester Pearson, founding father of Canada's diplomacy, has observed that 'striped pants are a state of mind'. Presumably therefore someone will occasionally be needed to valet them into sartorial and intellectual respectability. There is accordingly nothing new or shameful in the pedestrian, even sometimes menial, asides of diplomacy.

Among the dusty folders that serve me in lieu of a scrap-book, I even discovered a copy of the *Listener* dated 10 January 1952, in which our latter-day Lord Annan remarks that 'diplomacy, contrary to popular belief, is not spectacular. It is really a very dull, prosaic affair – you only have to talk to most diplomats to

[1] Barber, op. cit., p. 63

realize that.' Why then have diplomats always phlegmatically accepted that area of their function in which they play the intellectual equivalent of an air-hostess or a cleaning-lady? Perhaps because, as Annan goes on to say, 'What appears to be empiricism is really an infinite capacity for adjustment to the changing proportions of power.' The diplomat is in fact dealing in power, however decorously and vicariously.

And power is still an interesting coinage to handle, even in its small change, and especially in congenial company, which the diplomat usually is. Here, though he is unfashionable these days, I must quote Harold Nicolson – also from the *Listener* of 1952, but of a week later – which equally miraculously I find I have preserved. Of negotiation he comments that 'it is the art of discovering an equable exchange of interests between people who trust each other.' I have in fact been warned off Nicolson as a source more than once, on the ground that his version of diplomacy is superseded, ignoring the profession's present salutary diversion to and concentration on commerce. But in fact Britain's has always been a commercial diplomacy, as Nicolson – and Napoleon – well knew. Whatever the current diplomatic idiom, the achievement of durable economic relations will go on depending, just as much as ever, on the attainment of mutual trust. Despite a style mirroring its epoch, and a life-style entirely his own business and not mine, Nicolson's analysis of diplomatic principle endures. Trained for the 'Old Diplomacy', confronted with 'Diplomacy by Conference', I do not doubt that he would have coped more than adequately with the new summitry also.

In any event the diplomat has always been a tradesman, and an honest one, whether his commodity was the product of his country's workshops or the adjustment of a frontier. Out of another duty folder a note that I wrote on the fourth of December 1959, from my Latin days at the United Nations, says rather plaintively 'the UK are always asking something from the Latin Americans – votes, perhaps speeches. Yet we have so little to offer in return – our occasional moral and verbal support, as compared with the USSR's very substantial support on anti-colonial and economic issues.' Any success was therefore a trading success, depending – as the diplomat's always does – partly on bargaining skill, but mainly on substance, on the merchandise that he can offer. And for that he depends on his government.

So far as concerns the foreign policy of the diplomat's country, the more merchandise there is to show, the less skill – i.e. diplomacy – there seems now to be deployed in the bargaining. Dr Kissinger once made this abundantly clear to an interviewer well-known, if hardly of his stature. Total military and economic superiority had meant that the USA could always rely ultimately on solving its problems with last-minute 'crash programmes' – to which I can bear witness, having seen them in impressive action at both state and city as well as national level. However, the loss of the 'monopoly' of power in the free world, and of preponderance in global power, meant that the USA must now plan ahead. And international planning requires the diplomat, while the crash-programme does not. Hence no doubt the current resurgence, after some years of eclipse, of the American diplomat and State Department, and the use of 'channels' – a phenomenon also lately remarked on by a non-career United States ambassador to Britain.

Soviet foreign policy has never under-used its diplomats, nor wavered in the thrust of its diplomacy. Dr Kissinger was for his part always addicted to the 'pre-emptive concession'. By making a quick and huge concession he would reach his 'bottom-line' quickly, and stick to it. But how could the USSR's oriental heritage ever see it so? The pre-emptive concession would axiomatically, almost genetically, be taken instead as the first step in an endless vista of bargaining. So the USSR has had brilliant, strong, well-supported ambassadors, who speak directly not only to Foreign Ministers but to Heads of Government and State – to the Prime Minister in London, to the President in Washington. The standing of M. Dobrynin in Washington bears witness not just to his ability, but also to the effectiveness of the whole Soviet approach, as contrasted with the frustrations of his US counterpart in Moscow till 1979, Mr Malcolm Toon. There was never any doubt which of the two spoke with 'His Master's Voice'.

Perhaps the difference lies in the overall organic concept of Soviet foreign policy, with its inversion, or full-cycling, of the Clausewitz doctrine that 'war is an extension of politics . . .' For the USSR, as Afghanistan has illustrated, diplomacy is something totally integrated with military strategy; and her diplomats are formed, and armed, accordingly.

On all these and many other assumptions therefore it is hard to imagine a world which will need neither diplomacy nor diplomats. Admittedly of course such a prodigy might seem to have happened, and their nominal designation might briefly change if, for example, the world were surprisingly to become one place and, after all, nations and Foreign Ministries suddenly become things of the past. Even with this remotest of hypotheses however there would, by the nature of events, continue to be conflicts of interest between the different regions of this so long illusionary 'One World', and between the different ministries and departments administering it. For them full-time and highly professional conciliators would be needed, negotiators of differences, drafters of agreements, diplomats in all but name. At times they would arrive alone to negotiate with full powers. At others, in the event of problems of global dimensions, they would blend discreetly into the background, as expert advisers to superintending regional authorities and to the holders of major portfolios in the central government. Things, and people, would still be much the same, as indeed they are even with so imperfect a test-bench as the United Nations.

What the diplomat will not be – and has not been for some time – is the dilettante of largely hedonistic and social proclivity, of both legend and occasional fact. He – or, very importantly, she – will be much what he or she needs to be now – a person of above-average intelligence, energy and accomplishment, even more so perhaps than is produced by today's already rigorous selection procedures. The pressure of such competition within the Service will put a special and intensifying strain on one crucial factor of primordial if hitherto largely tacit significance – that of character. The rare and public exceptions to it have only served to prove its fortunately predominant rule. Especially will it be needed if, for a while, the personal hopes and satisfactions of reaching top official rank are eroded by national economic constraints, by 'summitry', or even by 'parachutism'. Such frustrations could impose a strain on a newly vulnerable grey area of professional integrity.

Already Britain's legendary Civil Service is the unfamiliar target of a new and refined cynicism; even a series of television comedies has not so much lampooned as adulated the more occult activities of those luminaries whose lives pivot around the twin suns of Whitehall and the Athenaeum. That the bamboozling and house-training of their political masters by the 'mandarins' is not merely an abstract theme for light comedy was brought home to me during a recent and mainly theological post-prandial exchange. It had been suggested that much recently apparent authoritarianism in the churches would be relieved if their potentates were exposed to the wholesome and democratic corrective of the 'Parliamentary Question'; nothing, apparently, so galvanizes a bureaucracy into fruitful activity. A former colleague of my own generation categorically refuted this thesis. To the contrary, he vouched for the once dreaded 'P.Q.' just as parodied in the television version – as the regular curtain-raiser for an elaborate top Civil Service charade, with unsuspecting cabinet ministers as officialdom's puppets.

I prefer a more naive interpretation. Much of course may depend on the sophistication of the Minister, or for that matter on the greater or lesser cynicism of his Permanent Secretary. More pertinent to the diplomat's future however is the recently identifiable relaxation by Whitehall of the attitudes governing the retirement of high-ranking civil servants. In the past a life in the public service usually prefaced a retirement in the public service; the one was the best preparation for, and indeed financed, the other. It is now however virtually standard procedure for such as are otherwise inclined to move over, on retirement and after a brief token interval, into full-time private employment in commerce, industry, banking or indeed all of them. Given the economic realities of Britain's present, and the 'comparabilities' accepted by our society, the level at which they cross over, while administratively equivalent to their former hierachical status, belongs financially to an entirely new dimension. Since such business appointments are generally approved and publicized well in advance of retirement, they have evidently been organized still earlier. In this way, it is said, an official can spend his last two years of officialdom planning his next ten years of retirement.

There is nothing new in the children of this world being shrewder than the sons of light, though admittedly St Luke gives them a retroactive absolution rather than an anticipatory green light. Even so, this is not a tendency that I should care to see encroaching on the particular vulnerabilities of diplomacy. At its most basic the diplomat is meant to be essentially mobile; the right man should always be on call for the right job. He will not be so if he has a particular type of post in view, tailored to equip his retirement with particular knowledge, experience and contacts, and ultimately an exceptional financial reward. The additional hazards of such metamorphoses – conflict of interest, deflection of motive, risk to confidentiality – are self-evident.

Obviously and legitimately the phenomenon of outstanding ability, experience and merit will always attract the attention of what are known as the 'headhunters'. Equally however the pressures and inadequacies of our society and epoch can all too easily encourage such talent to prepare and present itself as a willing quarry to the hunter, or indeed to reverse their roles. Between the two is the narrowest of margins. The present development is primarily a domestic innovation – legal, perfectly proper, but as unbecoming to those adopting it as to those sanctioning it. It needs to be steered well clear of diplomacy, if the career's most promising elements, the 'high flyers', are not to pursue from an early stage the right professional ambition for the wholly wrong personal reason. The recent Whitehall practice has already sufficiently coarsened the British official tradition and image, for a dubious return in national economic advantage and managerial efficiency. In the more sensitive areas of overseas representation it would be even more undesirable; the absolute difference between ambition and appetite is unmistakeable to any expert on the watch for such nuances.

So rather diffidently, and six hundred and more years after Bernard du Rosier, I have dragged morality back into my vision of diplomacy, and into my curriculum for the diplomat. Because of it I should not hesitate, despite all present imponderables, to counsel any anxious Mrs Worthington to put her daughter, as well as her son, on to the diplomatic stage. The monosex impartiality of their casting gives me the excuse to revert to yet another of those magnificent elderly ladies in and around the Foreign Office who, only lately, assured me that never in her long experience had she seen quite such splendid young people working for the FO – especially the girls, she added. She is quite right. Two of the young ladies my wife and I knew are now Her Majesty's Ambassadors. So also will be in due course their gifted and yet touchingly feminine young successors, whose identical merit is no longer in their case handicapped by novelty.

Selection, male and female, must then, I conclude, have been outstanding of late years. So courteous and sensible a generation is unlikely to grow either into cynics or into sentimentalists. I see them veering to neither pole – not to the Kissinger extreme, that morality is something between people and not between states – nor to the opposite – that it is obnoxious and Machiavellian for statesmen to have to choose, now and then, between evils. They will, I believe, wear with comfort and honour that invisible 'dog-collar' of the first Queen Elizabeth, which corresponds to a conscious, constant and self-chosen servitude of sorts. Like the soldier, the diplomat's first duty is to obey. He will advise, warn, disapprove; but finally he will do abroad as the elected leaders of his country instruct him through his masters at home. Even if such action is against his own judgement, he does at least know that he is not acting for a tyranny. And the young diplomat will find furthermore, to his great private comfort as the years go by, that diplomacy plus democracy add up to a total remarkably congenial to conscience and morality.

Particularly will this be so in the vexed area of the diplomatic recognition of obnoxious regimes. The occasional tendency to treat recognition as a moral accolade is, when not actually hypocritical, usually spurious and misguided. In most recent instances its withdrawal has been prompted not by the morality of the offensive regime but by considerations of political and ideological compatability and alignment. Meanwhile the normal business of life must go on between peoples – yet again that 'interface' – no matter how mutually detestable their regimes. Their governments must coexist without injury to each other's peoples. They can best demonstrate moral repugnance not by a general-post reshuffling between ambassadors and chargés d'affaires, but through the quiet, unconcealed contempt of their people and press for the other's ethic, or lack of it. On that criterion Britain has incidentally less to be ashamed of than most nations in the various recent permutations of recognition and morality.

The late Sir George Rendel's memoirs have already made their appearance in these pages as a yardstick of an earlier diplomatic 'style'. More importantly I have found them impressive by his setting of the diplomat's calling against an unchanging background of right and wrong. In his old age he recognizes that in various ways the diplomat's material prospects are not those of his youth. The peaks are less accessible, the pleasant posts fewer

– though like myself he considers the quality of recruitment higher. Above all however he sees in the diplomatic career, still persisting, a possibility of fulfilment ever rarer in an increasingly restrictive and predictable society. Just occasionally, he reflects, there can come for the diplomat that one chance of a lifetime – the averting of a conflict, the saving of a life – which will justify a whole career by one act.

Other ambassadors have reflected similarly, with as much urbanity if perhaps less philosophy. The distinguished Israeli ambassador Abba Eban has been reported as regretting, in his own diplomatic gloaming, that ambassadors no longer have the great importance of his early days; during all his ten years in Washington his Prime Minister went there only once, but does so now ten times a year. Then however he conceded that in no event could he have become a spokesman for Mr Begin; and the true diplomat is there to speak for the successive governments that he serves, which the politician turned diplomat never can. So perhaps all along Mr Eban had never been a real diplomat, but only a statesman after all.

A charming valedictory was also published by a retiring Italian ambassador to Britain, Signor Roberto Ducci.[1] He, like myself, has contemplated – not too seriously – the prospect that he belongs to a dying species, and gives many rueful instances of international relations proceeding merrily in the total absence of any diplomatic representation. His conclusion is that the ambassadors may well have to go. Thereafter however they might be replaced by something still uncommonly like a diplomat, once the incessantly travelling summiteers have found the merry-go round not so merry, or even dropped dead of exhaustion. In any case the process of making ambassadors redundant would, he expects, take nine hundred and ninety-nine years. During this interval they will not be at risk.

Ambassador Ducci's forebodings for the staying-power of the shuttle-diplomat have meanwhile found an authoritative clinical echo. Dr Hugh L'Etang's *Fit to Lead* (Heinemann 1980) surveys with professional misgivings the phenomenon of physical stress 'at the top'. In the more obvious correlation of mental health with political decision, many a layman must, like myself, have often

[1] *The Times*, 14 January 1980

239

wondered at the perversion of history by minds afterwards found to have been themselves disordered while ordering great events. For years we listen with bated breath to the leaders of great nations, only to recognize them later as having been unbalanced, to say the least, during much of their 'reign'; Mussolini, Hitler and Stalin are cases in point.

Physical ill-health and exhaustion may react less cataclysmically, yet in individual human terms just as tragically; Dr L'Etang instances the late Anthony Crosland, quite conceivably killed by his last few days' travel-and work-schedule as Foreign Secretary. The late Anthony Eden too is now seen to have been sick and in pain at the time of the Suez *débâcle*, and his efficiency correspondingly impaired.

Such cases abound among the world's leaders, in both legend and recent history; the conventional group photograph of the Yalta Conference is arguably a collective visual-aid making Dr L'Etang's point. And even if sound in mind and body it is perhaps expecting too much of political leaders that they should consent to function at the summit as mere figure-heads, sparing themselves by leaving all but the signature to the diplomats; stress is often self-inflicted. Yet those negotiations have most tended to succeed in which the leaders have not discarded the ancient skill of husbanding decision by maximum delegation. The resolution of the prolonged Rhodesia crisis was a model of this kind.

With the air-borne national leader, or Secretary of State, it is at times obscure whether by his prestige-visits he is supporting or eclipsing his representatives abroad. A recent and particularly competent Secretary of State for Trade demonstrates the assiduity of his Department by adducing the thirty trips overseas that he and his Minister of State had made in less than a year of office. Is however such a score-card the best index of efficiency? Between while no doubt the local ambassadors and High Commissioners have been carrying on with normal procedure. Whether for summitry or for prestige-visits, it is they who prepare the ground with the governments involved, who tidy up afterwards, and who provide continuity. What they can no longer provide, if mere agents of a new 'Concorde diplomacy', is the representational and plenipotentiary function; for to achieve direct contact at the highest level the element of prestige and full-power is, under the new dispensation, increasingly flown in from home. Is not then the new score-card interfering with the real score? And if this procedure becomes a regular practice, will not then the envoy's permanent spokesmanship and credibility inevitably atrophy?

For this reason flying incursions by Ministers from home are best reserved for emergencies, and for special good-will occasions when there can be no real alternative. As yet again the Rhodesia/Zimbabwe instance has shown, one such justifiable exception is when a major and specific act of national will is involved, and must be made manifest. During such a negotiation the immediacy and immensity of the wider political implications will undoubtedly take the leader himself – in this case the Foreign Secretary – into the front line. Even so, though leading his cohorts, he does not leave them behind; he takes them with him, and he does delegate. Nor does his government repeat the technique inordinately, thus devaluing its significance and negating its impact.

There is another reason justifying this reservation which impinges not so much on the long-term effectiveness of the ambassador on-the-spot as on the prestige of the eminent visitor himself, and therefore on the esteem in which his nation too is held. It is that the shuttle-diplomat, the diplomat-by-Concorde, risks not only becoming exhausted, but also on occasion being affronted. Not infrequently a visiting Minister, even a Head of State can, for possibly ephemeral reasons, be rebuffed by the receiving country. It has happened to a Chilean President visiting the Phillipines, and a British Minister of State touring the Arab emirates.

For a visiting statesman to return home having been made unwelcome, and not properly received, can be an affront. For an ambassador to be placed temporarily in local cold-storage is disagreeable, but a normal and usually transient occupational hazard only – a storm in a teacup. As I already said in Chapter IV, of FO vipers, the diplomat has a skin not so much thick as resilient. In consequence the ancient jibe that a diplomat is one who can smile in front while being kicked from behind leaves the professional unmoved. There is not one who, in his time, has not learned that, among his many roles, the function of safety-valve, even of scapegoat, must be taken in his stride.

Up to a certain point therefore a diplomat cannot be affronted, is indeed beyond personal affront. It is not quite so however when the recipient of the brickbats is not a diplomat, a professional intermediary, an almost impersonal institution, but a specially nominated envoy, giving himself the trouble of leaving constituency, desk and front-bench seat at home, to the glare furthermore of politically unpredictable publicity. These hazards of the new personal diplomacy are only just beginning to assert themselves. Meanwhile the diplomat, the present and future ambassador, will I suggest be well advised to keep his head and his sights down for a time. Already the pendulum is steadier, as diplomacy recuperates from the experience of seeming nothing more than a service-industry to summitry.

It is a consoling platitude that one can do a great deal of good by not caring who takes the credit. Overhanging it however is a large question-mark. Will international diplomacy continue indefinitely to attract the nation's best, if their only immediate prospect is to be 'continuity-man' in between successive 'summit-men'? I trust so, always assuming no over-hasty amputation of 'room at the top' and, in the case of the Foreign Office, given the fostering of a corporate spirit – the old *esprit de corps* – only waiting to be re-awakened.

The Foreign Office was always greater than the sum of its parts. Today somehow the whole seems less so; the individual excellence has for some years seemed greater than the total achievement. Perhaps a strong and committed Secretary of State was always a necessary catalyst. For the present however the British diplomat – no doubt like others becalmed and awaiting the shift of a world-wide breeze – will still have much to keep him busy and fulfilled. Externally the be-plumed envoy of tradition is perhaps turning into something more akin to the grey eminences of Whitehall's domestic corridors of power. Yet he is still doing much the same thing as always, though in a different style which, nevertheless, calls for much the same sort of man, or woman, to do it. He has the inward satisfaction of servicing something larger than himself – a country, a conviction, perhaps by extension mankind itself. And he is paying his way with them all by serving a craft whose ultimate purpose has always been the achievement and maintenance of peace.

Meantime he can be reasonably sure that the world will still esteem and need him – Ambassador, Counsellor, First Secretary, Archivist, Cypher-Clerk – when the Kissingers have had to stop, and the summits loom no more.

Short Bibliography

Arbuthnott & Edwards – *A Common Man's Guide to the Common Market* (Macmillan, 1977)

Barber, Peter – *Diplomacy* (The British Library, 1979)

Beaulac, Willard – *Career Diplomat* (Collier Macmillan, 1964)

Bell, Coral – *The Diplomacy of Detente* (Martin Robertson, 1977)

Boyle, Andrew – *The Climate of Treason* (Hutchinson, 1979)

Blakiston, Noel – *The Roman Question* (Chapman & Hall, 1962)

Bronowski, Jacob – *The Ascent of Man* (BBC, 1976)

Busk, Sir Douglas – *The Craft of Diplomacy* (Pall Mall Press, 1967)

Clark, Eric – *Corps Diplomatique* (Allen Lane, 1973)

Depetre, José Leon – *Derecho Diplomatico* (Manuel Porrua, Mexico City)

Duff Cooper, A. – *Talleyrand* (Jonathan Cape, 1932)

Garner, Joe – *The Commonwealth Office, 1925–1968* (Heinemann, 1978)

Garvey, Sir Terence – *Bones of Contention* (Routledge & Kegan Paul, 1978)

George-Brown, Lord – *In My Way* (Gollancz, 1971)

Gladwyn, Lord – *Memoirs* (Weidenfeld & Nicolson, 1972)

Gore-Booth, Lord – *With Great Truth and Respect* (Constable, 1974)

Grafftey-Smith, Sir Laurence – *Bright Levant* (John Murray, 1970); *Hands to Play* (Routledge & Kegan Paul, 1975)

Hankey, Lord – *Diplomacy by Conference* (Benn, 1946)

Hardinge of Penshurst, Lord – *Old Diplomacy* (John Murray, 1947)

Hayter, Sir William – *The Diplomacy of the Great Powers* (Hamish Hamilton, 1960)

243

Heller, Joseph – *Good as Gold* (Jonathan Cape, 1979)

HM Stationery Office – 1943 (Cmd. 6240) *Proposals for the Reform of the Foreign Service*. 1964 (Cmd. 2276) *Plowden Report*. 1968/9 (Cmd. 4107) *Duncan Report on Overseas Representation*. 1977 (Cmd. 7308) *Central Policy Review Staff Report on Overseas Representation*, with Blue Book.

Home, Lord – *The Way the Wind Blows* (Collins, 1976)

Hunt, Sir David – *On the Spot* (Peter Davies, 1979)

Kalb, Marvin & Bernard – *Kissinger* (Little, Brown & Co., 1974)

Kaufmann, Johan – *Conference Diplomacy* (Sijthoff/Oceana, 1968)

Kelly, Sir David – *The Ruling Few* (Hollis & Carter, 1952)

Kirkpatrick, Sir Ivone – *The Inner Circle* (Macmillan, 1959)

Kissinger, Henry – *White House Years* (Weidenfeld & Nicolson, 1979)

Kitzinger, Uwe – *Diplomacy and Persuasion* (Thames & Hudson, 1973)

Luna, Silva Armando – *El ABC del Diplomatico* (Montevideo, 1970)

L'Etang, Hugh – *Fit to Lead* (Heinemann, 1980)

McDermott, Geoffrey – *The New Diplomacy* (Hume Press, 1973)

Moorhouse, Geoffrey – *The Diplomats* (Jonathan Cape, 1977)

Morris, Roger – *Uncertain Greatness* (Quartet, 1977)

Moynihan, Daniel – *A Dangerous Place* (Secker & Warburg, 1979)

Nicolson, Harold – *Some People; Peacemaking* 1919; *Diplomacy* (Constable, 1927, 1933, 1939)

Page, Leitch & Knightly – *Philby* (André Deutsch Ltd, 1968)

Philby, Kim – *My Secret War* (Grove Press, 1968)

Queller, Donald E. – *The Office of Ambassador in the Middle Ages* (Princeton University Press, 1967)

Rendel, Sir George – *The Sword and the Olive* (Murray, 1957)

Satow, Sir Ernest – *Guide to Diplomatic Practice*, 5th Edition, edited by Lord Gore-Booth (Longman, 1979)

Scarisbrick, J. J. – *Henry VIII* (Eyre Methuen Ltd, 1968)

Seton-Watson, Hugh – *Neither War nor Peace* (Methuen, 1960)

Shawcross, William – *Sideshow* (André Deutsch, 1979)

Sykes, Sir Percy – *History of Persia*, 3rd Edition (Routledge & Kegan Paul, 1969)

Thompson, Sir Geoffrey – *Front Line Diplomat* (Hutchinson, 1959)

Trevelyan, Lord – *Diplomatic Channels* (Macmillan, 1973)
Public and Private (Hamish Hamilton, 1980)

Tuchman, Barbara W. – *A Distant Mirror* (Macmillan, 1979)

Wallace, Helen – *National Governments and the European Communities* (Chatham House PEP, 1973)

Wallace, Wallace, & Webb – *Policy Making in the European Community* (Wiley, 1977)

Webster, Charles – *The Art and Practice of Diplomacy* (Chatto & Windus, 1961)

Index

Freitas Valle, Cyro, 188, 189
Froissart, Jean, 128
Full-powers, 27, 151, 152, 155, 156
Fulton speech, Churchill's, 179

Gaddafi, President, of Libya, 225
Garner, Lord, 210 et seq.
Garvey, Sir Terence, 24
Gaulle, President Charles de, 22, 35, 37, 50, 64, 65
Giscard d'Estaing, President, vi, 21, 50
Gladwyn, Lord (formerly Sir Gladwyn Jebb), 5, 147, 178, 179, 192
Goethe, J. W. von, Kissinger as a Faustian figure, 32
Gore-Booth, Lord, 90, 133, 144, 147, 178, 221
Grafftey-Smith, Sir Lawrence, 145
Graham, Sir John, 76
Greene, Graham, 87, 90
Grotius, Hugo, (*Law of War and Peace*) 1625, 95, 96, 97, 152
Guadaloupe Summit, 1979, 131, 140, 231
Guatemala, 108
Gun-boat Diplomacy, *see* Diplomacy

Haldane, Lord, 139
Halifax, Lord, 63
Hammerskjoeld, Dag, 31, 184
Hankey, Lord, 138–142, 181, 184
Hardinge of Penshurst, Lord, 137, 138, 140, 144 et seq., 155, 162, 173, 208
Harlech, Lord, 64, 65, 74
Hasheesh, *see* Assassins, the
Havana Convention on Asylum, 6
Hayter, Sir William, 75, 76
Hazards, diplomatic, old and new, 3, 4, 6, 21, 26, 52, 92, 93, 98, 111 et seq., 146, 147, 171, 172, 241
Heath, Edward, 35, 65
Heath, Mark, 76
Hegel and the diplomatic triad, 7

Heller, J., portrayal of Kissinger's Washington, 32
Helms, Richard, 14
Henderson, Sir Nicholas, 49, 73, 74, 158, 160
Henry VIII, King, 21, 126, 128–131
'High-flyers', *see* Flyers
Hitler, Adolf, 134, 170, 240
Home, Lord (previously Sir Alec Douglas-Home), vii, 36, 53
Honours, attrition of diplomatic, 58
Honduras, 3
Hostage-taking, 111, 118; official, 127
Hot Springs Conference, 1943, 177
Hug, the diplomatic, 21–23, 131
Hundred Years War, 126, 127
Hunt, Sir David, 210
Hurd, Douglas, MP, 79
Hypochondria, diplomatic, 146, 147

Iceland, 47
Immunity, diplomatic, 3, 92 et seq., 115, 116, 118, 153, 165
Intelligence function, morality of, 88, 89, 156, 157, 158
Interchange between Diplomatic and Home Civil Service, 60
'Interface', 7, 19, 94, 165, 225, 238
International Law, inadequacy of protection afforded by, 117, 158
Inviolability of diplomatic premises, 95, 97, 99, 102, 117; breaches of, 98–102, 118
Inviolability, diplomatic, origins of personal, 3, 92
Iran, disturbances in, 67, 99, 109, 110, 173
Iran, terrorist occupation of London embassy, 111 et seq.
Iran, *see* also Persia
Iron Curtain, *see* Fulton speech, Churchill's

Jackson, Senator Henry, 152